The Portuguese-Speaking Diaspora

Joe R. and Teresa Lozano Long Series in
Latin American and Latino Art and Culture

~ DARLENE J. SADLIER ~

The Portuguese-Speaking Diaspora

SEVEN CENTURIES OF
LITERATURE AND THE ARTS

University of Texas Press AUSTIN

Requests for permission to reproduce material from this work should be sent to:
Permissions
University of Texas Press
P.O. Box 7819
Austin, TX 78713–7819
http://utpress.utexas.edu/index.php/rp-form

∞ The paper used in this book meets the minimum requirements of
ANSI/NISO Z39.48–1992 (R1997) (Permanence of Paper).

LIBRARY OF CONGRESS CATALOGING-IN-PUBLICATION DATA
Names: Sadlier, Darlene J., author.
Title: The Portuguese-speaking diaspora : seven centuries of literature and the
arts / Darlene J. Sadlier.
Series: Joe R. and Teresa Lozano Long series in Latin American and Latino art
and culture.
Description: First edition. Austin : University of Texas Press, 2016. Includes
bibliographical references and index.
Identifiers: LCCN 2016012936 (print) LCCN 2016015680 (ebook)
    ISBN 9781477310526 (cloth : alk. paper)
    ISBN 9781477311486 (pbk. : alk. paper)
    ISBN 9781477310533 (library e-book)
    ISBN 9781477310540 (non-library e-book)
Subjects: LCSH: Portugal—Emigration and immigration—History. Portugal—
Colonies—History. Portuguese—Foreign countries—History. Ethnicity—
Portuguese-speaking countries. Portuguese literature—History. Art,
Portuguese—History.
Classification: LCC DP534.5 .S23 2016 (print) LCC DP534.5 (ebook)
    DDC 909/.0466—dc23
    LC record available at https://lccn.loc.gov/2016012936

doi: 10.7560/310526

For Jim, as always

Contents

Acknowledgments

Many individuals provided me with important research assistance during the writing of this book. In Lisbon, I wish to thank Cláudia Castelo, Edmundo Rocha, and Tomás Medeiros for conversations about the Casa dos Estudantes do Império (CEI). Rose-Marie Medeiros put me in touch with Luiz Nazaré Gomes, who gave me permission to use João Pedro Cochofel's drawing of Amílcar Cabral. I am grateful to them both. Anabela Simão and Anabela Carvalho at the União das Cidades Capitais da Língua Portuguesa were most helpful in arranging permissions for use of artwork by Luandino Vieira and a photograph of students at the CIE. Photojournalist Alfredo Cunha graciously allowed me to use his photograph from the collection titled "Decolonization." Olímpia Pinto and Mário Matos dos Santos at the Fundação Casa de Macau were most welcoming, and I took full advantage of their excellent library resources. Over the years, Fernando Cristóvão has generously provided me with books and articles about travel narratives in the Portuguese-speaking world. He also introduced me into the membership of CLEPUL (Centro de Literaturas e Culturas Lusófonas e Européias), for which I am especially grateful. I also benefited from conversations with friends Teolinda Gersão, Bertina Sousa Gomes, Maria Isabel Barreno, and Maria Augusta Figueiredo. Ricardo Máximo and his colleagues at the Museu de São Roque were most helpful as I researched literature and arts about the Jesuits in Asia.

In Brazil, Cícero Sandroni called my attention to Brazilian author Salim Miguel's transatlantic correspondence in the 1950s with Lusophone African writers, several of whom were members of the CEI in Lisbon. Brazilian artist Goya Lopes was most receptive to my correspondence about her artwork on the diaspora, and she graciously allowed me to include images of her work in the book. In Macau, I was warmly welcomed by Father Artur Wardega and César Guillén at the Matteo Ricci Institute. Father Wardega was an inspirational and tireless guide to both the old and new parts of the city.

In Bloomington, my longtime colleague and friend Heitor Martins was a constant source of help and information, as indicated by the various references to him in the book. As always, Jim Naremore spent many a dinnertime listening to my ideas and providing loving support as well as giving me invaluable feedback on the manuscript. The book is dedicated to him.

I was fortunate to receive several research and travel grants from Indiana University to help write the book. I wish to thank the Office of the Vice President for Research for fellowships from the New Explorations and New Perspectives programs as well as a grant-in-aid; the Office of the Vice President for International Affairs for a summer research grant; and the College of Arts and Sciences' Arts and Humanities Institute (CAHI) for research and travel awards. Special thanks go to Becky Cape and the Lilly Library at Indiana for allowing me to curate an exhibit on the Portuguese-speaking diaspora and to Erika Dowell for creating the online version at http://www.indiana.edu/~liblilly/digital/exhibitions/exhibits/show/portuguese-speaking-diaspora.

The commentary on Walter Salles and Daniela Thomas's *Terra estrangeira* in chapter 7 is from a longer piece I wrote for a *symplokē* volume on cinema without borders (15, nos. 1–2, 2007). I am grateful to the journal's editor, Jeffrey R. Di Leo, for permission to include that commentary here.

Finally, I want to thank Sarah McGavick at the University of Texas Press for her help with the many illustrations that appear in the book. I am especially grateful to Jim Burr, my editor at Texas, for his support, excellent advice, and good humor.

The Portuguese-Speaking Diaspora

Introduction

This is a book about journeys to far-off corners of the world where travelers discover new peoples and landscapes, experience changes of identity, and yet feel longing for the places they left behind. It describes an attempt to conquer the earth but also the struggles, cruelties, and forced migrations that resulted from it. More specifically, it deals with literary and artistic representations of a long history of leaving home, losing home, or returning to a home that is no longer the same.

Long before the present-day economy of globalization, the Portuguese created a vast empire that encompassed Brazil and mid-Atlantic territories as well as parts of Africa, India, China, Southeast Asia, and Japan. Beginning with the 1415 siege of Ceuta in North Africa, an incipient diaspora took shape as sailors, merchants, and adventure seekers as well as criminals and other "undesirables" left Portugal, most with hopes of better lives. These expectations were nourished by letters, personal accounts, official reports, and other narratives, frequently illustrated, that regularly touted the beauty and wealth to be found in the new lands. The diaspora also included Jesuit priests who traveled widely to establish missions in accordance with the Treaty of Tordesilhas (1494), a papal bull that divided the non-Christian world between Spain and Portugal for the purposes of claiming territories and converting local inhabitants.

Ultimately, the costs of overseas expansion and the gradual loss of trade routes and market economies to the Dutch and British led to the empire's decline, although colonization efforts continued, along with African slave trafficking in the Atlantic—a heinous and seemingly endless enterprise that the Portuguese initiated in the fifteenth century. Following Brazilian independence in 1822, and throughout the nineteenth and most of the twentieth centuries, Portugal's economic stability relied heavily on emigration and remittances sent from the former colony and the remaining overseas provinces.[1] For political and economic reasons, migrations also occurred in the opposite direction, from former colonies to Portugal, especially after the April 25, 1974, Portuguese revolution and again when Portugal joined the European Union, in 1986. Portugal's global enterprise was the first and longest of any modern European nation's and lasted until 1999, when the Portuguese relinquished control of Macau to the Chinese.

According to *The Oxford English Dictionary*, the word *diaspora* means "dispersion" and originates in the Greek term *diaspeirein*, meaning "to sow or scatter." The word is usually applied to dispersions of specific groups of people. The Bible refers to the diaspora of Hellenic Jews and the diaspora of Christian Jews outside Palestine, but it is common to use *diaspora* to describe the dispersion of any kind of population, such as the black diaspora from the South to Chicago or Los Angeles. The diasporas or dispersions I discuss in this book are those having to do with the Portuguese-speaking groups that have been scattered throughout what was once the Portuguese empire.

Spanning seven centuries and several continents, my book covers literary and artistic works about diaspora and associated with the larger semantic field of diaspora as discussed by, among others, Tim Coles and Dallen Timothy in their volume *Tourism, Diasporas, and Space* (2004). For my purposes, this larger semantic field includes population travel and displacement resulting from colonization, adventure seeking, religious conversion, political exile, forced-labor movements, wars, economic migration, and tourism in the Portuguese-speaking world. For example, I discuss works about exploration and settlement by the Portuguese in different parts of the empire; about the black Atlantic slave population first shipped to Portugal and later to Brazil; about economic migrations that involved populations coming to as well as leaving Portugal; and about wars dating back to the early colonial period and ending with the African wars that sent Portuguese troops to Africa but also displaced local populations within the colonies. As I show in the later part of the book, a great deal of contemporary literature and film continues to focus on the reasons for and consequences of diaspora in the Portuguese-speaking world. Based on an array of written and visual materials, including historiographies, memoirs, poetry, fiction, cartographic iconography, painting, architecture, and film, the book offers a detailed analysis of the different and sometimes conflicting cultural productions of diaspora associated with empire and provides an important context for understanding the more complex and broad-based culture of movement by peoples from former colonies to postcolonial "homelands."

Drawing from a mix of archival materials, canonical and noncanonical literary texts, and examples from the visual arts, the book is the first comprehensive treatment of the Portuguese-speaking diaspora in English. Its interdisciplinary approach to the subject makes important connections between literature and the arts and the sociopolitical and economic realities responsible for population movements. Although there were significant migrations of Portuguese-speaking peoples to parts of Europe, North America, and Australia, my chief concern here is with texts and images based on diasporas between Portugal and areas occupied under the Treaty of Tordesilhas that came to be known as the Portuguese empire.

Within that constellation of territories, some receive more attention than others. Portugal figures prominently, especially in the early chapters dealing with literature and art about discovery, conquest, and colonization. This is the focus of chapter 1, "The Imperial Diaspora," which gives particular attention to *Os lusíadas* (1572) (*The Lusiads*), Luís Vaz de Camões's epic poem about Vasco da Gama's voyage to India in 1498 resulting in Portugal's command of the East-West spice trade. It is perhaps not as surprising as it might appear that such a small nation carried out a remarkable maritime feat. After all, in Roman times Lisbon was called Olisipo or Ulysses, after one of the world's most intrepid voyagers. Homer's *Odyssey* was a natural model for Camões, whose *Os lusíadas* refers to the people of the Roman province known as Lusitania. The mythical founding of Lusitania is attributed to Lusus, the son of Bacchus, the irascible divinity in Camões's poem who worries that the maritime triumphs of the Portuguese might make them divine.

In addition to *Os lusíadas*, in chapter one I examine literary materials such as plays, historiographies, and shipwreck narratives about the dangers and vicissitudes of overseas expansionism, as well as letters and other writings by Jesuits in India and the Far East. Artworks discussed in this chapter include fifteenth- and sixteenth-century Benin bronzes with their images of African *obas* (kings) alongside Portuguese soldiers; maps of the empire with the iconographies of conquest; and Japanese Namban screens with their colorful images of the Portuguese, who were also known as "southern barbarians" in Nagasaki.

Chapter two, "The Lusophone African Diaspora," begins with a discussion of the trafficking of thousands of the enslaved through the West African "door of no return" to ports in Portugal and Brazil. Like the Indian in Brazil, the African became an iconic figure in early representations of empire; however, unlike the Indian, whom Portuguese and other artists imagined and often drew along classical lines, Africans were everywhere evident in Lisbon and were more realistically represented. One of the topics addressed in this chapter is the so-called *cabeça de negro* (black slave's head), an image that appears on family coats of arms and such Manueline-style monuments as the Jerónimos monastery outside Lisbon. Other subjects studied in the chapter are Enlightenment-period essays on the treatment of slaves and personal salvation; the African-inspired *lunduns* of African-Brazilian poet Domingos Caldas Barbosa, who became a popular literary figure in eighteenth-century Lisbon; and images of slavery in nineteenth-century Brazilian poetry and prose by, among others, Antônio Gonçalves Dias, Joaquim Machado de Assis, and João da Cruz e Sousa.

Portugal's early relations with the Far East can be seen in the many luxury and utilitarian items produced in Asia for Portuguese consumption. Chapter three, "Oriental Imaginings and Travel at the Turn of the Twentieth Century," begins with a discussion of the blue-and-white Chinese porcelains with Portuguese coats of arms and the astrolabe and other navigational emblems that were first exported to Portugal in the sixteenth century. In fact, the nation's long-standing fascination with silks, screens, fans, and porcelains from Asia led to the rise of a chinoiserie industry in eighteenth-century Lisbon that survived well into the nineteenth century. But the chapter's main focus is nineteenth-century literary Orientalism and the works of three major Portuguese writers: José Maria Eça de Queirós, Wenceslau de Moraes, and Camilo Pessanha. Although Eça had never traveled to China, his protagonist in *O mandarim* (1880) (*The Mandarin* [1999]) does so, with unfortunate consequences when his imaginary expectations of the Orient fail to mesh with his experiences there. Moraes and Pessanha, on the other hand, lived most of their lives in Asia, and their often highly personalized accounts of China and Japan reveal a great deal about the customs and mores of lands and peoples largely associated in the Portugal imaginary with both the bygone days of imperial glory and the perceived "yellow peril" at the turn of the twentieth century.

In chapter four, "Into the Wilderness: The Race to Africa and the Promise of Brazil," I examine the travelogues of famous Portuguese explorers Alexandre Serpa Pinto and the team of Hermenegildo Capelo and Roberto Ivens, who were part of the larger nineteenth-century scramble by Europeans to explore and colonize Africa. In addition to discussing Serpa Pinto's and Capelo-Ivens's different strategies to protect and expand Portuguese sovereignty, I look at the role of newly created institutions like the Geographical Society of Lisbon and the Cartographic Commission in designating the 1885 "mapa cor-de-rosa" (rose-colored map), whose claims to territories between Angola and Mozambique were thwarted by the 1890 British Ultimatum. Among others who wrote about nineteenth-century travel in Africa was Eça de Queiros's fictional character and *touriste extraordinaire*, Carlos Fradique Mendes. The chapter examines Fradique's letters in Eça's *A correspondência de Fradique Mendes* (1900) (*The Correspondence of Fradique Mendes* [2011]) alongside his "secret" cache of missives about slave trafficking and racial mixing in Angola, subjects that appeared more recently in José Eduardo Agualusa's postmodern novel *Nação Crioula: A correspondência secreta de Fradique Mendes* (1997) (*Creole* [2004]). I also give attention to the importance and promise of Brazil for impoverished Portuguese in the late nineteenth and early twentieth centuries, especially as portrayed by José Maria Ferreira de Castro in his novels *Emigrantes* (1928) (*Emigrants* [1962]) and *A selva* (1930) (*Jungle* [1935]). Written in the late 1920s, these works introduced a new form of literary realism into Portugal akin to the emerging literature of social protest in 1930s Brazil.

Protest is also a prominent theme in *Mensagem* (Message), a bulletin published by the Casa dos Estudantes do Império (CEI, House of Students from the Empire) in Lisbon from the late 1940s until the early 1960s. The CEI was a government-sponsored social and cultural center for students who arrived from the colonies to attend universities in Lisbon, Coimbra, and Oporto. Although a considerable amount has been written about the history of the CEI and its various functions, very little critical commentary exists on *Mensagem*, which is the focus of chapter five, "The Casa dos Estudantes do Império and *Mensagem*." Among the earliest contributors to the bulletin, which featured poetry, prose, and essays, were Agostinho Neto, Viriato da Cruz, and Mário Pinto de Andrade, soon to become key figures in the African liberation movement. Featuring a range of literary styles and political views, *Mensagem* was the first and most important vehicle for the dissemination of African literature in Portuguese and called attention to authors such as Pepetela, Luandino Vieira, Luís Bernardo Honwana, Noémia de Sousa, and Alda do Espírito Santo, who are widely known today.

Chapter six, "A Lusotropicalist Tourist and Soldiers, East Indians, and Cape Verdeans on the Move," begins with a commentary on film adaptations of patriotic works about empire made in the 1930s and 1940s to elicit public enthusiasm for Estado Novo dictatorships in Portugal and Brazil. To reinforce Portugal's hold on the colonies, which came under attack at the United Nations after World War II, the Salazar government invited celebrated anthropologist and sociologist Gilberto Freyre to tour the then euphemistically called "overseas provinces" and defend their continued colonization by Portugal before the international community. I examine Freyre's travel narrative of that tour, *Aventura e rotina* (1952) (Adventure and routine), which supports, with some reservations, Portugal's sustained colonial presence, portraying it as vital to the "Lusotropicalist" mission of racial mixing. I also draw attention to government information booklets designed for soldiers in the colonies and to a former soldier's memoir about the ousting of the Portuguese military from India in 1961 and the soldiers' unhappy reception on returning to Lisbon. The chapter concludes with discussions of works by two Portuguese film directors about the Cape Verdean diaspora to Lisbon beginning in the 1960s. Pedro Costa's *Casa de lava* (1995) (*Down to Earth*) and his much-admired *Juventude em marcha* (2006) (*Colossal Youth*) focus on the consequences of leaving loved ones behind and the disillusionment of a promised land that despite its familiar language and customs is inhospitable and forever foreign. Fernando Ventrell's *Fintar o destino* (1997) (*Dribbling Fate*) contrasts life in the Cape Verdean archipelago, where the community is poor but united, with that of Lisbon, where the emphasis on wealth and individual success has an alienating effect.

In chapter seven, "War in Africa and the Global Economy: Leaving Home and Returning," I examine works about population movements resulting from the colonial wars, Portugal's entry into the European Union, and tourism. The chapter begins with a discussion of two of the earliest works to address the wars: Sarah Maldoror's film *Sambizanga* (1972) and the book *Novas cartas portuguesas* (1972) (*New Portuguese Letters*, [1975]) by Maria Isabel Barreno, Maria Teresa Hora, and Maria Velho da Costa. Although the two works have different perspectives, one African and the other Portuguese, both focus on the trauma of war for those who leave home to fight and, most importantly, on women's largely unsung roles in dissent and warfare. In many ways the wars became an even more sensitive topic in the years after the Portuguese revolution and African independence and are a central concern of João Botelho's groundbreaking film *Um adeus português* (1985) (*A Portuguese Farewell*). I examine its story, about a family that continues to suffer from a wartime loss, alongside Flora Gomes's film *Morta negu* (1988) (*Death Denied*), about Guineans who win the war only to return to new struggles in a liberated homeland. I comment as well on Miguel Gomes's *Tabu* (2010) (*Taboo*), a subtly ironic film about nostalgia for a colonial Africa of privilege and romance that elides the reality of a subjugated black majority.

An equally sensitive issue after the war was the *retornados* (returnees), colonials who fled their homes for Portugal after the African colonies were granted independence. In her novel *O retorno* (2011) (The return), Dulce Maria Cardoso writes about returnees' alienation and struggles in a land where those who never left are ambivalent about the homecoming of ex-colonials. Ambivalence as well as mistrust are at the center of Walter Salles and Daniela Thomas's *Terra estrangeira* (1996) (*Foreign Land*), a contemporary film noir about crime in Lisbon and uneasy encounters between the Portuguese and the Brazilian and Angolan migrants who have fled unstable homelands. Author José Eduardo Agualusa and filmmakers João Pedro Rodrigues and João Rui Guerra da Mata look back to the period of empire for narratives about contemporary Goa and Macau. In Agualusa's postmodern novella, *Um estranho em Goa* (2010) (A stranger in Goa) individuals from various Portuguese-speaking nations converge on the former cultural capital, now a favorite tourist destination where global trade in once valuable spices has given way to a black-market industry in imperial relics. Rodrigues and Guerra da Mata's film noir tribute, *A última vez que vi Macau* (2012) (*The Last Time I Saw Macao*), conflates memories about an idyllic childhood in the former colony with a fictional crime story in the world-famous tourist and gambling mecca. While the narrator despairs that Portuguese is no longer spoken and imperial landmarks have lost their significance, the film nevertheless shows the degree to which the Portuguese presence endures. There is a certain irony in the film's emphasis on loss in relation to China's omnipresence in the city. Portuguese language instruction in Macau as well as throughout China is now part of a boom industry created by China's economic interests in Portuguese-speaking countries, especially Brazil and oil-rich Angola—interests that Portugal looks to mediate more generally in the future.[2]

China's investment in Portuguese is a recent part of a centuries-long cultural mixing and diffusion of a language that traveled around the globe to become the lingua franca of regions and nations on four continents. As shown in the following chapters, the rich written and artistic record of that often problematic journey enables us to appreciate subsequent and more contemporary representations of people driven by different circumstances to leave home for other places in the larger homeland of the Portuguese-speaking world.

ONE

The Imperial Diaspora

Foi-s' o meu amigo d'aqui
na hoste, por el-rei servir,
e nunca eu depois dormir
pudi, mais ben tenh' eu assim
que, pois m' el tarda e non ven,
el-rei o faz que mi-o deten.

(From here my beloved departed
with the army to serve the king,
and I never could sleep after that,
but I feel that everything is all right
for, though he is late and has yet to return,
it is the king who keeps him from me.)

PERO DA PONTE, MID-THIRTEENTH CENTURY

Portugal's earliest poems were *cantigas*, songs written in Galician-Portuguese, a category of which, *cantigas de amigo*, were often plaintive lyrics spoken by a young woman about her beloved's absence. In the poem cited above, the woman speaks of her lover's delay in returning because of the *fossado*, obligatory military service to the king that often involved battles and ransacking of enemy territories.[1]

Following Pope Alexander III's acknowledgment of Portugal in 1179 as a nation under the king Afonso Henriques, the royal militias focused primarily on expelling the Moors, Muslims who had invaded the Iberian Peninsula in the early eighth century. By 1249, when troubadour Pero da Ponte was writing his *cantigas*, the Portuguese had driven out the Moors more than two centuries before their expulsion in Castile. Known as the Reconquest, the war against the Muslims was the subject of several medieval tales about valiant Christian warriors. For instance, in "A morte do lidador" (The fighter's death), the protagonist, Portuguese nobleman Gonçalo Mendes da Maia, celebrates his ninety-fifth birthday by riding with noblemen friends and troops into battle against the infidels and, though mortally wounded, striking down their infamous leader, Almoleimar.[2]

Once the enemy was expelled and the country's borders were secure, the Portuguese, under the command of the Infante Dom Henrique, also known as Prince Henry the Navigator, sailed to North Africa in 1415 and captured the port town of Ceuta, the nation's first overseas conquest.[3] The royal chronicler Gomes Eanes de Azurara, a close acquaintance of Dom Henrique's, praises the prince's navigational acumen and superlative land warfare in his Crônica da tomada de Ceuta (1449) (Chronicle of Ceuta's capture). This conquest was the first step in Portugal's empire building that by the mid-1500s would include Brazil, several Atlantic islands, and numerous coastal outposts and towns in Africa, India, China, Southeast Asia, and Japan.

The most renowned work about the Portuguese imperial diaspora is Luís Vaz de Camões's epic poem in ten cantos, Os lusíadas (1572) (The Lusiads). Often compared to Virgil's Aeneid and Homer's Odyssey, works cited in the poem, Os lusíadas celebrates Vasco da Gama's 1498 voyage around the Cape of Good Hope to India—a feat that gave Portugal enviable control of the lucrative spice trade in Europe. A distant relative of da Gama's and member of the lesser nobility, Camões was himself a participant in the expansionist enterprise and a prime example of a Renaissance soldier-writer who, in his case, was more devoted to wielding a pen than a sword.

A rebel, adventurer, and poet whose escapades far exceeded in kind and degree those associated with "doomed" romantic writers, Camões was initially deployed to Ceuta in 1549, where he lost an eye in battle.[4] He returned to Lisbon but left again in 1553, this time for Goa, the capital of Portuguese India, possibly as punishment for wounding a royal official. At the end of a three-year military stint, he accepted a job to oversee properties of the dead and missing in the Portuguese settlement of Macau, which was the first (and last) European colony in China.[5] Charged with malfeasance, Camões left Macau for Goa, where he lived for several years in impoverished conditions. He negotiated a loan for a return trip to Portugal with ship's captain Pedro Barreto and got as far as the Portuguese outpost on the island of Mozambique. Making his own way back to Lisbon via Mozambique, Diogo do Couto, a Portuguese soldier-writer and future royal scribe, happened across the penniless poet and acquaintance there. With financial support from Couto and others, Camões finally reached Lisbon in 1570. It is not clear exactly when during his seventeen years of travels and travails he began writing *Os lusíadas*, but after two years back home, he presented the finished manuscript to the young king, Dom Sebastião, to whom he dedicated the poem. Pleased with Camões's lofty portrayal of the country's overseas achievements and in keeping with the custom of the *alvíssara*, Sebastião awarded the poet a small pension.[6] Two years later, in 1572, *Os lusíadas* was published. Camões died in poverty on the eve of the Iberian Union. With Sebastião's death in the Battle of Alcácer-Quibir, Morocco, in 1578, and with no imminent heir to the throne, Portugal came under Spanish rule in 1580 and remained so for the next sixty years.

Os lusíadas casts the expansionist enterprise as a divine mission bestowed upon the Portuguese, who are both protected and undermined by various deities, most prominently Venus and Bacchus. Posed against a panorama of various mythological characters and their earthly interventions are Vasco da Gama, his mariner crew, and the local inhabitants they meet along the voyage as well as epic-heroic figures from Portugal's past whose brave deeds are recounted by various narrators at different points in the poem. Camões was not the first person to write about Portugal's expedition to India, and his poem has intertextual relations with several historiographies, such as João de Barros's two-volume *Décadas da Ásia* (1552–1553) (Decades of Asia) about "os feitos que os portugueses fizeram no descobrimento dos mares e terras do Oriente" (the deeds that the Portuguese carried out in the discovery of the seas and lands of the Orient) and Fernão Lopes de Castanheda's ten-volume *História do descobrimento e conquista da Índia pelos portugueses* (1551–) (History of the discovery and conquest of India by the Portuguese). Other works that circulated at the time were manuscript copies of Gaspar Correia's *Lendas da Índia* (Legends of India), based on the exploits of notables such as Vasco da Gama, Pedro Álvares Cabral, and Afonso de Albuquerque, an admiral and Portuguese India's second governor; *A suma oriental* (1512–1515), a fascinating report to Dom Manuel about lands and people from the Red Sea to Japan by the royally appointed apothecary Tomé de Pires; and commentaries by "horse traders" Domingos Paes and Fernão Nunes.[7]

There can be little doubt that Camões also was familiar with playwright Gil Vicente's canonical works, such as the farcical *Auto da Índia* (1509) (The India play), about the impact of expansionism on the homeland and, in particular, the marriage bed. A transitional writer between the

Middle Ages and the Renaissance, Vicente satirizes the *cantiga de amigo*'s abandoned and melancholic damsel in the figure of Constança, a soldier's pretty wife who is more than happy to be rid of her husband. During his three-year absence at sea, she is courted by a dim-witted Spaniard and a penniless, self-serving Portuguese. Unlike Ulysses's steadfast Penelope, Constança is not at all "constant" and encourages her paramours' attentions until her husband's inglorious return. Vicente also focuses on the *cobiça*, or greed, that comes with building an empire: despite the husband's years in the *fossado*, the lowly ranked soldier, unlike his superiors, has earned but a paltry sum. The playwright sidesteps issues of fidelity on the man's part, but as historian John Villiers has noted in "The Portuguese and the Trading World of Asia," the monsoons kept Portuguese fleets marooned for months in port towns, resulting in the creation of a significant mixed-race population (11).

Vicente's interest in the impact of the *fossado* on women left behind can be seen in his *A farsa de Inês Pereira* (1523) (The farce of Inês Pereira), in which the unwed Inês accepts a smooth-talking albeit penniless squire-songster over a dim-witted bumpkin with landowner expectations. Inês's much-anticipated and newfound freedom as a married woman is short-lived; before departing to battle the Muslims, her husband locks her in the house and gives his watchdog-servant the key. Inês gains her freedom when news of her husband's death arrives in a letter from her brother, who reports that he died not gloriously in battle but rather at the hands of a young shepherd boy in Africa. Ultimately Inês weds the country rube, now a landowner, who unknowingly facilitates her reunion with a former admirer by carrying her across a riverbed to where he resides. The play ends with a moral: "Mais quero asno que me leve que cavalo que me derrube" (I much prefer an ass that carries me than a horse that throws me). Vicente enjoyed royal patronage, and while his comedic images of war and expansionism were scathing, they generally focused on dubious and less than heroic types from the viewpoints of lovers and wives. Cuckolding was a regular topic in the *cantigas de escárnio e maldizer* (songs of scorn and name-calling), a category of medieval lyric that regularly described the marital consequences of the absent husband.

With the exception of Venus and other female deities, women play minor roles in *Os lusíadas*, and their images seem more compatible with the *cantiga de amigo* tradition. In Canto IV, wives and mothers (alongside older men and children) beseech male loved ones bound for India not to abandon them by risking their lives at sea.[8] Fearing the consequences of the women's collective plea, da Gama avoids the customary leave-taking celebration and solemnly sets sail. Camões's portrayal of women contrasts starkly with that of Vicente, who was more cynical about how women who were left behind viewed the men's absence. Expansionism for wives meant a loss of sexual activity, which was an expected part of the marriage contract. As we have seen in *Auto da Índia*, that loss is repaid by two besotted admirers. The wife's mistreatment and forced celibacy in *A farsa de Inês Pereira* happily end when her husband's absence owing to the *fossado* turns into something more permanent.

Adding to the solemnity of da Gama's departure in Canto IV of *Os lusíadas* is the appearance of the solitary, venerable Velho do Restelo, the Old Man of Restelo, who stands dockside and denounces the greed and vanity born of fortune seeking and fame. Comparing da Gama's expedition to humanity's fall from grace, he condemns the enterprise for prioritizing commerce (the apple) over religion and the mission to convert non-Christians. He complains that the fleet's departure leaves the homeland more vulnerable to occupation by infidels. The old man's reference to the proselytizing mission is a reminder that just three years prior to da Gama's voyage, the 1494 papal bull, or Treaty of Tordesilhas, granted Portugal and Spain the right to divide and seize non-Christian lands as long as they converted the inhabitants. This proclamation was the impetus for the proliferation of the Order of Christ cross that appeared on Portuguese ship sails, uniforms, and flags. The blood-red cross symbolized not only Christianity but also the sanctity and righteousness of Portugal's overseas cause.

But as *Os lusíadas* suggests and history has shown, the spreading of Christianity was rarely the priority for the Crown or even for Dom Henrique, a high official in the Order of Christ. His primary interest, like that of da Gama and other royally appointed expeditionary leaders, was claiming lands (and peoples) and establishing profitable commercial routes between them and Europe. *Os lusíadas* has relatively little commentary on Christianity except when da Gama and his mariners beseech God to protect them from storms or enemies. From Camões's perspective, the plot in *Os lusíadas* required less the presence of Christ and his teachings than a forum of strong-minded, pagan divinities who angle for control. This strategic decision meant a tribute to as well as comparison with the major literary works in the classical tradition. The gods' internecine battles, earthly deceptions, and supportive interventions provided just the kind and level of intrigue and suspense necessary for an epic rendering of da Gama's journey. The poetic use of the classical gods also served to link Portugal's greatness as a seafaring nation with great empires of Western culture.

Generally speaking, the gods' debates on the mariners' fate and Bac-chus's machinations are livelier and more compelling than the journey itself, with the exception of certain phenomena encountered by the marin-ers, such as Saint Elmo's fire and the Adamastor, the besotted giant turned rocky barrier whose tragic love story is one of the great moments in the poem.[9] Encounters with the African Other around the continent tend to be characterized by narrow escapes from deceptive and scheming Muslims. An important exception to the Muslim stereotype is the African leader who welcomes the Portuguese to Malindi, on the eastern coast, and pro-vides them navigational assistance to reach the Indian continent. What is significant about this particular encounter in Canto II and evident in con-tacts with even unfriendly locals is the African interest in knowing exactly who the Portuguese are. This is the case of the Malindi leader, whose curi-osity elicits da Gama's account of Portugal's achievements through ref-erences to its brave leaders (Cantos III–V). As more than one critic has noted, *Os lusíadas* is not about a single expedition but rather is about a na-tion whose empire and growing diaspora are implicit in Camões's render-ing of da Gama's voyage. Unlike the Malindi chief and others met around the African coast, the Portuguese express no historical, cultural, or ethno-graphic interest in the Other—an aspect of the poem that seems consistent with the early emphasis on maritime discoveries and commerce.[10]

Camões emphasizes this lack of interest in colonization in Canto VII, when the Portuguese finally reach Calicut, on the west Indian coast. Here da Gama greets the city's king by describing the trade routes now com-manded by the Portuguese: "do Tejo ao Nilo, / E desde a fria plaga de Zelanda, / Até bem de onde o sol não muda o estilo" (242) (from the Tagus to the Nile, / and from the frigid region of the low countries / to the Equa-tor), and proposing a business deal that would entail Portuguese firepower should enemies threaten their commercial dealings. Before responding to da Gama's proposal, the Indian leader wants to know more about the Por-tuguese. His representative, along with an interpreter, boards da Gama's vessel; there he sees a series of figures appearing on banners that pique his curiosity. Canto VIII begins as host and self-styled docent Paulo da Gama, Vasco's older brother, recounts the history of the more than two dozen legendary figures. He begins with Lusus, the man for whom the lands of Lusitania were named prior to the formation of the nation-state, and moves on to Ulysses, the purported founder of Lisbon (or Olisipo) for whom the city was originally named. Da Gama's lengthy homage to cen-turies of heroes and dedicated soldier-statesmen concludes with descrip-tions of Dom Henrique and other leaders, among them Count Pedro de

Meneses and Duarte de Meneses, all of whom secured strongholds in the North African campaigns.

While this remarkable pictorial exhibition described by da Gama predates the advent of the museum as we know it today, most if not all the heroic Portuguese described in this part of the poem were renowned portrait subjects before and during Camões's time; their names, stories, and images were as familiar to the Portuguese at home as the tale of Lisbon's founding by Ulysses. A prime example of their legendary status is the codex from Goa titled *Livro de Lisuarte de Abreu* (1563), with colorful, detailed illustrations varying from armadas to portraits of distinguished figures like Vasco da Gama (plate 1). In many ways, Camões's approach to imperial history strongly resembles the *Livro de Lisuarte de Abreu*'s gallery-style exposition in his book.

Even more interesting than portraiture contemporary with *Os lusíadas* is a play by the nineteenth-century writer Almeida Garrett, a ten-canto epic titled *Camões* (1825) about the poet's attempt to find a publisher for his poem after he returns home. Almeida's most famous play, the melodrama *Frei Luís de Sousa* (1843), adopts a portrait-gallery approach to hail the nation's achievements. In the play, individual pictures of Dom Sebastião and noblemen Dom Manuel de Sousa Coutinho and Dom João of Portugal represent the many who traveled afar, fought the Muslims, and disappeared at Alcácer-Quibir. The image of Dom João, Dona Madalena's first husband, is unknown to her daughter by her second marriage, Maria, who expresses curiosity about his identity. In a variation on the play's repeated reference to *sebastianismo*, a popular belief that Dom Sebastião was alive and would return from Africa to save the nation (initially from Spanish rule during the Iberian Union), Dom João suddenly appears after years in captivity. But instead of salvation, his return brings only tragedy to the family, especially to Maria, who is now recognized as the illegitimate child of Madalena's marriage to her beloved Dom Manuel de Sousa.[11] The play ends as a consumptive Maria dies of shame while her parents seek redemption by taking vows and entering a religious order. In this instance, military service to the king and the portrait of a nobleman brought back from the dead have tragic and fatal consequences for an entire family.

Like Almeida's much-later play, the pictorial exposition in *Os lusíadas* has dual functions: it supplements Vasco da Gama's earlier and more extensive oral history to the Malindi leader about heroes from the nation's past, and it enables Camões to honor the narrator Paulo da Gama alongside the many men whose praises he sings. A stalwart supporter of his younger brother Vasco and commander of the fleet's vessel *São Rafael*,

Paulo fell ill and died before their triumphal return to Lisbon. The poem's description of past Portuguese heroes adds to Camões's later, sharp critique of a contemporary sedentary and slothful generation that seems content to feed off the glory of its seafaring ancestors.

Os lusíadas is Camões's salute to the Portuguese mariners who ventured into the unknown to build what became one of the earliest, largest, and most enduring global empires. As he repeatedly reminds us, unlike Greek and Roman conquests, that feat went unheralded in verse over the years because of Portugal's failure to cultivate a national literature. If the story of Portugal's expansionism is to survive, he tells us, it requires a poet on the order of Virgil or Homer—a role he implicitly assumes. Camões's extraordinary interweaving of myth and history is evidence and substance for these and other metapoetical reflections. His own experiences abroad were far from epic or heroic, and though panegyric, his poem critiques the vicissitudes of empire, the lack of a strong lyric tradition, and the self-indulgence of his own generation. All the major Portuguese conquests were made by the time Camões wrote his epic work. His overseas experiences, coupled with an extensive literary knowledge and a measure of hubris, enabled him to imagine a remarkable voyage and a period that would never be duplicated. The centuries-long legacy of Os lusíadas is the image of a people on the move, undeterred by seemingly insurmountable forces. This portrait is celebrated to this day and is an indelible part of the national imaginary.

While royal scribes and chroniclers, ship captains, and soldier-writers like Camões were writing about Portuguese maritime adventures, artists at home were producing elaborately designed and colorful maps of the lands and sea routes being explored. In 1502, just three years after Vasco da Gama's return to Lisbon and two years after Pedro Álvares Cabral's founding of Brazil, an unidentified cartographer produced the 1502 Cantino planisphere (plate 2).[12] This and other beautifully illustrated maps of the period had no real practical navigational use but rather were artistic renderings of the empire, replete with iconographic representations of flora, fauna, and people in the newfound lands. Cantino's map is fascinating for what it tells us about the artist's conception of the empire that stretched from Brazil to India. Iconographies include forested tracts whose hardwoods were desirable for shipbuilding, lakes and rivers that supplied the passing fleets with fresh water, and birds of various species, most prominently Brazil's multihued parrots, which were shipped back to the homeland as exotica. On the African continent, the image of a lionlike figure appears next to the mountainous area marked "Serra Líoa" (Sierra Leone,

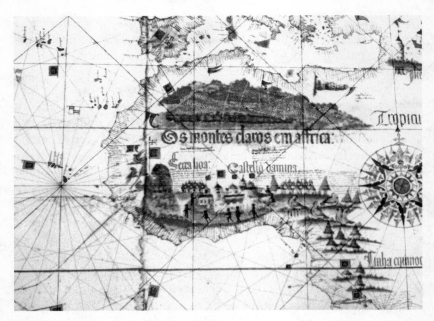

1.1. *Detail, Cantino planisphere (1502)*

literally Lion Mountain), while to the south, several tiny black figures stand in front of a warehouse-fortress, one of many around the coastline with flags bearing the Portuguese coat of arms; these buildings became central clearinghouses for African slaves shipped to Europe, the Atlantic islands, and Brazil. Large, centrally featured, and elaborately drawn, Africa is the cartographer's main focus and understandably so; by 1502, knowledge of the continent's coastline and trading centers there was well advanced, as suggested by the numerous place names inscribed on its border.

The Lopo Homem-Reinéis map of the Estado da Índia in the 1519 *Atlas Miller* is another product of Portugal's exceptional cartographic industry (plate 3). Dense with illustrations such as flags with the Portuguese coat of arms and fleets with the Order of Christ cross, the map calls attention to the breadth of Portuguese-controlled lands and sea routes. In addition to flora, fauna, and fortress iconography, the East African coast features a figure of a Muslim warrior on horseback, possibly a reference to enemies encountered there. Also prominent is the figure of Preste João (Prester John), the legendary Christian king of Abyssinia whom the Portuguese repeatedly tried to locate to extend their friendship and increase their commercial base. The reference to his large kingdom is marked "Arabia Felix" (Felicitous Arabia).

Especially important to cartographic images of expansionism were elaborately drawn and colorful *rosas dos ventos* (wind roses), or compasses. In the Cantino planisphere and other early maps, the compass's northern cardinal point is topped with a special decoration to orient the viewer. Noteworthy is the detail and evolution of these icons as the empire grew— they functioned as scientific markers of Portuguese expansionism but also as art. The Cantino planisphere has sixteen compasses spread from the Atlantic to the Pacific, with the largest and most detailed appearing at the center of the African continent. One of several imperial emblems, the *rosa dos ventos* was a reference to Dom Henrique and to Sagres, at the southwestern tip of Portugal, where a massive stone compass, uncovered by excavation in the early twentieth century, fronts the Atlantic. Critical to Portugal's overseas success, navigational experts working under Prince Henry collected up-to-date maritime travel information, produced sophisticated sea charts, and revolutionized sea travel with the design of a faster ship called the *caravela* (caravel). In Belém, Portugal, the site of the Old Man of Restelo's warning speech, and a Sagres simulacrum of sorts, is an enormous *rosa dos ventos* built into the ground—a gift from South Africa to Portugal in 1960. Just steps away from the Monument to the Discoveries, the wind rose was laid the same year to honor the five-hundredth anniversary of Dom Henrique's death. The design is unusual because the empire's cartographic image, on which small *rosas dos ventos* usually appeared, is

1.2. *Compass rose with map of Portuguese explorations in Belém. Courtesy of ROC2C.*

positioned within the compass's center. A possible interpretation for this inversion is that the memory of Henrique's navigational skill and imperial spirit was perhaps more important to the national image than that of its empire, which was a major financial drain on Portugal at the time. Within the year of that gift, a protracted colonial war began in the African colonies, ending with the 1974 revolution and the subsequent independence of all the Portuguese territories there.

While the Portuguese were negotiating African trading partnerships through peaceful means as well as by force, non-Christian Africans, or *cafres*, who appear in *Os lusíadas* as a single, homogeneous, and largely "barbarous" population, were producing finely wrought art objects that document the Portuguese presence. Among the best known are the Benin bronzes on which the region's leader, or *oba*, often appears in the company of his attendants.[13] Fashioned from *manilhas* (brass pieces, or bracelets), the plaquelike artwork often has Portuguese figures along with images of the brass items that the Europeans traded for gold, ivory, and other local goods.[14] The *oba* and his men are represented as warrior types with headdresses, multitiered necklaces, and lances. Their broad noses and thick lips contrast with the thinner features of the long-haired and bearded Portuguese, who wear helmets, mail, and armaments. Trade and art went hand in hand not just for sixteenth-century Europeans but also for west-coast Africans. Benin items especially fashioned for trade included finely carved ivory spoons and horns and saltcellars on which Portuguese figures often appear (plate 4). An especially beautiful saltcellar takes the form of an astrolabe or armillary sphere that was a symbol of Portuguese expansionism under King Manuel, whose motto, "Espera in Deo" (Hope in God), is carved on the sphere. The twisted ropes that form the saltcellar's legs and rounded base are other nautical emblems associated with sixteenth-century Manueline architecture, examples of which include the landmark Jerónimos monastery in Belém and the Convent of Christ window in central Tomar.[15]

The excitement created by Vasco da Gama's voyage and the opening of the maritime spice trade to Europe, along with advances in shipbuilding and navigational expertise, undoubtedly gave the Portuguese a sense that the world lay at their feet. Camões vividly depicts this attitude in Canto X of *Os lusíadas*, when Vasco da Gama is rewarded with a mountaintop view of the celestial "máquina do mundo" (world machine) and future discoveries to be made in the East (Southeast Asia and Japan) and West (Brazil).[16] Overseas accomplishment is at the heart of Simão de Oliveira's *Arte de navegar* (1606) (Art of navigation). A mathematician and cosmographer,

1.3. *Benin bronzes of* oba
and Portuguese soldier
(15th–16th century)

Oliveira's primer on cosmography and maritime travel explains the use of navigational instruments, with illustrations of the astrolabe, quadrant, and compass. The book's "how-to" section describes avoiding dangers at sea, reading the tides and lunar cycles, and understanding Corpo Santo, the Saint Elmo's fire phenomenon that confounded the sailors in *Os lusíadas.* It concludes with a prototype of today's GPS or MapQuest that provides detailed sailing instructions (replete with right- and left-hand turns) from Portugal to India. The king, Dom Manuel, was especially proud of his nation's overseas accomplishments, as can be seen in his 1507 missive to the bishop of Oporto titled *Gesta proxime per Portugalenses in India, Ethiopia et alijs orientalibus terris* (Recent deeds of the Portuguese in India, Ethiopia, and other eastern lands).

Other navigational accounts sometimes were reports by ships' pilots. Examples of this little-studied genre are the *Relato do piloto anónimo* (Report of the anonymous pilot) and *Carta do mestre João* (Letter from Master João), both written in 1500 about the founding of Brazil; Francisco Rodrigues's *Livro* (1511–1515), considered the first atlas of the modern world, which contains maps and charts from his expedition to Southeast Asia; Manoel de Figueiredo's *Hydrografia: Exames de pilotos* (1608) (Hydrography: Pilot exams), with Vicente Rodrigues's compass readings for travel between Portugal and India; Dom João de Castro's posthumously published *Roteiro de Lisboa a Goa* (1882) (Log book from Lisbon to Goa); and António Galvão's *Tratado* (1563) (Treatise) on the spice-trade routes. Galvão was the first to document all the Portuguese and Spanish discoveries prior to 1550.[17]

Frontispieces for the *Leitura nova* (New reading) collection commissioned by Dom Manuel for the Torre do Tombo and produced during his

1.4. *Astrolabe (1605)*

and his son João III's reigns (1502–1521 and 1521–1557, respectively) combine maritime and other imperial imagery. For example, in the uppermost tiers of the front-page illustration for *Livro 2 de Reis* (Book 2 of Kings) are a seashell, serpentine marine creatures, the crown atop the Portuguese coat of arms with its five shields and seven castles, and two astrolabes (plate 5). The page's side borders indicate that the artwork was done to celebrate the "most powerful King João III." The lower part of the frontispiece shows various divinities and sea creatures and two ships. A Portuguese vessel calmly rests under a goddess's watchful eye, while a ship with infidels (suggested by its prow figure) battles with a god-induced tempest and trident-carrying sea demons. Dated circa 1552, the illustration, by Fernão de Pina, son of the royal chronicler Rui de Pina, with its imperial and mythical references, might have inspired *Os lusíadas*.

During Dom João III's reign, Portuguese eyes were fixed firmly on "the Orient" and increasingly on Brazil, where the French were trading with Indians for the coveted brazilwood used to extract red dye for royal clothing. Pero Vaz de Caminha's encouragement to Dom Manuel to convert the indigenous habitants was finally answered in 1549, when Dom João III sent Jesuits to establish missions along the coast. He also sent Mem de Sá, the country's first governor-general, to oust the French from the area around Rio de Janeiro. Because Portuguese women largely remained at home and because colonization was a means to impede further enemy occupation, the Crown officially sanctioned unions between settlers and indigenous females.[18] As historian Alida C. Metcalf has observed, Jesuits functioned as mediators between Indian laborers and Portuguese colonists. Their religious teachings for settlers and Indians alike often took the form of verse plays written in Portuguese, Latin, and Tupi. Regarded as Brazil's first author, the Jesuit José de Anchieta wrote an epic poem, *De gestis Mendi de Saa* (1563), about Mem de Sá's successful war against the French colony known as França Antártica. In the tradition of Ignatius of Loyola, the founder of the Society of Jesus, Anchieta was also a prolific letter writer. His and his colleagues' letters from Brazil and other Portuguese territories, along with historiographic material produced by royal chroniclers and other scribes, were important sources of information about the growing imperial diaspora.

A characteristic of sixteenth-century literature in Brazil and elsewhere was *ufanismo*, the notable hyperbolic rhetoric used to praise newfound peoples and lands for the purposes of colonizing them. However, not every writer was enthusiastic about where the enterprise was headed. A good example is Diogo do Couto, author of nine volumes in the *Décadas da Ásia* series begun by the Crown's chronicler João de Barros.[19] Barros was a court favorite and given the prestigious post of treasurer of the Casa da Índia, de Mina e de Ceuta in Lisbon.[20] Dom Sebastião awarded him for his years of service with the Brazilian *capitania* of Maranhão, a land grant of enormous proportions that, like all but one, failed miserably because of absentee ownership or lack of experience in settling the new land. In his own *Décadas da Ásia* works, Barros describes the heady early years of expansionism as a just, righteous, and glorious cause, a view reiterated in his *Panegíricos*, dedicated to João III and the Infanta Dona Maria. Unlike his contemporary Fernão Lopes de Castanheda, Barros remained at home, writing about a bygone, idealized era in the classical style he knew so well rather than about unfamiliar realities and the rigors of daily life abroad.

Diogo do Couto was a less privileged member of the court who left Portugal for India at an early age. He spent close to sixty years there, with few return trips to Lisbon. Undoubtedly the most memorable of these journeys back to Portugal was in the company of a destitute Camões, whom he had met while both were soldiers in India. Literary historian Antônio Bragança has noted that Couto was no less patriotic than Barros, but he was an eyewitness to the mismanagement and greed of the privileged few soldier-privateers and merchants overseas who cloaked their misdeeds in the name of empire and king. Couto even states in *Décadas da Ásia* that circumstances did not allow him to disclose all the wrongdoings in his writings, but he adds that he would provide details if anyone were to inquire. In this regard, Couto was more forceful than Castanheda, who returned to Portugal with little fanfare and became a minor official at the Universidade de Coimbra.[21]

If Couto's readers were surprised by his remarks in *Décadas da Ásia*, several volumes of which were lost to fire and under other, less clear circumstances, his posthumously published treatise, *Observações sobre as principais causas da decadência na Ásia* (1790) (Observations on the principle causes of decadence in Asia), which is best known by its subtitle, *Diálogo do soldado prático, que trata dos enganos e desenganos na Índia* (The veteran soldier's dialogue that deals with the deceptions and disillusionments in India), and was later published as *O soldado prático*, was a more aggressive denunciation and a requiem of sorts to a promised land turned paradise lost. Critic Manuel Rodrigues Lapa, who wrote the preface to the 1937 edition, considered the book to be essential reading alongside *Os lusíadas*.[22]

Using dialogue form, a literary style later adopted by writers such as Antônio Fernandes Brandão in *Diálogos das grandezas do Brasil* (1618; *Dialogues of the Great Things of Brazil* [1986]) and Nuno Marques Pereira in *Compêndio narrativo do peregrino da América* (1728; Narrative compendium of the pilgrim from America) to celebrate Brazil, the book's conversations are between the soldier, a judge, and a nobleman and former governor of India. Looking to his interlocutors, who stand in for the Crown, the soldier seeks recognition and proper compensation for his many years of service in India. In doing so, he draws attention to the ineptitude, deceit, and corruption of certain overseas administrators responsible for the empire's moral decline since the glory days of Dom Manuel, who also was known as Lord of the Conquest, Navigation, and Commerce of Ethiopia, Arabia, Persia, and India. The soldier reinforces his complaint by telling his listeners that were Dom Manuel still living, he would die of disgust and shame at the state of things. Knowing full well that his book could result in serious retribution by the Spanish, who were then in control of Portugal, Couto retrofitted the dialogues so they take place when Dom Sebastião was on the throne, prior to the Iberian Union.

In many ways, Couto's book takes up where the diatribe by Camões's Old Man of Restelo left off. It is also a sober treatise on what Vicente, in his satirical *Auto da Índia*, describes as the rank and file's mistreatment by men of questionable noble lineage, such as officials in the Casa dos Contos (Accounting House) in Goa. Critical references to elitism and royal favoritism are everywhere in the volume: "[Muitos] fidalgos que são chamados a conselho . . . não têm experiência de nada; mas é esta maldição portuguesa tal, sua desconfiança tamanha, que homem que não é fidalgo não é chamado para nada: tendo exemplo em todas as outras nações em que se tem mais respeito à idade e experiência que no sangue e nobreza" (92). (Many noblemen who are called to advise . . . have absolutely no experience. But this Portuguese accursedness is such and so great is its distrust of others that any man who is not a nobleman is never called for anything: yet there are examples in every other nation where age and experience are more respected than a noble bloodline.) Denied respect and adequate compensation, Couto's soldier argues his case for justice and compensation.

Written later in life, O soldado prático is evidence of Couto's unabated dissatisfaction with what he viewed as an empire bereft of pride and moral virtue and whose mercantile interests overshadowed its proselytizing mission. Disillusioned, he turned his back on Lisbon and rarely left Goa, where he married, had a family, and died, in 1616. According to critic Álvaro Manuel Machado, Couto requested that the epitaph on his tombstone read, "Pátria ingrata, não possuirás meus ossos" (Ungrateful country, you shall not have my bones)—a final admonishment to his homeland.[23]

The power of Couto's Décadas da Ásia and O soldado prático derives from an in-depth knowledge of the quotidian workings of Portuguese rule in Goa. Couto's life there was relatively sedentary and contrasts sharply with that of his contemporary Fernão Mendes Pinto. Author of the celebrated Peregrinação (1614; The Travels of Mendes Pinto [1989]), Mendes Pinto was constantly on the move during his twenty-one years abroad, and his book is sweeping in its geographic focus. Written years after his adventures, at his home outside Lisbon, the volume offers a cornucopia of information about people and traditions in India, China, and Japan. Its chief virtue is its quasi-ethnographic commentary about local inhabitants, which is similar to, yet far greater in scope than, Caminha's letter about the indigenous people of Brazil.[24]

Oscillating between fact and fantasy, Peregrinação is a first-person account in the picaresque style of an antihero and his many adventures. The narrative also brings to mind the Stations of the Cross, a journey of immense suffering for a higher cause that in Mendes Pinto's case was considerably more material than spiritual. Like Couto, Mendes Pinto repeatedly comments on Portugal's failure to reward adequately those who served their country without the benefit of royal appointment. In fact, he concludes his book by describing the years futilely spent in Lisbon after his return in 1558, waiting for royal compensation:

> E vendo quão pouco me fundiam assim os trabalhos e serviços passados como o requerimento presente, determinei de me recolher com essa miséria que trouxera comigo, adquirida por mérito de muitos trabalhos e infortúnios . . . e deixar o feito à justiça divina, o qual logo pus por obra, pesando-me ainda por que o não fizera mais cedo, porque se assim o fizera, quiçá me poupara nisso um bom pedaço de fazenda. (2:362)

> (Recognizing that I, along with my works and past service, was so little valued, I decided to withdraw [from Lisbon to a country home] with the niggardly sum that I had brought with me and had acquired based on the merit of my many labors and misfortunes . . . and leave the matter to divine justice, which I did forthwith, regretting not having done so earlier and saving myself a good deal of money.)

His final words are not nearly as disdainful as Couto's dictum from the grave, but since no divine justice ever appeared, Mendes Pinto took the matter into his own hands and wrote his self-acclamation.

Critic Joan-Pau Rubiés has noted important distinctions to be made between Mendes Pinto's interests and those of Barros, Castanheda, and Couto. For these three royal chroniclers, local people and new lands served as background and color in narratives about empire.[25] For Mendes Pinto, locals were protagonists and often catalysts for events that occur in his book. Whether fictional or factual, his detailed topographic and ethnographic descriptions also call attention to civilizations removed from the coast. The hinterlands in India and other colonies were little known to the Portuguese, who were so closely identified with the sea that the Chinese in the sixteenth century compared them to "fish out of water" when they ventured onto land (Flores, "They Have Discovered Us," 192). A century later, a governor of the South China provinces Guangdong and Guangxi elaborated on this view, stating that "os portugueses não tinham terras, nem ainda que as tivessem as podiam nem sabiam lavrar" (the Portuguese had no lands and, even if they did, they would not know how to tend them) (in Barreto and Flores, *O espelho invertido*, 26).

Mendes Pinto is fairly equitable in his treatment of both pious and heinous acts committed by Europeans and Asians. He devotes 40 of *Pere-*

PEREGRINAÇAM

DE FERNAM MENDEZ
PINTO.

EM QVE DA CONTA DE MVYTAS E MVY-
to eftranhas coufas que vio & ouuio no reyno da China,no da Tar-
taria,no do Sornau,que vulgarmente fe chama Sião,no do Calami-
nhan,no de Pegù,no de Martauão,& em outros muytos reynos
& fenhorios das partes Orientais, de que neftas noffas
do Occidente ha muyto pouca ou
nenhũa noticia.

E TAMBEM DA CONTA DE MVYTOS CASOS PARTI-
culares que acontecerão afsi a elle como a outras muytas peffoas. E no fim della trata bre-
uemente de algũas coufas,& da morte do fanto Padre meftre Francifco Xauier,
vnica luz & refplandor daquellas partes do Oriente,& Reytor
nellas vniuerfal da Companhia de Iefus.

Efcrita pelo mefmo Fernão Mendez Pinto.

Dirigido à Catholica Real Mageftade del Rey dom Felippe o III.
defte nome noffo Senhor.

Com licença do fanto Officio, Ordinario,& Paço.

EM LISBOA. Por Pedro Crasbeeck. Anno 1614.
A cufta de Belchior ide Faria Caualeyro da cafa del Rey noffo
Senhor,& feu Liureyro.   Com priuilegio Real.
Eftà taixado efte liuro a 600 reis em papel.

1.5. Peregrinação *title page (1614). Courtesy of The Lilly Library, Indiana University–Bloomington.*

ginação's 226 short chapters to a first-person account by privateer and doppelgänger António de Farias, whose cruelty contrasts sharply with the antihero's sufferings.[26] The book contains another twenty chapters on a psychopathic Brahmin king who is the opposite of the chivalrous Siamese leader Xemindó. Although Mendes Pinto is not the first to comment on the "civilized" Chinese, he provides the reader with information on their conduct, governance, commerce, and arts as the basis for his evaluation of their superior society. His enthusiastic commentary on Peking resembles the rhapsodic *ufanismo* of sixteenth-century writings on Brazil:

Afirmaram-nos os chins que tem esta cidade oitocentos mil vizinhos e
vinte e quatro mil casas de mandarins, e sessenta e duas praças muito
grandes, e cento e trinta casas de açougues, de oitenta talhos cada uma,
e oito mil ruas, de que seiscentas, que são as mais nobres, têm todas
ao comprido, de uma banda e da outra, grades de latão muito gros-
sas, feitas ao torno. . . . Todas estas ruas nobres têm arcos nas entra-
das, com suas portas que se fecham de noite, e as mais delas têm chafa-
rizes de água muito boa e são em si muito ricas e de muito grande trato.
. . . O pescado deste rio é tanto, em tanta quantidade . . . que parece
impossível dizer-se, o qual se vende todo vivo, com juncos metidos
pelos narizes por onde vêm dependurados, e afora este peixe pescado
fresco, o seco e salgado que vem do mar é tambem infinito. Afirmaram-
nos mais os chins, que tinha dez mil teares de seda, porque daqui vai
para todo o reino . . . e que rendia esta cidade a el-rei todos os dias dois
mil taéis de prata, que são três mil cruzados, como já disse muitas vezes.
(*Pereginação*, 1:247–248)

(The Chinese inform us that the city has eight hundred thousand
inhabitants, four thousand homes occupied by Mandarins, sixty-two
enormous central squares, one hundred thirty slaughterhouses, each
with eighty butcher blocks, and eight thousand streets, six hundred of
which are majestic and bordered with brass latticework that stretches
their entire length. . . . All these streets have archway entrances whose
doors are closed at night, and most of them have richly styled and well-
tended fountains with very good and healthy water. . . . The fish from the
river are so many and in such great quantity that it seems impossible to
imagine, and they sell them still alive, with hooks through their noses
from which they are hung, and besides this fresh fish, there are dried and
salted fish from the sea that are of infinite number. The Chinese also tell
us that the city has ten thousand silk looms that produce all the silk for
the realm . . . and that every day the city pays two thousand silver taels
[coins] to the king, which is the equivalent of three thousand cruzados,
as I have repeatedly observed.)

It is noteworthy that most of the narrator's attention is on material as opposed to natural wealth, which was the principal subject of early writings
on Brazil. Large monetary transactions are especially good indicators of
a civilized society; here, as elsewhere in the book, the narrator carefully
records them and provides exchange-rate valuations for his readers.

Mendes Pinto also refers in his memoir to Tomé Pires, who was scribe, accountant, and controller of drugs in India and Malacca between 1511 and 1516; *A Suma oriental*, 1:xxv). Although of humble origins, Pires was a royally appointed ambassador to China; *A Suma oriental* includes ethnographic commentary on the Chinese that is interesting to read alongside *Peregrinação* as well as documents such as Pero Vaz de Caminha's letter on Brazil, that appears in *Os três únicos testemunhos do descobrimento do Brasil*, edited by Paulo Roberto Pereira. Pires begins his narrative on China as follows:

> Segundo o que as nações de que deste levanter contam, fazem as coisas da China grandes assim na terra como gentes riquezas pompas estados & contas outras que mais se creriam com verdade a verem-se em nosso Portugal que não na China. É grande a terra da China de fermosos cavalos & mulas, segundo dizem, e em grande número.
>
> O Rei da China é gentio de grande terra e gente. É a gente da China branca da nossa alvura. Vestem os mais panos pretos de algodão & disso trazem saios de cinco de nesgas assim como nós, somente saem muito largos. Trazem na China nos invernos feltros nas pernas à maneira de peúgas e em cima botas bem obradas que não chegam do joelho para cima & trazem suas roupas forradas de peles cordeiras & de outras pelitarias. Trazem deles pelicas. Trazem coisas de rede de seda redondas como peneiras pretas de nosso Portugal. Tem um jeito de alemães: tem na barba trinta [ou] quarenta cabelos [e] calçam sapatos franceses de ponto de ladrilho muito bem feitos.
>
> Comem todos os chins porcos[,] vacas e de todas outras alimárias bebem gentilmente de toda sorte de beberagens. Gabam muito nosso vinho. Embeberam-se grandemente. É gente fraca & para pouco. Esta que se vê em Malacca são de pouca verdade & furtam isto a gente baixa. Comem com dois paus & altamija ou porcelana na mão esquerda junto com a boca & com os dois paus sorver esta é a guisa da China.
>
> As mulheres parecem castelhanas. Têm saias de refuegos e coisas & sainhos mais compridos que em nossa terra. Os cabelos compridos em rodilhados compridos põem gentil maneira em cima da cabeça e lançam neles muitos pregos de ouro para os ter & ao redor da pedraria quem há tem e sobre a moleira jóias de ouro e nas orelhas & pescoço. Põem muito alavaiade nas faces e arrabique sobre ele e são alcoforadas que Sevilha lhe não leva a vantagem. E bebem como mulheres de terra fria. Trazem sapatos de pontilha de seda e brocados. Trazem todas abanicos na mão; são da nossa alvura & delas têm os olhos pequenos e outras grandes. E narizes como hão de ser. (*A suma oriental*, 252–253)

(According to what the nations here in the East say, things of China are made out to be great, riches, pomp and state in both the land and people, and other tales which it would be easier to believe as true of our Portugal than of China. China is a large country with beautiful horses and mules, they say, in large numbers.

The king of China is a heathen with much land and many people. The people of China are white, as white as we are. Most of them wear black cotton cloth, and they wear sayons of this in five pieces with gores, as we do, only they are very white. In the winter they wear felt on their legs by way of socks, and on the top well-made boots which do not reach about the knee, and they wear their clothes lined with lambskin and other furs. Some of them wear pelisses. They wear silk net caps like the black sieves we have in Portugal . . . They are rather like Germans. They have thirty or forty hairs in their beard. They wear very-well made French shoes with square toes.

All the Chinese eat pigs, cows and all other animals. They drink a fair amount of all sorts of beverages. They praise our wine greatly. They get pretty drunk. They are weak people, of small account. Those who are to be seen in Malacca are not very truthful, and steal—that is the common people. They eat with two sticks and their earthenware or china bowl in their left hand close to their mouth, with the two sticks to suck in. This is the Chinese way.

The women look a lot like Spanish women. They wear pleated skirts with waistbands, and little loose coats longer than in our country. Their long hair is rolled in a graceful way on the top of their heads, and they put many gold pins in it to hold it, and those who have them put precious stones around, and golden jewelry on the crown of their heads and in their ears and on their necks. They put a great deal of ceruse on their faces and paint on the top of it, and they are so made up that Seville has no advantage over them; and they drink like women from a cold country. They wear pointed slippers of silk and brocade. They all carry fans in their hands. They are as white as we are, and some of them have small eyes and others large, and noses as they must be.) (*The Suma Oriental*, 1:116–117)

For Barros, Camões, and the increasingly disenchanted Couto, India was a promised land for trade as well as the spread of Christianity among those who, like Caminha's Tupi, were thought to be ripe for conversion.[27] Of humble stock and without royal connections, Mendes Pinto hired on with different expeditions in seeking his fortune; like many other Portuguese in Asia and explorer-*bandeirantes* (flag bearers) in Brazil, he served the imperial cause by opening new territories for commerce. Toward the end of his travels, he met the Jesuit Francisco Xavier (later canonized as Saint Francis Xavier) and was a novitiate in the order for a few years. Mendes Pinto served on missions to Japan, and though the achievement is discounted today, he laid further claim as the first European to set foot on Japanese soil.[28]

The Christian God is everywhere present in *Peregrinação*, and the recognition of sin and the desire for salvation are constants. A self-proclaimed sinner, Mendes Pinto thanks God for seeing him through shipwrecks, thirteen captivities, and the seventeen times he was sold into slavery. In a final commentary, he praises God for sparing him to write his "rude e tosca" memoir. Rebecca Catz has noted that by the end of the seventeenth century, Mendes Pinto's "crude and uncultured" book had passed through nineteen editions in six languages (introduction, xxvii), a bestseller more widely read in Europe than Cervantes's *Don Quixote*. *Peregrinação*'s historiographic value lies in its portrait of empire not as one of complete subjugation but rather as one of human interaction and acts of "diplomacy and negotiation" that far supersede "the epic thrust of a single nation or a single system of beliefs" (Rubiés, "Oriental Voices," 42). The exploits of its anti-hero are necessary reading for anyone interested in the Portuguese empire and the Luso-Asiatic encounter. Albeit posthumously, Mendes Pinto finally gained the recognition he sought — ironically, not as a veteran in the service of his country but as a writer of autobiographical fiction.

Although *Peregrinação* is not an example, many writings about the diaspora incorporated elaborate representations of lands and peoples by artists who often never left Portugal and therefore had no real knowledge of their locations in the world or characteristics. At the same time, artisans in Africa, India, and Asia were producing extraordinary works that testify to the Portuguese presence. In Angola, the Kongo people fashioned crucifixes and missionary figurines out of brass pieces traded by the Portuguese. Colorful sixteenth-century miniatures from Goa depict well-to-do or "honored" Portuguese men and women alongside Indian companions who are Christian converts and wear European dress (plate 6). These works are especially significant in representing the presence in India of Portuguese women, whose population was inordinately small.[29]

As the Portuguese capital in India, Goa was a center and crossroads for Hindi artists and others who, though not of the Catholic faith, were hired to carve façades and paint religious scenes for Jesuit churches and schools.[30] Among local items produced for religious orders as well as for

1.6. Ceylon-Portuguese casket (18th century)

export were beautifully carved oratories, filigree-style crosses, and lacquered chests and altar pieces in teak and ebony with ivory and mother-
of-pearl inlays (plate 7).[31] Furniture was often embellished with Catholic
icons, the symbolic *quinas* (shields), or a nobleman's coat of arms. Religious figurines were especially desirable trade items, and some of the finest
came from Macau. Ming Dynasty artists also created delicate porcelains
decorated with maritime symbols and Latin inscriptions that attested to
the Catholic presence (plate 8). Images of the astrolabe were often incorporated into porcelain designs and woven into tapestries.[32]

Few artworks of the period compare in size and beauty with the multi-
paneled folding screens produced in Japan by Kanō Naizan, Kanō Domi,
and others, a number of which, fortunately, have survived. Among the
subjects in these pictorials are the Namban—Portuguese men also known
as "southern barbarians"—departing Goa and arriving in Nagasaki, the
name given to the Portuguese diocese; Jesuits and other religious figures
in prayer or walking along streets; and Portuguese merchants engaged in
trade.[33] Because trade required laborers and slaves, their presence is also
richly documented. Most appear to be locals, but several are Africans. The
Japanese traveled from miles around to witness the Portuguese presence,
Mendes Pinto observed: "vinham de quinze léguas de distância . . . depois

1.7. Chinese Ming Dynasty Virgin Mary (16th century)

1.8. Afro-Indo-Portuguese chair (16th century)

recebiam-nos em ceremônias (in M. Mendes Pinto, *Biombos*, 14) (they came from fifteen leagues away . . . [and] then received us ceremoniously).

Portuguese traders are readily identifiable because of their billowing *bombachas (pantaloons)*, shirts, and tall hats often symbolic of practitioners of the Christian faith. The Portuguese were often referred to as "homens de chapéu" (hat-wearing men); hats are prominent in Asian iconographies of them as well as other Europeans in the period (Barreto and Flores, *O espelho invertido*, 30). The screens show the Portuguese and their entourages as active figures who parade along streets while engaging in conversation or transporting goods. Some appear on horseback, overseeing the loading and unloading of ship goods, and others are doing business in local shops. Depicted in delicately designed and colorful robes, Japanese shopkeepers and their families tend to be represented mostly indoors, peeking from windows and doorways at the passing foreigners (plates 9 and 10). Other examples of Namban artwork are iron stirrups with inlaid brass and silver and red lacquer on which Portuguese figures appear (plate 11). According to historian Michael Cooper, Japanese nobles who owned objects such as Namban stirrups and saddles with Portuguese iconography wanted to show their acceptance of Europe and modernity.[34]

Iconic images of the Portuguese in Asia appear on dinnerware, ceramics, porcelain, and even weaponry that were produced in China and Japan.

1.9. *Portuguese ship arriving in Nagasaki. Namban screen (late 16th century).*

1.10. Replica of Saint Lawrence cannon (1627), with Portuguese shield and cross

One of the most artistically lavish of large weapons is the 1627 Saint Lawrence bronze cannon produced by the foundry of Manuel Tavares de Bocarro in Macau, which was often referred to as the Cidade do Nome de Deus (City whose name means God). Christian figures, the *quinas*, and a cross appear on the cannon alongside two dragonlike sea creatures that represent the Asiatic presence.[35] All the large cannons produced by the foundry were positioned on the hilltop fortress, Fortaleza do Monte (now the Macau Museum), to protect the city, and each was named after a Catholic saint. During World War II, they were sold by the government of Macau to the Japanese in exchange for rice.[36] Cannon replicas now grace the former fortress exterior, one of which is pointed at the garishly opulent Grand Lisboa, a huge lotus-shaped hotel-casino and the tallest building in Macau.[37]

THE JESUIT PRESENCE IN THE FAR EAST

Chinese and Japanese artists generously illustrated the Portuguese missionary presence; on one Namban screen panel, for example, dark-robed priests sit under a covered shelter with their heads bowed in prayer.

Other missionary imagery is of churches and an oratory with a cross.[38] While Portuguese illustrations often represented New World natives as classical-style cannibals, Japanese works seem less hybrid in their presentation of Occidentals and Africans, although merchants and priests on Namban screens have Asiatic eyes. In a category of its own is sixteenth-century artwork that features an Orientalized Francis Xavier, the charismatic Apostle of the Indies who preached in the Far East and whose dedication to the Christianizing cause in Japan resulted in his canonization, along with that of his friend and Society of Jesus founder Ignatius of Loyola, just seventy years after Xavier's death.[39]

Xavier's letters home are important testimonies to the imperial mission and the Portuguese diaspora during what was known as the *século cristão* (Christian century).[40] In a letter dated October 20, 1542, shortly after his arrival in India, he urged his superior to increase the Jesuit presence there to avoid the defection of local converts whose communities had no priests. He expressed concern that university study—especially among fellow Jesuits at the Sorbonne—had eclipsed the importance of missionary work. In a letter to his superior, he advocated that his colleagues adopt a selfless attitude and pray to God to be sent wherever God felt the need,

1.11. *Print of rubbing from original cannon (1627)*

1.12. *View from Museu de Macau toward Grand Lisboa casino*

1.13. *An Asiatic Saint Francis, Francisco Xavier (1600)*

even as far away as India. In 1549, on his way to Japan, Xavier reiterated his concern in a letter to Padre Simão Rodrigues back in Lisbon:

> Escreverei . . . principalmente à de Paris, para lhes lembrar que não vivam em tanto descuido, fazendo tanto fundamento de letras, descuidando-se da ignorância dos gentios.
>   Espantarão muitos meus amigos de fazer uma viagem tão comprida e tão perigosa, e eu me espanto mais deles, em ver a pouco fé que têm; . . . pois N. Senhor tem poder sobre as tempestades do mar da China e

Japão, e baixos que são muitos conforme ao que dizem, aonde se per-
dem muitos navios, e sobre todos os ladrões do mar, que há tantos que
é coisa de espanto. . . . E como Deus N. Senhor tenha poder sobre todos
estes, a ninguém tenho [medo] senão a Deus, que me dê algum castigo
por ser negligente em seu serviço, inhábil e inútil para acrescentar e
estender o nome de Jesus Cristo entre gente que o não conhece.
(In Fróis, *História de Japam*, 1:19–20)

(I'll write . . . especially to those in Paris to remind them not to be so
dedicated to the study of letters that they forget the needs of the natives.
  My friends are amazed by the idea of making such a long and dangerous voyage, yet I am astonished by them and the little faith they have;
. . . as Our Lord has power over storms in the China and Japan seas,
which are greater now than ever before, and over the winds and shoals
that are considerable and, according to sources, have destroyed many of
our ships, and over the sea-faring robbers, who are so many it is fright-
ening. . . . And since God Our Father has command over all these things,
I fear only Him that he might punish me for being negligent and failing to carry out His mission to spread the name of Jesus Christ among
people who do not know him.)

Xavier cut a huge missionary swath through Asia, through India,
Malacca (Malaysia), China, and Japan. According to Jesuit historian
Andrew C. Ross, Xavier's success in Japan can be partially attributed to his
interest in incorporating aspects of the local language and culture into his
proselytizing mission; as such, he demonstrated a level of curiosity about
the Other that was characteristic of the intellectually inclined Jesuits but
far from commonplace among builders of the empire (*Vision Betrayed*,
19–20).
  Xavier's letters home, which were printed and circulated widely, are
no doubt partly responsible for the mystique that Japan in particular held
for Portuguese writers such as Wenceslau de Moraes in the nineteenth century.[41] In a letter dated 1552, Xavier wrote,

Esta terra de Japão é muito grande em extremo. São ilhas. Em toda esta
terra não há mais que uma língua, e esta não é muito difícil de tomar. Há
oito ou nove anos que foram descobertas estas ilhas de Japão pelos Portugueses. São os japões gente de muita opinião em lhes parecer que em
armas e cavalaria não há outros como eles. Gente é que tem em pouco a
toda a outra gente estrangeira.

. . . É gente de grande cortesia entre eles ainda que com estrangeiros não usam aquelas cortesias, porque os têm em pouco. Em vestidos, armas e criados, gastam tudo quanto têm, sem guarder tesouros. São muito belicosos e vivem sempre em guerras, e quem mais pode é mais senhor. É gente que tem um só rei, porém há mais de cento e cinquenta anos que lhe não obedecem, e por esta causa continuam as guerras entre eles. (In Paulino and Oliveira e Costa, eds., *O Japão visto pelos portugueses*, 40)

(This land of Japan is very large in extension. They are islands. Throughout the land there is but one language and that is not very difficult to learn. These islands of Japan were discovered by the Portuguese eight or nine years ago. The Japanese people are very opinionated, believing there are no others as experienced in weaponry and equestrian skill. These are people who show little respect for all other foreigners.

. . . They are a people that show great politeness among themselves, although they do not extend the same courtesies to foreigners who think little of others. They spend everything they have on clothing, weapons, and servants because they have so few of them. They are very bellicose and are constantly at war, and whoever has the most power is the one who wins out. They have only one king, but for the last one hundred and fifty years they have not obeyed him, and this is why they continue to fight among themselves.)

Xavier also comments on the innate intellectual curiosity of the Japanese:

São tão curiosos e importunos em perguntar, tão desejosos de saber, que nunca acabam de perguntar e falar aos outros as coisas que lhes respondemos às suas perguntas. Não sabiam eles [que] o mundo é redondo, nem sabiam o curso do Sol, perguntando eles por estas coisas e por outras como dos cometas, relâmpagos, chuva e neve e outras semelhantes, a que nós respondendo e declarando-lhas, ficavam muito contentes e satisfeitos, tendo-nos por homens doutos, o que ajudou não pouco para darem crédito a nossas palavras. (Ibid., 41–42)

(They are so curious and inopportune in their questions, so desirous of knowledge that they never stop asking and speaking to others about things that we tell them in response. They did not know that the earth is round, nor did they know the rotation of the Sun, asking us about these and other things, such as comets, lightning, rain and snow and the like. They appear very happy and satisfied with our responses, and consider us educated men—a fact that has helped no little in giving credence to our words.)

Native curiosity is a characteristic likewise ascribed by Camões to the foreign Other in *Os lusíadas*.

A sixteenth-century Japanese point of view of the Occidental Other is worth noting here from a work titled *Teppo Ki* and later translated as *Crónica da espingarda* (1606). Like the Xavier letters immediately above, it is quoted in O *Japão visto pelos portugueses*, published in 1993 by the Comissão Nacional to commemorate Portugal's former colonial reach:

> Estes homens, bárbaros do Sudeste, são comerciantes. Compreendem até certo ponto a distinção entre superior e inferior, mas não sei se existe entre eles um sistema próprio de etiqueta. Bebem em copo sem o oferecerem aos outros; comem com os dedos, e não com pauzinhos como nós. Mostram seus sentimentos sem nenhum rebuço. Não compreendem o significado dos caracteres escritos. São gente que passa a vida errando de aqui para além, sem morada certa, e trocam as coisas que possuem pelas que não têm, mas no fundo são gente que não faz mal. (Ibid., 37)

> (These men, barbarians from the Southeast, are merchants. They understand to a certain point the distinction between superior and inferior, but I do not know if a proper system of etiquette exists among them. They drink from a cup without offering it to others; they eat with their fingers and not with sticks as we do. They show their feelings openly. They do not understand the meaning of written characters. They are a people who spend their lives wandering from here to there, and they exchange their possessions for things that they do not have. But on the whole, they are not a bad people.)

Among Jesuits inspired by Xavier's call for missionaries was Padre Luís Fróis, who lived in India and later Japan. He wrote invaluable reports on Xavier's as well as his own Far East experiences; these were collected and published centuries later as the five-volume *História de Japam*.[42] His commentary on Xavier's healthy debates with *bonzos* (Buddhist priests) gives a sense of the future saint's more accommodating approach to missionary work in Japan.[43] Fróis's history portrays the rugged life of a traveling Jesuit, although he adds from time to time a pinch of humor. In a 1550 report, he describes the rigors faced by Xavier in his winter journey to Miaco (Kyoto):

> E muitas vezes eram as neves tão grandes, que lhe davam em partes pelos joelhos, e em outras daí para riba. Acertando de encontrarem com um homem, que ia enfadado da neve, lhes disse: "Se vós outros sois do Tengicu (que quer dizer os templos dos céus), porque não dizeis lá em riba que não deitem cá tanta neve?" E era, de noite, o frio tão intenso e penetrante que, pela roupa ser pouca que levavam, às vezes o Pe. Mestre Francisco deitava em cima de si os tatamis com que estava esteirada a caça, e ainda com isso não podia receber quentura. Passavam rios fridigíssimos, uns lhe davam pelos joelhos, e outros quase pela cinta; e o Padre ia descalço, até que se embarcaram em um porto para dalí irem ao Sacai. (1:35)

> (And oftentimes the snows were so great that in some areas they were up to the knees, and in others, they reached even higher. Coming across a man who was complaining about the snow, they asked him: "If you all are from Tengicu (which means the temples of the heaven), why can't you tell them up above not to drop so much snow?" And at night the cold was so intense and penetrating that, lacking sufficient clothing, Padre Francisco lay under the straw mats on which the fruits of the hunt were stretched out, and even that did not warm him. They walked through extremely icy rivers, with waters up to the knees, and other times up to their waist. And the padre went barefoot until they left the port city to go to Sacai.)

By the end of the sixteenth century, several religious primers had been translated into Japanese, among them Luis de Granada's *Guía de pecadores* (Guide for sinners), which was published in Nagasaki in 1599. The Italian-born Jesuit Alessandro Valignano, who was appointed to oversee the mission in Japan and about whom Fróis writes extensively, adopted conversionary tactics that included training priests in the local language, an approach that Portuguese Jesuits in Brazil had already adopted in their work with the Tupi.[44] One of the important publications to appear as a result of Valignano's accommodating methodology was a Latin-Japanese-Portuguese dictionary that became the model for a Japanese-Spanish version.[45] Valignano also led a delegation of four young Japanese ambassadors to Portugal in 1582, who came back bearing a printing press with movable

1.14. *Japanese "hidden" Christians in Portuguese dress (16th–17th century)*

type; shortly after their return, the young men entered the order (Teixeira, "Japoneses em Macau," 204). Other important works that appeared as a result of Valignano's efforts were Padre João Rodrigues's *Arte breve da língua japoa* (1604–1608, Brief art of the Japanese language), the first Japanese grammar to be written, and *Vocabulário da língua de Japão com a declaração em português, feito por alguns padres e irmãos da Companhia de Jesus* (1603, Vocabulary of the language of Japan with commentary in Portuguese by some priests and brothers of the Society of Jesus), both of which were published in Nagasaki.[46] By the beginning of the seventeenth century, when these books first appeared, there were approximately one-half million Catholics in Japan, or slightly more than 6 percent of the population.

Reports of enslaved Japanese, forced conversions, and transgressions against Japanese tradition gradually led the Japanese to expel the Jesuits and other missionaries in 1641; two years earlier, the Japanese had cut off all trade with the Portuguese in Macau. Priests who remained in Japan risked crucifixion, and some were crucified before the order's official expulsion. A letter by the Jesuit Domingos de Brito lists other forms of execution used and the number executed, among them thirty-two who were slowly burned to death, eighteen who were hung upside down, and three who were decapitated.[47] A diaspora made up of priests and Christian converts headed to Manila, Macau, Siam, and elsewhere (Teixeira, "Japoneses em Macau," 210). In 1640, an official Portuguese delegation was sent to Nagasaki to try to convince the Japanese to repeal the trade embargo. After arriving, most of the envoys were seized, jailed, sentenced to death, and decapitated. The story of their martyrdom is the subject of Jesuit António Francisco Cardim's *Relaçaõ da gloriosa morte de quatro embaixadores portugueses, da cidade de Macao, com cinquenta e sete cristãos de sua companhia, degolados todos pela fé de Cristo em Nagasaki, cidade de Japão, a três de agosto de 1640: com todas as circunstâncias de sua embaixada, tirada de informações verdadeiras e testemunhas de vista* (1643) (Report on the glorious death of four Portuguese ambassadors, from the city of Macau, accompanied by fifty-seven Christians, all of whom were decapitated for their Christian faith in Nagasaki, city of Japan, on the third of August 1640: with all the circumstances of their embassy, based on true information and eyewitnesses).

Cardim's document provides detailed information on the preparation of the delegation's execution, which, in addition to the four Portuguese noblemen-ambassadors, included seamen and others from Spain, India, China, Timor, and Malabar. Thirteen in the mission were spared and returned to Macau in a small boat. According to their accounts, the Japanese wanted to ensure that they reported everything that happened in Nagasaki. Their accounts focused on their seizure and treatment by the Japanese and the company's last days in prayer, "até os negros boçais entre si" (10) (even the black slaves among them). Cardim reports that the four ambassadors were the first to be executed, and he describes in detail the increasing number of blows required as each one queued up to be beheaded. The victims ranged in age from eight to sixty-eight years. Their severed heads were nailed to boards and later destroyed along with their ship. Addressing his narrative to Dom João IV, Cardim ends the document solemnly with the names and short biographies of the deceased.[48] A Latin version of this report includes an engraving that depicts the imminent decapitations.[49] Japanese-Portuguese commercial and diplomatic relations did not resume until 1860.

RELAÇAÕ
DA
GLORIOSA MORTE
DE QVATRO EMBAIXADORES
Portuguezes, da Cidade de Macao, com sincoen
ta, & sete Christaõs de sua companhia, dego
lados todos pella fee de Christo em Nan-
gassaqui, Cidade de Iappaõ, a tres de
Agosto de 1640.

COM TODAS AS CIRCVNSTANCIAS
de sua Embaixada, tirada de informaçoës verdadeiras, & testemunhas de vista.

PELLO PADRE ANTONIO FRANCISCO
Cardim da Companhia de IESV Procurádor
géral da Prouincia de Iappaõ

EM LISBOA.

Com todas as licenças necessarias.

Na Officina de Lourenço de Anueres Anno de 1643.

Taxão esta Relaçaõ em vinte & sinco reis em papel.
Lisboa. 14. de Ianeiro de 1643.
Meneses.   Coelho.

1.15. *Frontispiece of* Relação da gloriosa morte *(1643).*
Courtesy of The Lilly Library, Indiana University–Bloomington.

THE INQUISITION, THE JEWISH DIASPORA, AND SHIPWRECKS AT SEA

In addition to soldiers, administrators, adventurers, and Jesuits, the diaspora included Jews and "New Christians" (Jews who had undergone conversion), who fled the Conselho Geral do Santo Ofício (General Council of the Holy Office)—the Inquisition—established in Portugal in 1536 by Dom João III. While Jesuits abroad were busy converting locals and trying to keep Portuguese colonizers from exploiting the native population, the Inquisition denounced and punished New Christians and others who were suspected of secretly practicing "heretical" faiths. In Portuguese colonies such as Goa, the Inquisition carried out investigations of Jewish, Hindi, and Muslim converts. (Apparently Xavier's 1545 and later pleas to the Crown to send officials to protect the converts from slavery and other exploitations by the Portuguese were partially responsible for the Inquisition's 1560 installation in Goa.[50]) Punishments at home and abroad ranged from interrogations and torture to jail terms, deportation, and autos-da-fé, in which individuals were burned at the stake. The Inquisition also censored materials published in the realm and ultimately grew to influence nearly every aspect of life in Portugal.

Among the victims of the Inquisition in Goa was Garcia de Orta, a New Christian who authored one of the most important volumes to appear in the sixteenth century. Born of Jewish parentage in 1501 in Castelo de Vide, Orta studied medicine in Spain and in 1526 moved to Lisbon, where he became one of Dom João III's physicians. He left for India in 1534 as the personal physician to Martim Afonso de Sousa, a captain and later governor of India, and settled in Goa, where he befriended Camões and conducted pioneer medical research using tropical plants. In 1563, he published *Colóquios dos simples, e drogas e coisas medicinais da India e assim dalgumas frutas: achadas nela onde se tratam algumas coisas tocan-*

1.16. *Execution of the condemned by the Inquisition at Lisbon's Terreiro do Paço (1722)*

tes a medicina, prática, e outras coisas boas para saber (Colloquies of reme-
dies and drugs and medicinal things from India and also of some fruits:
Found there where things pertaining to medicine, practice, and other good
things to know are discussed). Translated into Latin in 1567, his study was
acclaimed throughout Europe as a primer for scientists and physicians.
Historian Charles R. Boxer wrote in his personal copy of the first edition:
"[This is] the gem of printed books in my library. . . . It is the most interesting book published by the Portuguese in India, and one of 2 or 3 compiled
by a layman in the 16–17th centuries."[51]

The colloquies are structured around fifty-nine dialogues between
Orta and his recently arrived physician-friend, Ruano, as they discuss the
nature and variety of local plants and herbs. Although the principal topics are botany and pharmacology, the dialogues often veer into geography,
animal life, and politics. Orta not only describes specific herbal treatments
for different maladies but also gives derivations and translations of the
names of plants and herbs into other languages. His discussion of cardamom has its Arabic translation, *cacolla*. Ruano asks: "E em latim como lhe
chamaremos ou em grego?" (And in Latin, how do we call it, or in Greek?)
Orta's reply emphasizes the significance of his findings: "Os gregos nem
os latinos antigos não conheceram cardamom" (46). (Neither the ancient
Greeks nor the Romans were acquainted with cardamom.) Here and elsewhere, Orta demonstrates his considerable knowledge of the classics.

Colóquios is often cited by literary scholars because its preface contains the first-ever-published poem by Camões. An ode dedicated to the
count of Redondo, who at the time was Francisco Coutinho, the viceroy
of India, the poem celebrates the count's military achievements, which
Camões compares with those of the ancient Greeks, and praises India's
rich botanical *orta* (garden, and an obvious reference to the book's author)
as part of the "campos lusitanos" (Lusitanian fields). Camões claims that
"o gran volume / Que agora em luz saindo, / Dará a Medicina um novo
lume, / e descobrindo irá segredos certos / A todos os antigos encober-
tos" (15) (the great volume / now coming to light / will bring new insight
to Medicine, / uncovering certain secrets / unknown even to the ancients).

Despite his medical expertise, political connections, and wide recognition as the author of *Colóquios*, which the Holy Office censors approved
back home, Orta and members of his family were investigated by the Inquisition in 1565. Orta died three years later, in 1568, before the Inquisition
could interrogate and prosecute him. His sister, who also lived in Goa, was
less fortunate; the year after his death, she was denounced, found guilty
by the tribunal, and burned at the stake. In 1580, the year of the Iberian

Union's inception, the Holy Office executed Orta in (partial) absentia by exhuming his remains that were buried in Goa and incinerating them in an auto-da-fé.[52]

The long arm of the Inquisition extended to new lands, including Brazil and the West African island of São Tomé, which were favored destinations for Jews fleeing from Portugal. A large number of Jews settled in Pernambuco in the Brazilian Northeast, where they lived in relative peace under the Dutch occupation and a governor who practiced religious tolerance, Prince Johan Maurits. There they became involved in the Dutch East India Company and were soon trading partners with Jews who had left Portugal for the Netherlands. The first synagogue in the New World was built in Recife, the Dutch capital in Brazil.

Much has been written about the seventeenth-century Jesuit firebrand António Vieira and his struggle with the Inquisition as he traveled between Portugal and his posts in Bahia and Maranhão. Vieira stands as an important reminder that the Society of Jesus was separate from and not always in agreement with the Holy Office. Vieira suggested to his patron-king Dom João IV that the Jewish mercantile class, which had been banished along with all other Jews in the late fifteenth century, be welcomed back to Portugal and be made exempt from paying taxes, as were all other citizens (Novinsky, "Padre António Vieira," 152); he also asked that New Christians be protected from the Inquisition's wrath. For Vieira, both initiatives were vital for shoring up a post–Iberian Union economy that was in steep economic decline.[53] Taken from his mission in Bahia, he was put on trial and imprisoned by the Inquisition from 1665 to 1667 for teachings and writings partly inspired by Judaism and partly by Sebastianism, which prophesied the coming of a savior and the creation of a Portuguese spiritual "Fifth Empire."

Following Vieira's reconciliation with the political and religious powers in Lisbon, he traveled to Rome. There he argued against Portugal's 1673 Law of Extermination, which ordered the expulsion of New Christians along with their families, with the exception of children under the age of seven, should the converts be found guilty of practicing Judaism (Novinsky, "Padre António Vieira," 155). In defiance of the Inquisition, he pleaded the New Christians' cause directly to the pope, who brought about a temporary suspension of the Holy Office's persecutions, including the auto-da-fé.[54] Despite his success in Rome as a diplomat, scholar, and teacher, Vieira's arguments on behalf of the Jewish people were unsuccessful. He returned to Lisbon for a time before traveling back to Brazil, where he worked on his collected *Sermões* (Sermons). In the meantime, the Inquisition resumed its work. In 1759, Portugal's prime minister, the marquis of Pombal, expelled the Jesuits from all Portuguese territories because they had become, in areas like Brazil, a landowning force with considerable political power; years later, in 1773, Pombal abolished the autos-da-fé and put a halt to New Christian persecutions. The Inquisition as an institution was finally dismantled in 1921, as part of the liberal reforms instituted by Portugal's First Republic (1910–1926).

Politics, religion, and trade continued to propel a diaspora that was traveling to and from Portugal as well as within the overseas colonies and between trading outposts. The spread of Christianity by Jesuits, Benedictines, Dominicans, and Franciscans in the empire created a surge in the production of religious decorative arts by both Portuguese and indigenous artisans, while local laborers and slaves built churches that were graced with architectural flourishes, some of which have survived.[55] In his essay "The Arts in Brazil before the Golden Age," art historian Nuno Senos writes about the scholarly neglect of early Brazilian colonial art prior to the emergence of *mineiro* Aleijadinho (Antônio Francisco Lisboa) and his stunning baroque statuary, paintings, and church façades in the eighteenth century. Not surprisingly, the oldest surviving wood carvings, tiles, statuary, and architectural vestiges in Brazil tend to be religious in nature.

A considerable number of expansionist-period maps, woodcuts, engravings, and paintings feature the Portuguese caravel and its successor, the *nau* (carrack), both of which regularly appear in full majesty with their billowing sails and Order of Christ cross.[56] That image of seafaring greatness and exploration can also be found in early stanzas of poet Garcia de Resende's long poem in "Miscelânea e variedade de histórias" (1545) (Miscellany and Variety of Stories):

> Nisto que posso dizer
> que não seja todo dito?
> também não posso escrever
> tais coisas, sem se fazer
> um processo infinito.
> que grandes povoações!
> que grandes navegações!
> que grandes rios! que riquezas!
> que costumes! que estanhezas!
> que gentes e que nações! (21)
> . . .
> Outro mundo nós vimos

per nossa gente achar
e o nosso navegar
tão grande, que descobrimos
cinco mil léguas por mar,
e vimos minas reais
de ouro, e de outros metais
no reino se descobrir;
mais que nunca vim saber
engenho de oficiais. (64)

What can I say about this
that hasn't already been said?
I also cannot write
about such things without making it
a never-ending task.
What incredible populations!
What incredible navigations!
What incredible rivers! What riches!
What customs! What strange sights!
What peoples and what nations!
. . .
We saw another world
founded by our people
and our navigating was
so vast that we discovered
five thousand leagues of sea,
and we saw royal mines
of gold and other metals
discovered in the realm;
more than ever we came to know
our leaders' intelligence.

But Resende's poem also comments on the consequences of nation-building and the diaspora, not to mention an influx of captives taken from the colonies:

Vimos muito espalhar
portugueses no viver,
Brasil, ilhas a povoar,
e às Indias ir morar,

natureza lhes esquecer:
vemos no reino meter
tantos cativos crescer,
e irem-se nos, naturais,
que se assim for, serem mais
eles que nós, a meu ver. (67)

We saw the dispersion
of Portuguese who went to live in
Brazil, who populated islands,
and who went to India to reside,
forgetting their origins:
we saw so many captives
come to our realm and grow in numbers
while so many Portuguese went out,
that to my way of seeing
there's more of them here than us.

By the late sixteenth century, images of exploration and conquest were gradually being eased aside by preoccupations with the nation and empire's economic decline and commercial and personal losses, especially in the East. In the early 1600s, the Dutch East India Company, a chartered company with stockholders, gained a solid foothold in the spice trade; its approach to commerce in the East was successful, and the Portuguese ultimately lost command of maritime trade in the State of India.[57] Adding to the loss of capital was loss of lives. In "Miscelânea," Resende briefly comments on shipwrecks, but he is even more concerned with the loss of local foodstuffs:

Vi grandes perdas no mar,
más novidades na terra,
muitas mudanças no ar:
nos verões, no invernar,
vemos já também que erra:
pão, carnes, frutas e vinho,
e os pescados marinhos,
azeites, e todo o que há
se nos vai de Portugal,
e não sei por que caminhos. (75)

I saw great losses at sea,
bad news traveled the land,
many changes in the air:
in the summer, in winter,
we see still other problems:
bread, meats, fruits and wine,
fish from the sea,
olive oil and every other thing
are taken from us in Portugal,
and where it goes from here, I have no idea.

The Jesuit Francisco Xavier wrote in his letters back home that many Portuguese sailors, officials, adventurers, and priests, as well as those from other countries who accompanied them, died at sea.[58] In the literature of the time, this topic is often associated with Camões's poem about a young, dark-skinned slave named Bárbara who was supposedly his East Indian mistress. It is among the poet's most compelling verses about the power of love, and it challenges traditional notions of ideal female beauty by praising Bárbara's blackness. The story behind the poem has to do with the shipwreck that Camões survived off the coast of Ceylon, now Sri Lanka. According to several sources, the poet saved himself and his manuscript of *Os lusíadas* while allowing his lover to drown.[59]

Around the time that Camões experienced this particular disaster, a series of startling eyewitness and "as told to" accounts were circulating back home in pamphlet form on the travails of other Portuguese, including women and children, who were lost at sea or perished as castaways or captives on foreign soil. The images of discovery and riches associated with the *nau* were increasingly conflated with ones of risk and loss. While inclement weather and enemy vessels commonly caused ships to go down, the pamphlets publicized lesser-known and more troubling causes, such as sloth, ignorance, and greed, which were implicitly attributed to the Crown. That level of critique may be why certain pamphlets were published anonymously. Still others were written by respected authors, such as Diogo do Couto, João Batista Lavanha, and Bento Teixeira Pinto. Twelve of the narratives from the period 1562 to 1602 appear in Bernardo Gomes de Brito's two-volume *História trágico-marítima* (1735, 1736) (*Tragic History of the Sea*), a source that constitutes an important trilogy along with *Os lusíadas* and *Peregrinação*.

Of the narratives in *História trágico-marítima*, some of which are extremely long, the first and most-cited is the "Relação da muito notável perda do Galeão S. João" (1552) (Report of the very notable loss of the galleon St. John), about the suffering and deaths of Captain Manoel de Sousa Sepúlveda and his family in Africa. It is one of the several anonymously written reports based on survivor and eyewitness accounts.[60] Typical of this subgenre and of most prose writing of the time is the focus on the nobility or individuals with royal connections and their families and associates. Although hundreds of nameless individuals suffered and perished, they serve only as background information or collateral damage.[61] Despite their tragic outcomes, these narratives continue the epic-heroic tradition of much earlier tales like *A morte do lidador*, except that instead of Muslims or other "heathens," the main enemy, as Camões's giant Adamastor suggests, is the sea. Regardless of blood or social class, no one in these accounts escapes its wrath.

But there still are other enemies to consider, as is clear in the narrative about Captain Sepúlveda's demise. Greed is the principle culprit. Whether presented directly or implicitly, greed is a factor in nearly all the prose pieces studied here and a central motif in the works by Camões, Resende, and Vicente. What is unusual about the Sepúlveda story is the degree to which greed, as much as or more than the sea, is responsible for significant loss of life. Approximately five hundred people were on the *São João* when it left India for Lisbon, and only a handful of its passengers survived. The author's indictment of the disaster appears in the first pages and reads like a legal brief: the ship's maximum cargo capacity was ignored and exceeded; the sails on the ship were in poor condition and did not fit properly on the masts; and there were no reserve sails should the ones in use be destroyed. Constant repairs meant delays that in turn meant dealing with inclement weather. The ship had leaks, and perhaps most damaging of all, the main rudder lacked sufficient nails and ultimately broke apart. When the sails finally collapsed, the passengers constructed makeshift substitutes out of their own clothing. An attempt to repair the rudder failed. Lifeboats were few and ill equipped. Lack of proper navigational training added to misjudgments about the ship's capabilities and course. All these elements led to the ship's breaking into pieces before sinking. Without food, water, or adequate clothing, the passengers who made it to shore were stranded on a desolate southern African coast.

Although God is not a factor in all the writings of the time, his presence is seen in early epic-heroic literature about the Reconquest, in chronicles such as *A tomada de Ceuta* and in Jesuit-authored works. What makes Sepúlveda and other characters heroic is the portrayal of their trust in God, which takes the form of acts of strength and charity in difficult times, as well as their feelings of inadequacy, humility, and guilt in situations out of their control. The descriptions of their suffering are not so different from those of martyred Christians. Faith is consoling, and they pray as they face death. The report on the Sepúlveda disaster even notes that African slaves aboard ship prayed along with the Portuguese Christians. After days of wandering and starvation, the Sepúlveda entourage, greatly reduced in number, came under attack by locals. They were stripped of their clothes, and Sepúlveda's persevering but pious wife was loath to display her nakedness to others, so, using her hands, she dug a little cove in the ground to conceal her body, refused to get up, and shortly afterward died. Sepúlveda's death was less heroic but nonetheless poignant: his mind addled by hunger and the death of his wife and children, he wandered naked into the bush and was never seen again. Although he might have been saved had he stayed with the few who ultimately survived, the narrator disagrees: "parece que foi assim melhor para sua alma, pois Nosso Senhor foi servido" (22) (it seems it was better for his soul this way, for Our Lord was served).

The narrative ends on an interestingly high and slightly humorous note. Pantaleão de Sá, a survivor of the shipwreck and attack, roamed the countryside until finally discovering a village, to which he turned for help. The community agreed to take him in and not kill him if he cured their ailing king, who suffered from a putrefied leg wound. Although lacking medical expertise of any kind, Sá had no option but to agree; he made a mud plaster for the wound. Miraculously, the leg healed and the king offered him half of his realm if he stayed. Wanting nothing more than to return to Portugal and his family, Sá declined the generous offer. Laden with gifts of gold and precious stones, he was escorted to a Portuguese settlement in Mozambique.

The period of exploration and conquest that to this day is celebrated in Portugal is far more complicated than monuments, special publications, holidays, dedications, and festivities may suggest. An examination of the literature of the time reveals the incredible accomplishments of a small country on the move but also the disappointments, frustrations, and failures that characterized the imperial enterprise and that have often been overlooked or minimized. As for the arts, art historian Luís de Moura Sobral has stated that they mirror the "unsystematic, scattered nature of the so-called Portuguese empire" ("Expansion and the Arts," 390), which seems a very good way of thinking about the range of works that were produced. I would add that a considerable amount of the art as well as architecture of the time is hybrid in nature and reflects in various ways a synthesis between vastly different cultures and the Portuguese world as travelers went back and forth freely in the expanding empire. However, not everyone who traveled within the empire was free to do so, as we shall see in the next chapter.

~ TWO ~

The Lusophone African Diaspora

Quem cativar será ele também cativo.

(Let whosoever takes captives also be a captive.)

FERNANDO OLIVEIRA, *A ARTE DA GUERRA DO MAR*, 1555

Although the Reconquest involved the capture and enslavement of "infidel" North Africans, or Moors, the siege of Ceuta in 1415 marks the beginning of a slave-trafficking enterprise that shipped thousands of Africans from the western sub-Sahara region to Portugal. Historian Vitorino Manuel Godinho has stated that in the first decades of the empire, approximately 2,000 Africans were transported annually and that between 1441 and 1505, at least 140,000 had been taken to Lisbon, the requisite port of entry for all slaves (*Os descobrimentos*, 161). There they worked as domestic and court servants, as street vendors, and in various other jobs in the growing urban economy. They also toiled in the countryside, clearing and planting the land, and their presence and labor enabled rural Portuguese to seek more exciting and profitable lives at sea or in the city (Tinhorão, *Os negros*, 83). Slaves who readily accepted conversion were often schooled and returned to their sub-Saharan homelands, where they helped the Portuguese win favor with local tribes; acquire information about gold, ivory, and a possible sea route to India; and barter for more captives. Ultimately, the slave trade eclipsed gold and ivory as the most lucrative enterprise. To accommodate the growing commerce in slaves, in 1482 the Portuguese built a fortress at Amina, or Elmina ("the mine"), on the Gold Coast (present-day Ghana) that served as a clearinghouse for the millions of captives who were shipped to the New World.[1]

Also called the Castelo da Mina, the fortress became a popular cartographic icon that artistically defined the empire's magisterial image and its occupation of West Africa. The castle on the Cantino planisphere of 1502 (figure 1.1), the oldest surviving Portuguese map, looms when compared to the lion icon that represents the whole of Sierra Leone. On the planisphere, the castle's pastoral guise in a forested landscape where African figures stand at ease outside its walls belies the actual business inside of receiving and processing captives, who were housed in dungeonlike cells until dispatched through the "porta sem retorno" (door of no return) to awaiting cargo ships.[2] An even more benign image can be found on a map in the *Atlas de Lázaro Luís* (1563), on which the castle looks more like a forest cottage with a tiny winding pathway than a processing center for gold and slaves (plate 12). A less colorful image of the fortress appears in Sebastião Lopes's *Atlas Universal* (ca. 1565), where it and a Portuguese flag represent the empire in West Africa (plate 13).[3]

Sixteenth-century Portuguese art and architecture regularly used Africans as emblems of overseas conquest and commerce, proselytization and acculturation, and the primitive and the exotic. Appointed by Dom João II to lead the nine-galley expedition that built the Castelo da Mina, Diogo de Azambuja was laid to rest in 1518 in a tomb with African bas-reliefs by artist Diogo Pires-o Moço. Sculpted figures include a tableau of four slaves at work. Resembling cherubs with short, wooly hair, the sculpted slave figures engage in tasks associated with the extraction and refinement of gold and are hemmed in by imposing carved *quinas* (shields) that were symbols of the empire. An earlier fifteenth-century example is the *cabeça de negro* decoration by Diogo Pires-o Velho on the tomb of Fernando Teles de Menezes, a Portuguese nobleman who served in Ceuta. With eyes shut tight and teeth biting what appears to be a rope, the African figure wears a pained, tragic expression on his face; a profusion of carved tropical fruits and plants surrounding his head has a smothering effect, as do the *quinas* that surround the figures on the Azambuja tomb.

The seafaring Manueline style that characterized the high point of Portuguese expansionism includes the Azambuja tomb, but a far more prominent example is the Jerónimos monastery, whose exterior features a dramatic bas-relief of a *cabeça de negro* in profile.[4] With eyes closed and a slight smile on his face, the profile is tilted slightly upward, as if he were dreaming or in pleasant repose. A carved garland of nautical rope circles

2.1. *African head on Teles de Menezes tomb, Igreja do Mosteiro de São Marcos, Coimbra*

and tightly frames his image, as if to suggest that escape is impossible even in sleep (or death). Other examples of this figure are on a Mina family coat of arms with three identical *cabeça de negro* profiles on a shield and a fourth perched at the top. In this instance, the figures are open-eyed and wear gold, symbolizing one of Mina's most precious commodities and the family's proudest possessions.

These and other period renderings of Africans did not suffer the Europeanization imposed on early representations of the Brazilian indigenous population, whose physical features were deemed more European than African.[5] Portuguese artists saw Africans on a regular basis, but they had to imagine New World inhabitants based on hearsay and writings by authors such as the German Hans Staden and the Frenchman Jean de Léry, both of whom wrote about living among the Tupinambá. A good early example of this different approach to the colonized Other is Grão Vasco's painting *Adoração dos Magos* (1501–1506), in which an African figure is still stylized but more realistic than the classically styled Tupi warrior (plate 15). In Jorge Afonso's sixteenth-century *Adoração dos Reis Magos*, the African is the focus of the painting as a whole, while the Virgin and Child are set slightly off to the side (plate 16). Richly dressed and bejeweled, the African stands tall above his European and vaguely Asian-looking companions as he doffs his crown to the mother and child; although adoring, he seems reserved in comparison to the other two kings, who kneel before the Christ Child with their hands clasped in reverence and prayer. Their body language suggests the total acceptance of Christ, while the African has yet to be fully convinced.[6]

The African presence appears in other Portuguese religious paintings of the period in which the Virgin Mary appears. Like the three magi, a trio of women attends the birth of the Virgin in Garcia Fernandes and Jorge Leal's *Nascimento da Virgem*. One of the women is African and stands at the bedside between the other two, who are European. Although the woman on the far right wears a colorful, fancy headdress, a cloth-covered basket draws the viewer's eye to the black woman, who balances the receptacle on her head. Like the two kneeling magi in Afonso's painting, the two European women seem especially adoring of the birth: one rests her hand on the new mother's chest while the other looks directly at her and offers the gift of a fowl. Possibly a servant, the African is more subdued, but she is treated pictorially as an equal, and her bearing is proud as she steadies the basket with her hand. In Gregório Lopes's *Bandeira Real da Misericórdia de Alcochete* (Royal banner of the blessing of Alcochete), numerous European figures surround the Virgin, including bishops and friars, noblemen and women, along with two black figures—an African king and a soldier in European military garb.

Much later, in 1756, when slave trafficking was at its zenith, a popular votive painting titled *Milagre de Nossa Senhora do Rosário do Castelo a Francisco de Sousa Pereira* (Miracle of Our Lady of the Rosary of the Castle to Francisco de Sousa Pereira) took a different view of the relationship between the Virgin and African peoples. Here the Virgin and Christ Child protect a slave master who has named his ship after her and whose prayers for her intervention against a mass slave uprising onboard are answered. The votive most likely refers to the slave trade that no longer shipped Africans to Portugal but rather shipped them through the more direct Africa to Brazil route. (In 1761, the marquis of Pombal abolished the importation of slaves to Portugal.) The transporting of more than three million slaves to Brazil, not counting the many Africans who lost their lives at sea, took place over a period of more than three hundred years. According to this votive, that centuries-long enterprise of enslavement enjoyed, at least on one occasion, divine protection.

Gregório Lopes's painting is an important reminder that although the vast majority of blacks labored as domestic or field slaves, many served the king on maritime expeditions or as combat soldiers on land. Their enemies were invaders or anyone who defied the Portuguese Crown, which could

include their African kinsmen. In Brazil, Henrique Dias, the son of purportedly freed slaves, and his black troops were instrumental in driving
out the Dutch from Pernambuco, with major victories at the first and second battles of Guararapes, in 1648 and 1649. Earlier, in 1638, Dias received
the title of *fidalgo* from King Felipe III for his successful military campaign
against the Dutch in Bahia. He was also named supreme commander of the
black regiment "terço da gente preta," which also fought against fugitive
slave uprisings in the *quilombos*. Despite his renown as a warrior on both
sides of the Atlantic, Dias wrote to Dom João IV on August 1, 1650, to regis-
ter a complaint against the commander-in-chief and governor of Pernambuco, General Francisco Barreto. He begins the letter by summarizing his
years of military service to the Crown, despite the loss of a hand, and then
proceeds with his grievance:

> E ora, pelo Mestre de Campo General Francisco Barreto, que governa,
> sou tratado com pouco respeito, e com palavras indizentes à minha pes-
> soa, nem me conhece por soldado, e que não sou nada nem venço soldo,
> [e] a este respeito outras muitas moléstias, que todos geralmente pade-
> cem, até que sua Majestade seja servido mandar remediar tantas fal-
> tas, pelo que convém à conservação deste Estado. (In Camargo, *O negro
> escrito*, 25)

> (And now Field Marshal General Francisco Barreto, who governs, treats
> me with little respect and uses unspeakable words against my person,
> nor does he acknowledge me as a soldier, and for being unrecognized,
> I receive no payment. In this respect I suffer, along with the many other
> annoyances that others generally suffer, until Your Majesty is served by
> rectifying these many injuries, according to what is fitting to maintain
> the welfare of this State.)

Dias's letter had its desired effect; in 1656, he traveled to Lisbon, where
the queen regent Dona Luísa de Gusmão awarded him a knighthood in
the Order of Christ.[7] She also approved the continuation of the black mili-
tia, along with salaries and pensions for his soldiers. In his *Antologia do
negro brasileiro* (1950), Edison Carneiro cites Dias's added demand for the
manumission promised for slaves who had fought in his regiment. A law
passed in 1657 by the Conselho Ultramarino (Overseas Council) granted
his request (Mattos, "'Black Troops,'" 19).

Historian Hebe Mattos states that many slaves, referred to as "africanos" or "etíopes" (Ethiopians), were brought to Brazil from Mina and

Angola, where they initially honed their battle skills against the Dutch occupation (1641–1648) ("'Black Troops,'" 15). Mattos translates the eighteenth-century historians Diogo Lopes de Santiago and José António Gonçalves de Mello's vivid description of the Africans' indefatigable warrior prowess on Brazilian soil:

> E eram tão quotidianas as pendências, que tanto que os holandeses saíam a buscar cajus, e outras frutas do mato, os negros minas logo lhes caíam de improviso, e com as vidas lhas faziam largar; e eram tão bárbaros estes minas, que não lhes queriam dar quartel, mas antes cortavam as cabeças aos que matavam e vinham com instrumentos bélicos a seu modo e ao de sua terra com buzinas e atabaques, fazendo muita festa, dizendo que aqueles os foram cativar às suas terras, sendo eles forros. (Santiago and Mello, *História da guerra*, 526)

> (Conflicts were so commonplace that as soon as the Dutch went out to collect cashew nuts or other fruits from the forest, the Mina blacks soon fell upon them and took their lives, and these Minas were such barbarians that they did not want to spare them [further], but rather cut off the heads of those whom they killed. [They] came with their own instruments of warfare from their land with horns and drums, making merry, saying that the Dutch had gone to capture them in their homelands where they were free.) (In Mattos, "'Black Troops,'" 15)

Because of the black soldiers' superior battle capability, the Portuguese government even returned them to Africa to rout the Dutch from Angola. The returning troops included an entire company from Dias's regiment (Mattos, "'Black Troops,'" 16–17).

There are several portraits of Henrique Dias, but his image is best associated with a 1758 anonymous votive painting of the first Battle of Guararapes in which he and his black regiment appear in the foreground (plate 17).[8] Here, unlike in the *Milagre de Nossa Senhora* painting, the Virgin and Christ Child look down favorably on the armed blacks and protect them. Vítor Meirelles's dramatic 1879 painting of the same battle shows Dias and his soldiers in combat, but their figures are recessed and overshadowed by the white commanders on horseback. Dias also appears in the Brazilian neoclassical poet José de Santa Rita Durão's epic poem *Caramuru* (1781), about the shipwrecked Portuguese Diogo Álvares Correia, who lived among the Tupinambá and helped colonize Brazil in the early sixteenth

2.2. Batalha dos guararapes *(1879)*, *by Vítor Meirelles*

century. Canto IX in the poem focuses on Caramuru's Indian wife, Para-guaçu, who has a vision of the future Dutch invasion of Brazil and the call to arms of "Henrique Dias, / capitão dos etíopes valente" (Henrique Dias, valiant captain of the Ethiopians). Diogo Lopes Santiago and José António Gonçalves de Mello wrote at length about Dias in their *História da guerra em Pernambuco* (1634) (History of the war in Pernambuco), but they had a peculiar way of describing the relationship between the leader's physical appearance and his valor: "negro na cor, porém branco nas obras e no es-forço" (118) (black in color, however, white in his works and effort). This attitude extended to Dias's valiant troops: "ainda que negros, eram os sol-dados d'el-rei" (139) (although black, they were soldiers of the king).

One of Durão's contemporaries, the poet José Basílio da Gama, wrote a transatlantic tribute to an Angolan captain who served the Portuguese in Africa.[9] The poem *Quitubia* (1791) celebrates Domingos Ferreira Assun-ção, who fought in the "guerra preta" (black war) against Queen Ginga, who was his aunt, in the area around present-day Luanda.[10] The poem's epigraph, "Faccia pompa d'Eroi l'Africa ancora" (Let us show that Africa also has its heroes), is a quote from Metastasio's 1750 opera *Attilio Regolo* about the Roman senator and military leader who commanded the Roman troops in Africa.

Da Gama writes passionately of Assunção's selflessness and his radi-ance in battle—an acknowledgment of his African name, Quitubia, which means "fire." Following several bloody battles and after defeating Queen Ginga's forces, he sailed to Lisbon, where he was first received by a tearfully grateful marquis of Pombal and then by Queen Maria I. In the midst of describing this moving royal reception, da Gama interjects the following lines about Quitubia's military triumph and his race: "Com o seu sangue compraste a glória. / Que ainda que essa cor escura o encobre" (With your blood you bought glory. / Despite the dark color that envelops you). This line makes patently clear that glory was incompatible with being black unless one's actions (blood) were of a kind and level deemed to be white. The poem concludes with Quitubia's celebrated return to his wife and family as a recipient of the Order of Christ, whose red cross he wore as his reward for protecting the empire.

An occasional resident and advocate of Brazil, the eighteenth-century Portuguese poet António Dinis da Cruz e Silva celebrated da Gama's tribute to the unsung African hero in a sonnet titled "A José Basílio da Gama, Autor do poema intitulado Quitubia" (*Poesia*, 4) (To José Basílio da Gama, author of the poem entitled Quitubia). The poem commends da Gama's perspicacity of subject matter and his challenge to the stereotypic image of Africa as a land that produced "só cruéis feras, só monstros" (only cruel beasts, only monsters). Apparently he had no argument with da Gama's line about the incompatibility of glory and black skin and most likely read it as further praise for the African's accomplishments. Silva ends with a play on the Metatasio epigraph that opens da Gama's poem:

Hoje do bom Quitubia à gente cega
A fé pintado e o grão valor, demonstra
Que também tem heróis África ardente.

(Today the faith and great valor of
The good Quitubia are known to those once blind,
Showing that ardent Africa also has its heroes.)

An oil painting titled *Chafariz d'el Rei* (The king's fountain) from the mid- to late sixteenth century that is believed to be the work of a Dutchman is a remarkable portrait of the Alfama in Lisbon (plate 14). It shows a large number of blacks among the white Portuguese near a public fountain in the oldest part of the city. For the most part, they appear as servants and vendors. There are also a boatman, a musician, and a man who looks as if he is dancing an African *lundum* and performing the *umbigada* (belly bump) with his white female partner. Another man on horseback who dons a plumed hat and rich robes with the cross of the Order of Christ suggests that Quitubia was not the only African to be a member of the military order.[11]

The historic significance and lyric praise given to individuals like Henrique Dias and Quitubia were an exception to the norm that the great majority of Africans and their descendants experienced in their contacts with the Portuguese. In the mid-seventeenth century, the Jesuit António Vieira preached sermons in Brazil against the mistreatment of slaves by landowners and farmers who prevented them from attending Sunday Mass; he also preached to the slaves about the heavenly rewards they would receive after this misery on earth, their "doce inferno" (sweet hell). But as Raymond Sayers rightly points out, Vieira's attitude toward slavery was inconsistent and full of contradiction: "[A]s a literal humanitarian who defended the Jews, he had of necessity to sympathize also with the Negroes; as a Jesuit, he had to support the position of his order, which defended the Indians at the expense of the Africans; and as a statesman, one of the greatest of restored Portugal, he saw the need for Negro slaves in the economic development of Brazil" (*The Negro*, 42). Vieira suffered the wrath of the Inquisition for his unpopular position that Portugal needed the Jewish population for its economic well-being as well as for his messianic writings about Portugal as a future spiritual Quinto Império (Fifth Empire). However, as Sayers and others have noted, he took a more sanguine approach to African slavery because it spared the indigenous populations from enforced labor and freed them for the Jesuit missions.

A century prior to Vieira, however, the priest, naval pilot, soldier, grammarian, and intellectual Fernando Oliveira condemned slavery and called for its eradication in his *A arte da guerra do mar* (1555) (The art of war at sea). His was a unique voice until the advent of the abolitionist movement in mid-nineteenth-century Brazil. He was also brutally frank about Portugal's heinous enterprise and the business of forced religious conversion:

> Tomar as terras, impedir a franqueza delas, cativar as pessoas daqueles que não blasfemaram Jesus Cristo, nem resistem à pregação de sua fé, quando com modéstia lha pregam, é manifesta tirania. . . . Nós fomos os inventores de tão mau trato, nunca usado entre humanos. Não se achará, nem razão humana concide, que jamais houvesse no mundo trato público e livre de comprar e vender homens livres e pacíficos,

como quem compra e vende alimárias, bois, cavalos e semelhantes.
Assim os tangem, assim os constrangem, trazem e levam e provam e
escolhem com tanto desprezo e ímpeto, como faz o magarefe ao gado
no curral. Não somente eles, mas também seus filhos, e toda geração,
depois de nascidos cristãos nunca tem remissão. (24–25)

(To seize lands, to impede their freedom, to capture people who neither
blaspheme Jesus Christ nor resist with the preaching of their faith, when
they modestly profess it, is manifest tyranny. . . . We were the inventors
of such evil never before used among human beings. One will not find,
nor will human reason allow, that there was ever in the world a public
and free contract for the buying and selling of free and pacific men as
if buying and selling foodstuffs, oxen, horses and the like. They [Portu-
guese] prod them, they constrain them, and take them back and forth,
examining and selecting them with such scorn and impetus, just like
butchers toward cattle in the corral. Not only they but also their children and every succeeding generation born Christian will never gain
remission.)

A arte da guerra do mar was denounced by the Inquisition, and
Oliveira was persecuted. This was not his first run-in with the Inquisition,
and he spent several years of his life in jails, either for his opinions about
religion (he refused to denounce the Protestant faith) or as a captive soldier of enemy armies. His attitude on what constitutes a "just war" especially provoked the ire of officials of the Inquisition, who saw it as a gross
offense against Church and empire. He wrote, "Não podemos fazer guerra
justa aos infiéis que nunca foram cristãos, como são mouros, e judeus, e
gentios, que conosco querem ter paz, que não tomaram as nossas terras,
nem por alguma via prejudicaram a cristandade" (23). (We cannot make
a just war against infidels who were never Christians, such as the Moors
and Jews and native inhabitants, who want to make peace with us, who
did not occupy our lands or in any way harm Christianity.) It is not clear
if Oliveira was opposed to slavery as a brutal enterprise or because it was
counter to the Christian faith and jeopardized the possibility of salvation.
Regardless, his opposition to slavery was unequivocal, and because of his
opinions, he was removed from his academic post at the Universidade de
Coimbra.

   In 1758, the Portuguese priest Manuel Ribeiro Rocha, who resided in
Bahia and practiced as a lawyer, published *Etíope resgatado, empenhado,*

sustentado, corrigido, instruido, e libertado. Discurso teológico-jurídico, em que se propõem o modo de comerciar, haver, e possuir validamente, quanto a um, e outro foro, os pretos cativos africanos, e as principais obrigações, que correm a quem deles se servir (Ethiopia redeemed, engaged, supported, corrected, instructed, and liberated. Theological-juridical discourse in which are proposed the manner of commerce, the having and valid possession of African captives, according to one and other courts of law, and the primary obligations of those whom they serve). Similar to Vieira, Rocha did not contest the institution of slavery, but he defended the African slaves' right to dignity and argued against their mistreatment. He also discussed four ways by which slaves could secure their freedom: by paying in full whatever funds the owners had invested in them; by serving the requisite number of years to match the funds invested; by being released from years still to be served by the owners' death and granting of freedom in the will; or via the slaves' own death. The first way was undoubtedly the most difficult to achieve, while the last was likely the most commonplace, until 1888, when slavery was finally abolished in Brazil.[12]

The ideals of the Enlightenment played an important role in the writings of Rocha and others at the time who felt compelled to focus on the evils of slavery in the empire. Undoubtedly Pombal's 1761 decree that ended slave trafficking to Portugal—but not to the rest of the empire—raised an awareness of problems associated with the enterprise. We can see this in a number of works of the period, including the anonymous 1764 pamphlet titled "Nova e curiosa relação de um abuso emendado, ou evidências da razão, expostas a favor dos homens pretos em um diálogo entre um letrado e um mineiro" (New and curious account of a corrected abuse, or proofs of reason, offered in support of black men in a dialogue between a lawyer and a miner); like Rocha's book, the pamphlet's author argues for the better treatment of slaves.[13] In this case, however, the subject is fictionalized and arises out of a dialogue about the *mineiro*'s earlier promise to grant his slave freedom. Unhappy with the slave's reaction to this unfilled promise, the miner now wants to sell the slave and ship him to Brazil, although the slave now has the protection of the Irmandade da Nossa Senhora do Rosário dos Homens Pretos (Fraternity of Our Lady of the Rosary of Black Men), whose members cannot be sold overseas. In their dialogue, the lawyer parries with the *mineiro* over reasons why he should keep his word; he also calls attention to the abuses committed against slaves in Brazil and the moral imperative to recognize their humanity and curtail all mistreatment. To do otherwise, he says, is a sin that would weigh heavily on a true believer's conscience. In keeping with the enlightened spirit of their debate and despite his skepticism, the miner follows the counselor's advice and remunerates him for his services.

Another figure in the debate was Luís de Santos Vilhena, a Portuguese professor of Greek who accepted a teaching position in Bahia in 1787. There he saw firsthand the widespread human scourge of slavery and its ill effects on Brazilian society as a whole, which he described to a friend in a letter that appears in his *Recopilação de notícias soteropolitanas e brasílicas, contidas em XX cartas* (1802) (Compilation of Salvadoran and other Brazilian news, contained in XX letters). His attitude toward blacks, especially "uppity" blacks and mulattoes, is racist and reminiscent of views of the seventeenth-century Bahian poet Gregório de Matos. For his part, Vilhena argues forcefully for an end to slavery, if only to eradicate inhumane acts carried out by slave owners. In this passage, reason becomes the arbiter for his position on the subject:

> É sem dúvida uma grande obra de misericórdia o libertar os nossos irmãos cativos, mas parece mais conforme a razão e justiça o ficarem os libertos desta natureza, e qualidades responsáveis sempre a um tutor, ou director que coativamente os desviasse do mal, e os digirisse para o bem, e não deixá-los entregues à sua brutal vontade. Não se faz certamente a injúria em chamar deshumano a quem pelo não sustentar lançar fora de sua casa um escravo, que no seu serviço cegou ou estropiou, de forma que não pode mais servir, tendo sido mais afortunados os bois dos israelitas, do que escravos de senhores tais, e se estes merecem o nome de deshumanos, ignore o que se deve dar àqueles que conservando no cativeiro escravos cegos, e aleijados, sem dar-lhes sustento algum, os mandam mendigar pelos fiéis, para que no fim de cada semana lhe pagam quatrocentos e tantos réis, sob pena de áspero castigo. (In Moura, *Dicionário da escravidão*, 271)

> (It is undoubtedly a great mercy to free our captive brothers, but it seems more in keeping with reason and justice for them to be freed and remain so under the responsible eye of a tutor or director, who would forcibly keep them from evil and guide them toward goodness, and prevent them from acting on brute will. It is certainly not an injustice to call inhumane the one who, for lack of funds, throws out a house servant who can no longer work because he was blinded or crippled while during his service. The oxen of the Israelites were more fortunate than

slaves of such a master. And if these men deserve to be called inhumane, I cannot fathom what name is deserving of those who keep captive both blind and crippled slaves, giving them no support whatsoever, and who send them to beg among the faithful and at the end of the week exact four hundred réis or more under penalty of harsh punishment.)

Vilhena's contemporary José da Silva Lisboa took a more overtly racist approach in *Memória dos benefícios políticos do governo d'El Rei Nosso Senhor D. João VI* (1818) (Memoir of the political benefits of the government of Our King Dom João VI). Here he argued that São Paulo and Rio Grande do Sul were making economic strides while cultivating a lighter-skinned population because of a growing Portuguese population and a reduction in the number of African slaves. He was especially adamant that Brazil not replicate what had happened in the Caribbean and become, to use his wording, a "Negroland" (in Serrão and Marques, *Nova história*, 372).[14]

AFRICA-BRAZIL-PORTUGAL: THE POETIC JOURNEY OF DOMINGOS CALDAS BARBOSA

Ai céu!
Ela é minha iaiá
O seu moleque sou eu.

(Oh heavens!
She is my missy
And I'm her black boy.)

DOMINGOS CALDAS BARBOSA, *VIOLA DE LERENO*, 1826

While neoclassical poets Santa Rita Durão and Basílio da Gama wrote briefly in praise of heroic blacks, and Rocha and others were proposing better treatment of slaves, reducing their numbers, or even giving them their freedom, the African-Brazilian poet Domingos Caldas Barbosa was penning classically influenced and popular verses at the Jesuit school in Rio. Following his schooling, he entered the military and was sent to Sacramento, near the Rio Plata, to support the 1750 Treaty of Madrid that reconfigured Spanish and Portuguese landholdings and borders. His enlistment ended after Spanish and Portuguese troops wrested control of the area from the Jesuits and their Guarani mission community.[15] The son of an Angolan slave and a Portuguese man, Caldas Barbosa was born as his parents crossed the Atlantic to Brazil or shortly after their arrival in Rio. The year of his birth is disputed by historians (either 1738 or 1740). Unlike many children of such unions, he was formally recognized by his father, who worked in a treasury office in Angola and supported his son after he left Brazil to study at the Universidade de Coimbra in 1763.[16] With his father's death and the loss of his allowance, the young man roamed penniless and suffered a period of intense penury. His verses to commemorate royal events were finally noticed, and ultimately he secured two noblemen-patrons. Through his contacts with the nobility, he also secured a clergy position and a salary. Like poets of his time, Caldas Barbosa wrote odes and sonnets in the neoclassical mode, but he was more interested in composing *cantigas*, which he sang to the accompaniment of his viola. He was a regular guest and popular performer at soirées and salons, where he entertained high society with his compositions called *lunduns* and *modinhas*. In 1790, he founded the short-lived Nova Arcádia, along the lines of Lisbon's earlier Arcádia Lusitana (1756–1776), which promoted linguistic simplicity and bucolic themes over the Baroque's ornate and often complex style. But as Heitor Martins has noted, the lighter, playful content of Caldas Barbosa's *cantigas* might best be described as closer to the rococo.[17] In 1798, two years before his death, Caldas Barbosa published *Viola de Lereno*, his first volume of *cantigas* under the name Lereno Selinuntino, the neoclassical pastoral name he adopted and by which he was widely known. A second volume of his *cantigas* appeared posthumously in 1826.

Like his mixed racial and cultural identity, Caldas Barbosa's poetry and music represent the merging of Africa, Brazil, and Portugal. He introduced Portuguese upper-class society to the Brazilian sung *lundum*, whose African-based rhythms and dance arrived in Brazil with the Angolan slave trade.[18] His *lunduns* are linguistically accessible and melodic, with frequent word repetitions and refrains. They often take place in or suggest a *locus amoenus*, the preferred setting for neoclassical poets. Although many shepherd-poets tended to be stoic and restrained in their emotive impulses, Caldas Barbosa wrote about love in more delicate ways—that it can be cruel and unrelenting but also pleasurable, inspired, and even divine.[19] In this respect, his sung verse is reminiscent of the medieval *cantiga* and the troubadours' declarations of love's wonder, delight, and *coita* (suffering).[20]

Music historians tell us that sensuality, if not lasciviousness, charac-

terized the African *lundum*, whose dance steps included the *umbigada* between partners. The Portuguese eighteenth-century poet Tomás Antônio
Gonzaga, who resided in Brazil before his exile to Mozambique for his role
in the plot to overthrow the Portuguese monarchy in Brazil known as the
Inconfidência Mineira (1789), seems to have agreed with this attitude, as
can be seen in the sixth verse epistle from his *Cartas chilenas*:

Aqui lascivo amante, sem rebuço,
À torpe concubina oferta o braço;
Ali mancebo ousado assiste e fala
À simples filha que seus pais recatam:
A ligeira mulata, em trajes de homem
Dança o quente lundum e o vil batuque.
E, aos cantos do passeio, inda se fazem
Ações mais feias, que a modéstia oculta. ("Carta 6," 33)

(Here a lascivious lover, without disguise,
Offers his arm to the sordid concubine;
There an audacious youth enters into conversation
With a modest daughter, whom the parents try to protect:
The light-footed mulatta, dressed as a man,
Dances the hot lundum and the vile batuque.
And at the edges of the dancing, even uglier actions
Occur that modesty prevents me from disclosing.)

Ricardo Cravo Albin has noted that Portuguese high society adopted the
lundum once curtsies and bows (*mesura*) replaced the *umbigada*, while in
Brazil, poor and working-class whites and blacks continued to perform the
bump (*Dicionário*, n.p.).

Caldas Barbosa's *lunduns* greatly appealed to both elite and popular classes, who enjoyed his pleasant rhymes and light wit. They were also
charmed by his use of the exotic in the guise of African and Tupi words, repeated references to Brazil, and his own Luso-African-Brazilian heritage:[21]

Eu tenho uma Nhanhazinha
A quem tiro o meu chapéu;
É tão bela, tão galante,
Parece coisa do céu.
    Ai céu!

Ela é minha iaiá
O seu moleque sou eu. (II, 2:32)

. . .

Eu tenho uma Nhanhanzinha
De quem sempre sou moleque;
Ela vê-me estar ardendo
E não me abana c'o leque.
  Ai céu!
  Ela é minha iaiá
  O seu moleque sou eu. (II, 2:33)

(I have a little missy
To whom I take off my hat.
She's so polite, so pretty,
She's like a gift from heaven.
  Oh heavens!
  She's my missy
  And I'm her black boy.

. . .

I have a little missy
For whom I am always a black boy;
She sees I'm burning with desire
Yet she fails to cool me with her fan.

Here Caldas Barbosa plays with the idea of unrequited love, but the class distinctions in medieval verse between the lovesick poet and the indifferent lady of the court are supplanted by the "black boy" in relation to his "little missy," references that evoke the racial distinctions and social hierarchy within plantation society. In the poem "Aqui está que todo é teu," (Here it is, for all is yours), the word *escravo* connotes both his "love slave" status and his ties to a people born free and then sold into servitude:

Para ser teu Nhanhazinha
Não deixei nada de meu,
Té o próprio coração
Aqui está que todo é teu.

Se não tens mais quem te sirva
O teu moleque sou eu,

Chegadinho do Brasil
Aqui está que todo é teu.

Eu era da Natureza
Ela o Amor me vendeu;
Foi para dar-te um escravo
Aqui está que todo é teu. (II, 2:19–20)

(To be yours Nhanhazinha,
I left nothing of myself,
Even my own heart
Here it is, for all is yours.

If you no longer have anyone to serve you
I'm your black boy,
Just arrived from Brazil
Here it is, for all is yours,

I was born of Nature who
Sold me to Love;
Just to give you a slave
Here it is, for all is yours.)

One of Caldas Barbosa's more complex *lunduns* is titled "Lundum em louvor de uma brasileira adotiva" (Lundum in praise of an adopted Brazilian), in which the poet registers his surprise at seeing a young Portuguese woman who performs the dance as well as a Brazilian:

Quem me havia de dizer
Mas a coisa é verdadeira;
Que Lisboa produziu
Uma linda Brasileira.
Ai beleza
As outras são pela patria
Esta pela Natureza. (II, 2:29)

(Who could imagine
But the thing is true;
That Lisbon produced

A pretty Brazilian.
Oh beauty
The others are born to the dance
She is by her Nature.)

In some respects the poem anticipates the *saudade* theme that the Brazilian romantic Gonçalves Dias developed in "Canção do exílio" to describe his longing for his country while living in Portugal. Dias's poem is
a good example of the nativist attitude in Brazilian literature that praised
Brazil's natural wealth over that of Portugal. Caldas Barbosa's poem is
more complex; while the sight of the *lundum* triggers the poet's thoughts
about his homeland, the dancer's execution is so surprisingly Brazilian
that he takes delight and joy in its performance. He does note an important cultural difference, one that was in keeping with the *mesura* adopted
by the Portuguese: "É nas chulices de lá / Mas é de cá nas mudanças." That
is, while flirting is part of the dance in Brazil, no such suggestive moves appear in the Portuguese version.[22]

In addition to the *lundum*, Caldas Barbosa introduced a Brazilian version of the light verse form known as the *modinha*, whose lyrics, often accompanied in Portugal by more complicated musical scores (and, later,
dance steps along the lines of the waltz), were entertainment for the upper
class. The Brazilian *modinha* was more popular in themes, music, and
dance style, ultimately segueing into the *samba-canção*; and according
to Cravo Albin, it was the first popular musical form to be successfully
exported from Brazil and disseminated to the outside (*Dicionário*).[23] Not
everyone, however, was a fan of Caldas Barbosa's *lunduns* and *modinhas*;
this was especially true of the Portuguese elite, including intellectuals such
as Gonzaga and the linguist and historiographer António Ribeiro dos Santos, who wrote disparagingly about them and states,

Hoje pelo contrario só se ouvem cantigas amorosas de suspiros, de
requebros, de namoros refinados, de garradices. . . . Esta praga é hoje
geral, depois que o Caldas começou de pôr em uso os seus rimances,
e de versejar para mulheres. Eu não conheço um poeta mais prejudicial à educação particular e pública do que este trovador de Venus e de
Cúpido: a tafularia do amor, a meiguice do Brasil e em geral a moleza
americana, que faz o carater de suas trovas, respiram os ares voluptuo-
sos de Paphos, e de Citera, e encantam com venenosos filtros a fantasia
dos moços e o coração das Damas. Eu admiro a facilidade dos motivos

que toma para seus cantos, e o pico e a graça com que os remata; mas
detesto o assunto, e mais ainda a maneira porque ele o trata. (In Braga,
Filinto Elísio, 616–617).

(Today on the contrary all one hears are amorous *cantigas* with sighs,
sentimental wording, perfect lovers, [and] bubblings. . . . This scourge
is everywhere today, after Caldas [Barbosa] introduced his little songs
and started singing verses to women. I don't know a poet more harm-
ful to private and public education than this troubadour of Venus and
Cupid: the sweetness of love, the gentleness of Brazil, and in general,
the American indolence that characterize his verses which breathe
the voluptuous air of Paphos and Cythera and enchant with venom-
ous magic potions the fantasies of young men and the hearts of ladies.
I admire the informality of the motifs that he sings, and the spirit and
grace with which he refines them; but I detest the subject matter and
even more the way he reasons to treat it.)

The nineteenth-century romantic interest in collecting and transcrib-
ing ballads on both sides of the Atlantic shows the degree to which Caldas
Barbosa's lyrics became part of the popular songbook—so much so that
this work seemed truly folkloric in both Portugal and Brazil. In his *História da literatura brasileira*, Brazilian poet, essayist, and literary critic Sílvio Romero wrote about his 1860s and 1870s travels in northern Brazil in
search of local songs. To his surprise, he realized that many of the lyrics
being sung were from Caldas Barbosa's *cantigas*:

O poeta teve a consagração da popularidade. Não falo dessa que adqui-
riu em Lisboa, assistindo a festas e improvisando na *viola*. Refiro-me a
uma popularidade mais vasta e mais justa.

　Quase todas as *cantigas* de Lereno correm de boca em boca nas
classes plebéias, truncadas ou ampliadas. Formam um material de que
o povo se apoderou, modelando-o a seu sabor. Tenho desse fato uma
prova direta.

　Quando em algumas províncias do Norte colegi grande cópia de
canções populares, repetidas vezes colhi cantigas de Caldas Barbosa
como anônimas, repetida por analfabetos.

　Foi depois preciso compulsar as obras do poeta para expurgir da
coleção anônima os versos que lhe pertenciam. É o maior elogio que,
sob o ponto de vista etnográfico, se lhe pode fazer. (1:305)

(The poet was popularly acclaimed. I am not talking about the fame he acquired in Lisbon, attending parties and improvising on the *viola*. I'm referring to a wider and more just popularity.

Almost all Lereno's *cantigas*, either truncated or elaborated, passed from one mouth to the other among the lower classes.

They formed the material that the people took over and fashioned to their own tastes. I have direct proof of this fact.

When I was in the northern provinces, collecting a large sample of popular songs, I often recognized songs by Caldas Barbosa that were thought to be anonymous and were repeated by people who were illiterate.

Later I had to consult the poet's work to expunge verses that were his from the songs by anonymous authors. From an ethnographic point of view, this is the highest praise one can give.)

Like his African ancestors, Domingos Caldas Barbosa brought to Portugal a part of that rich hybrid culture that, in this instance, passed through Brazil. In Portugal his songs circulated widely and crossed back in the nineteenth century with Portuguese emigrants to the land where he was born. In recent years those songs have come to the attention of scholars and are an excellent example of the imperially produced hybridity that is characteristic of lusophone culture.[24]

As part of the transplanted African culture, the *lundum*, as well as the *batuque* and capoeira, also captured the attention of artists who traveled to Brazil. Arriving in Rio in 1822, the year of Brazilian independence, the German Johann Moritz Rugendas painted numerous works during his three-year stay that portray the African experience. Among the most compelling are his small, ethnographic-style portraits of different African groups in Brazil, including slaves from Benguela, the Congo, Mozambique, Mina, Cabinda, and Quiloa—all of whom passed through Valongo, the principal slave port in Rio. In his illustrated study titled *Malerische reise in Brasilien* (1835) (*Viagem pitoresca através do Brasil* [1941], Picturesque voyage through Brazil), Rugendas commented on the range of African communities to be found in Valongo: "Num só golpe de vista o artista podia conseguir resultados que na África só atingiria depois de longas e perigosas viagens a todas as regiões daquela parte do mundo" (*Viagem pitoresca*, 118) (In one glance, the artist could get results that in Africa could be achieved only after making long and perilous journeys to every region in that part of the world). In addition to the *lundum* and other African performance

2.3. Lundu *(1835), by Johann Moritz Rugendas*

2.4. Valongo Desembarkment *(1835), by Johann Moritz Rugendas*

arts, Rugendas documents the harsh reality of slave life with paintings of slaves in the dark hold of a ship, in cells awaiting auction, in the mines and fields, and in ultimate distress on whipping posts. Rugendas seems to have been affected by what he saw, stating at one point that Brazil "é o único país onde o comércio dos escravos continua a praticar-se sem nenhuma espécie de restrição" (118) (is the only country where the business of slavery continues to be practiced without any sort of restriction). The impact of that freewheeling transatlantic commerce continues to resonate in the present day, as can be seen in the colorful, poignant artwork of Brazilian Goya Lopes (plates 18 and 19).

THE AFRICAN IN NINETEENTH-CENTURY BRAZILIAN LITERATURE

I have written elsewhere about the appropriation of the Indian as noble savage and symbol of the Brazilian nation by nineteenth-century authors. With few exceptions, the African was absent from literary works at that time.[25] Exceptions include Gonçalves Dias's early prose work *Meditação* (1846) (Meditation) and his poem "A escrava" (1846) (The slave), whose theme of exile and longing is reminiscent of his "Canção do exílio." In fact, both poems appear in *Primeiros cantos* (1846) (First songs), a first volume whose verses were inspired by his wanderings, as he notes in the prologue: "[F]oram compostas nas margens viçosas do Mondego e nos píncaros enegrecidos do Geres—no Doiro e no Teia—sobre as vagas do Atlântico, e nas florestas virgens da América" (They were composed on the lush banks of the Mondego [Portugal] and the darkened peaks of Gerês— on the Douro e Teia—on the waves of the Atlantic and in the virgin forests of America [Brazil]).[26] In "A escrava," Alsgá pines for the Congo, as idyllic a place as Brazil is in "Canção do exílio" except that Africa also represents freedom. The idea of longing, *saudade*, in "A escrava" develops from the poem's epigraph from the tragic opera *Marino Faliero* into a poem about a lost land, a lost love, and a lost identity. Alsgá has a name in her homeland, but in Brazil she is simply a "mísera escrava" (miserable slave).

Although the poem is not dated, it was written after the 1831 law that granted freedom automatically to any African brought to Brazil and that punished those involved in slave trafficking within the country. While the legislation had a brief impact, external and internal trafficking continued to the point that during the 1840s, when Gonçalves Dias published *Pri-*

meiros cantos, the number of Africans brought to Brazil exceeded 350,000. To curtail the flow, in 1845 the British instituted the Aberdeen Act, which prohibited all slave trafficking between Africa and the Americas. The historic alliance between the Portuguese monarchy and England resulted in this particular legislation, which was widely referred to as "para inglês ver" (for the English to see). With its passage, the British navy frequently stopped and inspected Brazilian ships on the high seas that were believed to be transporting slaves. These inspections led to heinous actions by traffickers to conceal their human cargo, such as throwing captives overboard and hiding them in barrels, where they often perished from suffocation. In 1850, Brazil enacted the Eusébio de Queirós Law, which abolished trafficking to Brazil altogether, although slaves continued to be brought in clandestinely through remote port towns.

The focus of "A escrava" is in keeping with Enlightenment-inspired works that promoted the humanity of slaves and demanded their better treatment. Alsgá is not the epic-heroic African imagined by Basílio da Gama, yet she is treated as an individual whose longings have emotional and psychological depth. However, unlike the popular noble savage figures of the period, whose real-life counterparts had long disappeared, Alsgá represents a population whose misery was everywhere evident in Brazil. In Alsgá, Gonçalves Dias created a romantic figure whose yearnings evoke sympathy and compassion. She is also a tragic figure because she is enslaved and, as we soon learn, her master is not enlightened. The poem ends as Alsgá's memories of the "doces terras d'além-mar" (sweet lands beyond the sea) are suddenly halted by the "voz irritada [do] ríspido Senhor" (the harsh Master's angry voice), and she is returned to "sofrer cruento" (*bloody suffering*, my emphasis) as a nameless "mísera escrava."

Ten years prior to the publication of *Primeiros cantos*, Domingos José Gonçalves de Magalhães published the poem "Invocação à saudade" (Invocation to longing) in his collection *Suspiros poéticos e saudades* (1836) (Poetic sighs and longings). Although its treatment of the slave is not individualized as in "A escrava," the images of longing and suffering as well as a specific reference to the "miserável Africano" suggest its importance for Gonçalves Dias's own poem. It is a strongly worded work that critiques the imperial greed that drove the slave trade and portrays Brazil as a land that will flourish only after everyone is free:

> Oh terra do Brasil, terra querida,
> Quantas vezes do mísero Africano

Te regaram as lágrimas saudosas?
Quantas vezes teus bosques repetiram
Magoados acentos
Do cântico do escravo,
Ao som dos duros golpes do machado?

Oh bárbara ambição, que sem piedade,
Cega e surda de Cristo a lei postergas,
E assoberbando mares, e perigos,
Vais infame roubar, não vãs riquezas,
Mas homens, que escravizas!
Mil vezes o Senhor, para punir-te,
Opôs ao teu baixel ondas, e ventos;
Mil vezes, mas embalde,
Nas cavernas do mar caiu gemendo.
Á voz do Eterno obediente a terra
Se mostra austera e parca,
Que a lágrima do escravo esteriliza
O terreno que orvalha.
A Natureza preza a Liberdade,
E só franqueia aos livres seus tesouros.

Oh suspirada, oh cara Liberdade,
Descende asinha do Africano à choça,
Seu pranto enxuga, quebra-lhe as cadeias,
E adoça-lhe da pátria a dor saudosa. (348–349)

(Oh land of Brazil, beloved homeland,
How many times did
The suffering African's tears of longing
Replenish you?
How many times did your woodlands
Reverberate with the mournful modulations
Of the slave song
With the sound of the machete's hard blows?

Oh barbarous ambition, blind and deaf to Christ,
You pitilessly disregard the law.
And overcoming the seas and dangers,

You infamously steal not vain riches,
But men, whom you enslave!
To punish you, a thousand times God
Opposed your fleet with waves and winds;
A thousand times, yet in vain,
Into the depths of the sea they sank, groaning.
Obedient to the Eternal's voice,
The land appears austere and barren,
For the slave's tears sterilize
The ground they water.
Nature prizes Liberty,
And only bestows its treasures on those who are free.

Oh desired and cherished Liberty,
Lower your wing over the African in the hovel,
Dry his tears, break his chains,
And soothe his painful longing for home.)

The poems by Gonçalves de Magalhães and Gonçalves Dias exemplify two distinct attitudes toward the slave trade. "A escrava" laments the situation of the slave, while "Invocação à saudade" denounces the institution of slavery and is one of the earliest examples of Brazilian abolitionist poetry. It is also important to consider the possible connection between "Invocação" and Gonçalves Dias's prose work *Meditação*, in which he explicitly attacks the institution of slavery. Both works were written prior to the 1850 law that prohibited slave trafficking to Brazil and, in the case of "Invocação," thirty years before Castro Alves wrote his celebrated "Navio negreiro" (1868) (Slave ship), whose narrator describes the abuse meted out to slaves in transit and his horror over the fact that the flag under which the ship sails is Brazilian.[27]

Also before "Navio negreiro" and other abolitionist works written by Castro Alves along the lines of his "Vozes d'África" (Voices from Africa) and "O negro bandido" (The black bandit), the poet Luís Gama, who was born free, was sold into slavery by his father, and ultimately became a court advocate for those illegally enslaved, wrote *Primeiras trovas burlescas de Getulino* (1859) (First burlesque verses by Getulino). Gama's unique approach included satirizing the middle and upper classes, especially the faux nobility who tried to pass as white. For Gama, everyone was a *bode* (goat), a pejorative term used to refer to mulattoes, and he created the neologism *bodarrada* (goat herd) to describe the African-based heritage of Brazilian society as a whole. His poem titled "Quem sou eu?" (Who am I?) is wonderfully ironic and pokes fun at all sorts of people who claim to be white and whom he calls his "parentes" (relatives). His jocular diatribe also deftly jabs at those who trafficked in slaves in what was supposedly the "century of reason":

Que no século das luzes,
Os birbantes mais lapuzes
Compram negros e comendas,
Tem brasões, não—das *Kalendas*,
E, com tretas e com furtos
Vão subindo a passos curtos. (In *Luís Gama*, 178)

(That in the century of lights,
The coarsest scoundrels
Buy blacks and titles,
They have no coat of arms—from the calends,
And through skullduggery and thieving
They rapidly climb the social ladder.)

Gama was unique in his challenge to poetic convention. Not only did he ridicule racial passing, stupidity, and machinations, but he also used classical forms to denounce them. References to Homer, Dante, and Camões as well as to Greek and Roman gods and heroes abound in his verse, although Gama uses them to conjure up the epic if not sublime nature of a society's connivance, pretense, imbecility, and malfeasance. In his ode to snuff, "A pitada," he combines the erudite and vulgar to praise its substance, application, and results:

Vem de engenho sublimado;
É capaz de tirar monco
Do nariz mais confinado (In *Luís Gama*, 130)
. . .
Oh! Pitada milagrosa,
Pitadinha portentosa!
Eu quisera ser um Dante,
Ter uma harpa ressonante,
P'ra cantar a tua glória (131)

(Derived from sublime invention;
[Snuff] is capable of extracting snot
From the most constricted nostril.
. . .
Oh! Miraculous snuff,
Dear wondrous snuff!
I wish I were a Dante,
With a resonant harp,
To sing your glory)

Gama's collection also contains a few poems that address in more somber fashion the African experience in relation to other topics, including nature, romantic love, and his mother, whom he looked for after gaining his freedom but never found. Like Gonçalves Dias's "A escrava," Gama's "Coleirinho" opens with an epigraph, in this case, from the Latin poet Tibullus, whose elegiac verses include a line about a slave in chains who sings. The word *coleirinho*, the diminutive form of *coleiro*, is an endearing reference to a little bird and is the name given to the slave by the poet, who exhorts him to sing to ease his longing for his country and the family that suffers his absence. Although the theme of *saudade* is central to both poems, Alsgá's dreams of Africa occur as she looks across the ocean, while Coleirinho is in chains and caged like a pet bird on a perch. As Gama acknowledges, to survive such inhumane conditions requires a song to break the pain—"o mal quebranta" (156)—the elegiac poem that we are reading. What gives Gama's composition greater political force is his emphasis on slavery's separation of family members and its impacts on the child who, "sem pai, no agreste ninho, / Lá ficou sem ti, sem vida" (157) (without a father, in the wilderness nest, / Remained [in Africa] without you, without life). Like most of Gama's poems, "Coleirinho" might be read as a commentary on his own experience as a child separated from his mother, a slave; who lost his rightful freedom when sold into servitude; and who suffered a lifetime of harsh treatment because he was outspoken and black. His endurance as a "provisional lawyer," without a diploma, who repeatedly challenged the judicial system and defended those illegally enslaved, undoubtedly owed much to his songs, or *trovas*, about racial prejudice and injustice, which are unlike anything written in Brazilian literature.[28]

MACHADO DE ASSIS ON RACE

O melhor modo de apreciar o chicote é ter-lhe o cabo na mão.

(The best way to appreciate the whip is to have the handle in one's hand.)

MACHADO DE ASSIS, *QUINCAS BORBA*, 1891

While Luís Gama published poems as well as newspaper articles that critiqued Brazil's attitude toward its African heritage and slavery, Joaquim Maria Machado de Assis, the country's most distinguished author and a mulatto like Gama, rarely turned his attention to race or slavery despite his friendship with abolitionists of the period, including Joaquim Nabuco, with whom he founded the Academia Brasileira de Letras. Machado was far more interested in dissecting the foibles of the bourgeoisie, especially the *bacharel* (college graduate in law), whose pretensions and failures were the focus of his subtly eviscerating works. In many ways his playful, ironic attitude toward the middle class has much in common with Gama, although Gama's character Getulino, who always self-identified as black, wielded race as his weapon against the blunderingly hypocritical and pretentious individuals who denied their heritage and proclaimed themselves to be white.

Literary critics often mention Machado's apparent lack of interest in writing about race or the problems of the Brazilian nation, although both of these topics appear in "Sabina," a long poem from his volume of poetry titled *Americanas* (1875).[29] Published just four years after the Lei do Ventre Livre (Law of the Free Womb), which declared that children of slaves born thenceforth would be free, *Americanas* is the first book to treat all three races as Brazilian. The storyline in "Sabina" is all too familiar: a beautiful house slave is seen bathing by the young master of the house, Otávio, who is on break from his university studies. Their attraction is mutual, and they make love over several days. He returns to the city and his classes, while Sabina, who learns she is pregnant, awaits his return. When Otávio next appears, he is accompanied by his young bride. Sabina decides to kill herself near the same spot where she and Otávio first made love, but her "instinto materno" (maternal instinct) prevents the act.

Like Machado's early novels, the poem has all the emotional trappings of romantic literature: a couple's attraction, their passion, the consequences of their lovemaking, a long separation, the presence of another woman, heartbreak, and a near-suicide. Nature also plays a fundamental role as the idyllic setting for the couple's encounter and for the tragic heroine's planned escape from unrequited love. If "Sabina" is read strictly as a romantic poem, Sabina ultimately survives love because of motherhood. By contrast, José de Alencar's famous Indian maiden character, Iracema, gives birth but perishes from longing for the Portuguese Martim, the child's father. Readers at the time might also presume that Sabina's child would be born free, which may be implicit in the poem's ending. But the poem is far more complex in its use of romantic imagery and might also be understood as an indictment of society's treatment of domestic slaves like Sabina who are deceived into believing they are not enslaved but rather members of the family. The poem's initial stanzas describe Sabina as stylishly dressed and far removed from those who live in the slave quarters. The poem notes that her smooth hands are unmarked by fieldwork and that she grew up "entre carinhos e afeições" (among tenderness and affection) in the big house, whose *iaiá* (little missy) was her cherished playmate and whose young master is now the object of her passion.

But Sabina *is* a slave, and Otávio's desire, as the poem's narrator informs us, stems from *cobiça* (greed), the same vice criticized by earlier Portuguese poets and one that Sabina fails to perceive. In his passionate speech to seduce her, Otávio suggests that they are equals: "No livre peito / De seus senhores tens a liberdade" (Because of your masters' heartfelt freedom, you are free). The irony builds when he adds, "A melhor liberdade, o puro afeto / Que te elegeu entre as demais cativas, / E de afagos te cobre!" (The best freedom is from the pure fondness / That chose you from all the other slaves / And covers you with affection!) Riddled with false claims about her actual status as a slave, his hollow romantic speech paves the way to her physical surrender.

Machado's portrait of Otávio is an early example of his disdain for the pompous and duplicitous *bacharel* figure that appears in many of his later works. His tongue-in-cheek description of Otávio suggests that regardless of intellect, the diploma in hand is sufficient to guarantee him a place in government or, in Machado's subtly ironic words, "Os curvos braços da feliz cadeira / Donde o legislador a rédea empunha / Dos lépidos frisões do Estado" (The curved arms of the felicitous chair, from which the legislator grasps the reins of the State's sprightly horse). The youth's superficiality and frivolity are also the source of a pun by the poet, who describes the adoring and fawning Otávio as a *cativo* (captive) of the city girl whom he meets and marries. Sabina's fate is sealed by romantic innocence, and perhaps Otávio's is as well, but he and his bride are embraced by the family, while Sabina faces alone the consequences of the family's "liberties."

In September 1887, one year prior to the abolition of slavery, Machado took up the issue of emancipation in no. 29 of his ironic chronicles, which appeared in the Rio-based *Gazeta de Notícias* under the series title *Gazeta da Holanda* (1886–1888).[30] The poem satirizes the years of debate about slavery in Brazil over whether "[o] escravo inda é escravo ou gente" (the slave is still to be considered a slave or a human being). The first-person narrator expresses wonder that members of the slave community, or *interessado* (interested party), whom he sees everywhere in the streets, have been left out of these discussions. Hailing a passing vendor, the conversation, with all its irony, is as follows:

E disse-lhe: "Pai Silvério,
Guarda as alfaces e as couves;
Tenho negócio mais sério,
Quero que m'o expliques. Ouves?"

Contei-lhe em palavras lisas,
Quais as teses do Instituto,
Opiniões e divisas.
Que há de responder-me o bruto?

—"Meu senhor, eu, entra ano,
Sai ano, trabalho nisto;
Há muito senhor humano,
Mas o meu é nunca visto.

"Pancada, quando não vendo,
Pancada que dói, que arde;
Se vendo o que ando vendendo,
Pancada, por chegar tarde.

"Dia santo nem domingo
Não tenho. Comida pouca:
Pires de feijão, e um pingo
De café, que molha a boca.

"Por isso, digo ao perfeito
Instituto, grande e bravo:
Tu falou muito direito,
Tu tá livre, eu fico escravo." (*Cronicas*, 392–393)

(And I said to him: "Father Silvério,
Keep your lettuce and collards;
I have a more serious issue,
I want you to explain it to me, hear?"

I told him in even words,
What the Institute's arguments were,
Their opinions and slogans.
And what did the brute have to say in reply?

— "Well, sir, I think on this
Year in and year out;
There are plenty of humane owners
But mine has yet to be seen.

"A beating when I don't sell,
A beating that hurts, that burns;
If I sell what I am hawking,
Then I get a beating for getting back late.

"Neither saint's day nor Sunday
Do I get off. Food: very little;
A small plate of beans and a drop
Of coffee that barely wets the mouth.

"For that reason I say to the perfect
Institute, so grand and brave:
You talk very well
But you're free, and I'm still a slave."

Machado's references to and occasional attacks on slavery are also embedded in his larger portrait of bourgeois society. For instance, in his story "O caso da vara" (1891) (The case of the switch), Damião, a young seminarian, seeks the support of the widow Sinhá Rita to convince his father that he is better off leaving the seminary. The wily Damião reasons that if he pleads with Rita, who is the woman friend of his weak-willed godfather, she will succeed in forcing him to secure Damião's irascible father's consent. Damião's supplications contrast with the silence of the *crias* (poor children raised in well-to-do households) to whom Rita teaches sewing for her income. One of them, a small black girl called Lucrécia, timidly laughs when Damião, now optimistic about his bid for freedom, tells Rita an amusing story. The girl's laugh earns her Rita's displeasure and the promise of the switch if she fails to complete her task. Damião feels pity for Lucrécia, who is sickly and bears the marks of captivity, and he decides to protect her from Rita's wrath if she fails to finish her work. Later, when Rita tells Damião to retrieve the switch for Lucrécia's whipping, he pauses and reflects on his pledge. Knowing his chances of freedom, like the girl's fate, are squarely in Rita's hands, he hands her the switch.

Like Luís Gama, Machado distanced his literary persona from the middle-class characters whom he satirized. Unlike Gama, however, he never self-identified as an African descendant or mulatto and spoke with a quasi-aristocratic voice to critique bourgeois stupidities and malice. That his protagonists are often slaveholders adds to his critique of a society that, as Gama often observed, allowed idiots, fools, and even criminals to own and abuse slaves. As Machado's narrator in the novel *Quincas Borba* ironically notes and the sadistic Sinhá Rita plainly demonstrates, the whip has a satisfying feel and empowering capability—as long as the handle is in one's hand.

Machado published *Quincas Borba* and "O caso da vara" in 1891, three years after the emancipation of slaves. The short story begins with the narrator's inability to date the event described, although he asserts it happened prior to 1850, the year slave trafficking was officially abolished.[31] Machado's narrators often engage in this kind of fudging of facts that ultimately reveals an important relation between the past and present. What the reader of "O caso da vara" is told is that Lucrécia is black (*negrinha*) and has suffered physically, from the burn on her hand and the scar on her forehead to her frequent cough and overall frail condition. Although she is described as Rita's *cria* and *discípula* (student) and not a slave, Lucrécia labors long hours under Rita's watchful eye, and if the daily quota is not met, as is frequently Lucrécia's lot, she is beaten. What remains unspoken is Lucrécia's attention to Damião's tale and the fact that she laughs despite her subjugation. Her laugh also mirrors Rita's own reaction as if they were equals.

Damião's rationalizations that lead him to retrieve the switch illustrate the way self-interest so often trumps professed good intentions. They are pure Machado in his ironic assessment of those who look to gain. A more sobering image is Lucrécia, who has no agency and whose fate, as the narrator implies, is ineluctably tied to the sharper end of the switch. In Machado's earlier chronicle, Pai Silvério comments indirectly on this fact: good intentions by those who are free have no meaning for the enslaved as long as the latter are beaten daily. As late as 1891, Machado was writing about the whip as part of Brazil's identity and heritage as a slave-owning society, a heritage that continued to be upheld by the best of Brazilian society.

QUESTIONS OF RACE

"A abolição é a aurora da liberdade; esperemos o sol; emancipado o preto, resta emancipar o branco."

(Abolition is the dawn of liberty; let us await the sun; once blacks are free, what remains is to free the whites.)

PAULO, IN MACHADO DE ASSIS, *ESAÚ E JACOB*, 1904

Machado's tongue-in-cheek commentary about emancipation is spoken in the voice of the liberal Paulo Santos, who, unlike his conservative twin brother, Pedro, supports freeing the slaves and the republican cause. However, not every Brazilian abolitionist was liberal, and not every conservative was against emancipation. Joaquim Nabuco is a good example of this seemingly contradictory position. A diplomat and monarchist who left Brazil after the installation of the republic, in 1889, he was a major voice in the fight to free the slaves alongside Castro Alves and the lesser-known but important José do Patrocínio, a monarchist and co-founder with Nabuco of the Sociedade contra a Escravidão (Society against Slavery), in 1880, and the engineer-journalist André Rebouças, who collaborated with Nabuco and Patrocínio in the abolitionist cause.

One of Nabuco's most rousing attacks on slavery appears in his book *O abolicionismo* (1883), in the twelfth chapter, titled "A escravidão atual." He argues that while Brazil promotes itself to other nations as a country that has abolished slavery as a result of the Free Womb legislation, newspapers in Brazil show the opposite to be true:

Em qualquer número de um grande jornal brasileiro — exceto, tanto quanto sei, na Bahia, onde a imprensa da capital deixou de inserir anúncios sobre escravos — encontram-se, com efeito, as seguintes classes de informações que definem completamente a condição presente dos escravos: anúncios, de compra, venda e aluguel de escravos, em que sempre figuram as palavras *mucama, moleque, bonita peça, rapaz, par-*

dinho, rapariga de casa de família (as mulheres livres anunciam-se como *senhoras* a fim de melhor se diferenciarem das escravas); editais para praças de escravos . . . ; anúncios de negros fugidos acompanhados em muitos jornais da conhecida vinheta do negro descalço com a trouxa ao ombro, nos quais os escravos são descritos muitas vezes pelos sinais de castigos que sofreram . . . ; notícias de manumissões, bastante numerosas; narrações de crimes cometidos por escravos contra os senhores, mas sobretudo contra os agentes dos senhores, e de crimes cometidos por estes contra aqueles, castigos bárbaros e fatais, que formam, entretanto, uma insignificantíssima parte dos abusos do poder dominical.[32]

(In any number of the greatest newspapers in Brazil—except, as far as I know, in Bahia, where the capital newspapers stopped inserting notices about slaves—one can find, in effect, the following types of information that fully define the present-day condition of slaves: ads for buying, selling and renting slaves, in which appear the words *mammy, black boy, pretty piece, boy, little brown boy, family servant girl* (free women describe themselves as *ladies* to distinguish themselves from slaves); ads for slave markets . . . ; ads about fugitive slaves accompanied in many newspapers by the well-known image of a barefoot slave with a bundle on his shoulder, in which slaves are many times described by the marks from punishment that they suffered . . . ; notices of a fair number of manumissions; stories about crimes committed by slaves against their owners, but especially against the owners' agents, and crimes committed by the latter against the former, barbarous and fatal crimes that constitute only a very insignificant number of abuses carried out by dominical power.)

The chapter ends with a list of the numerous crimes and infractions committed against slaves, and it constitutes one of the nation's most forceful arguments on behalf of emancipation in Brazil. As a member of a wealthy and high-powered Northeastern family and as a rising man of letters, Nabuco had access to the political leadership and became the spokesperson and standard-bearer for the abolitionist movement.

At the same time, a subsequent chapter in *O abolicionismo*, titled "Influência da escravidão sobre a nacionalidade" (Influence of slavery on nationality), strikes a different note with regard to the African legacy in Brazil. Nabuco agrees with scientific theories at the time about superior and inferior races and argues that racial mixing of whites and blacks (as with masters and slaves) had produced a less civilized population that in his words was "a primeira vingança das vítimas" (the first revenge by the victims).³³ For Nabuco, miscegenation was the penalty and cross to bear because of the "vícios do sangue africano" (vices of African blood) that included "desenvovimento mental atrasado," "instintos bárbaros," and "superstições grosseiras" (arrested mental development, barbarous instincts, and crude superstitions). Nabuco subscribed to the idea that Brazil would have been better off, more homogeneous, if it had been discovered three centuries later or if other colonizing forces, including the Dutch, had remained and propagated to ensure a larger European presence. He also imagined a Brazil more along the lines of the United States or a more robust Brazil populated without mixing of Europeans and free Africans. For Nabuco, the legacy of slavery, or "payback" by the slave, is the mulatto, a hybrid figure disdained by whites, Africans, and Brazilian blacks in the nineteenth century. This is the same figure, or *bode*, whom Luís Gama wrote about as the unstated racial identity of all Brazilians.³⁴

Opinions like Nabuco's about Brazil's mixed-race population are addressed in Aluísio Azevedo's *O mulato* (1881), a widely read and popular novel about a young man's return from Europe to his native land and his cool reception by closed, Portuguese-descended middle and upper classes in São Luís, capital of Maranhão. Raimundo only vaguely remembers his father and has no memory of his mother. Following his father's assassination, he was sent to Portugal, where he was educated and graduated from the university in Coimbra. He has only recently arrived from Europe by way of Rio to sell his father's lands. Except for Manuel, his father's brother and the town leader, local society keeps Raimundo at arm's length. He finds the people's aloofness curious but passes the time reading and talking with his cousin Ana Rosa, with whom he gradually falls in love. When he asks Manuel for her hand in marriage, his uncle refuses; only after Raimundo insists does Manuel reveal that Raimundo's mother was his deceased father's slave and that she and Raimundo were granted their freedom shortly after his birth. The revelation staggers Raimundo, who has never questioned his race, although he has long been curious about his mother's identity. Secure in his reasoning and feelings, he continues the courtship, and he and a pregnant Ana Rosa make plans to flee to Rio.

Like most love-on-the-run melodramas, *O mulato* ends badly for the couple. Raimundo is ambushed and shot dead by Luís Dias, Manuel's wily Portuguese accountant and preferred son-in-law candidate, despite the fact that Ana Rosa despises him. Luís conspires with the sly prelate Diogo, who suspects that Raimundo knows about his murderous past. Traumatized by Raimundo's killing, Ana Rosa miscarries and falls deathly ill. Unlike the women in most stories of *amour fou*, she survives Raimundo's death, the loss of their child, and her own illness. The novel ends a few years later, with a surprising glimpse of Ana Rosa affectionately addressing Luís, who is accompanied by their three children. This unexpected conclusion is Azevedo's ironic commentary on the strength of the status quo, which survives by erasing all traces of Raimundo's hybrid presence.

In *O mulato*, Azevedo portrays an insulated community that prides itself on its religious practices and beliefs, its Portuguese heritage, and the apparent absence of racial mixing that characterized Northeast plantation society.[35] Azevedo's anticlericalism is evident in the character of the sly and murderous Diogo, and his abolitionist stance is explicit: Dona Bárbara, Manuel's aptly named live-in mother-in-law, is vile in her racist rants and harsh treatment of slaves; ostentatiously pious, she surrounds herself with statues, candles, and other trappings of the Church. But just as her piety is false, her religious beliefs reveal her to be a hypocrite: despite her Catholic zeal, she wears a *figa*, the African symbol for good luck, to protect her from the evil eye. Bárbara and other women in the novel are especially villainous types, but male characters are also intolerant.[36] Manuel's friend, the boorish and self-important Freitas, rails against blacks, especially female domestic servants, whom he denounces for passing along "indecent stories" and "immorality" to their young white mistresses. His extreme fastidiousness in manner and dress seems fueled by his fascination with tales of sordidness. He states, "Sei de outro caso de uma escrava que contagiou a uma família inteira de empigens e dartros de caráter feio!" (95). (I know another case of a slave who infected an entire family with her ugly character's ringworm and skin sores!)

While Manuel obligingly shelters his nephew for purported family reasons, his real motivation is capitalist greed. He keeps Raimundo close to ensure his brokering of Raimundo's inherited property to earn a tidy profit. Reactions of townspeople toward Raimundo vary to the extreme; despite rumors of his heritage, young, eligible women like Ana Rosa are attracted by his dark good looks and polished manners, which seem different and exotic in the insular Maranhão context. Men like the pompous Brito display a wholly different attitude. Observing Raimundo from a distance, Brito confides to his friend Bento, "São assim estes pomadas cá da terra dos papagaios! E ainda se zangam quando queremos limpar-lhes a raça, sem cobrar nada por isso!" (122). (That's what those full-of-airs types from this parrot land are like! And what's more, they fume when we want to cleanse them of their race, without even charging for our services!) The Lusophobe character Sebastião de Campos repeatedly laments that the Dutch lost the War of Guararapes and were ousted from Brazil (101). Azevedo makes a brief tongue-in-cheek reference to a "pale mulatto" who joins in the town gossip when Raimundo suddenly departs his uncle's house. Following speculation that Manuel has asked him to leave, the fellow remarks, "É muito bem feito, não consentirem que estes negros se metam conosco!"(245). (Very well done, people shouldn't allow those blacks to mix with us!) Here the dominant ideology leads not only to passing but also to self-negation and discrimination against one's own race.[37]

While several Rio literary critics responded positively to Azevedo's indictment of Maranhão's racial intolerance, the novel's reception in Maranhão was fiercely negative—so much so that Azevedo moved to Rio, where he later published his celebrated *Casa de pensão* (1884) (Boardinghouse) and *O cortiço* (1890) (*A Brazilian Tenement* [1926]) prior to abandoning writing altogether for the diplomatic service.[38] But as Gilberto Freyre once observed, Azevedo's critique of Maranhão could also be read as a commentary on Brazilian society at large, including the urban centers of the Central-South, where social Darwinism, French positivism, and an ideology that equated Brazil's mixed-race population with tropical disease and societal degradation were also apparent (Peard, *Race, Place*, 84). This is clearly the case in Nabuco's lament about miscegenation and national identity. In the 1930s, Gilberto Freyre changed the terms of that particular discourse in his *Casa grande e senzala*, in which he views Brazil's racially mixed population as a sign of its progress as a "social democracy." But that narrative was also problematic and generated its own set of racial stereotypes consistent with the language of eugenics and the politics of "whitening" in the nineteenth century.

Perhaps the strongest but least read indictment of racial prejudice at the turn of the twentieth century is a long prose poem by the symbolist poet João da Cruz e Sousa titled "Emparedado" (Walled in). Appearing at the end of his book *Evocações* (1898) and published a decade after emancipation, it is a prose-poem manifesto attacking social determinism and discriminatory practices that prevented blacks from gaining full participation in Brazilian society. Born to former slaves in Santa Catarina, Cruz e Sousa received an excellent education with the support of a patron but was rejected for administrative positions for which he was eminently qualified. He and his poetry attracted slings and arrows from prominent literary critic Araripe Júnior, who disparagingly described the poet, recently arrived to Rio, on the order of a gape-mouthed primitive. Cruz e Sousa's blackness also became the measure by which Araripe Júnior compared the "combative" nature of Cruz e Sousa's volume *Missal* (1893) with the "psychological acuity" of his contemporary Raul Pompéia's poems in *Canção sem metro* (Songs without meter):

> Entre as *Canções sem metro* e a obra do poeta catarineta, há uma grande diferença determinada pela raça e pelo temperamento de cada um. Raul Pompéia possui a acuidade dos psicólogos da nova geração e um espírito profundamente inclinado à filosofia sugestiva, de sorte que os seus escritos aparecem sempre impregnados disso a que Proudhon chamava *l'expression de l'avenir*: tendências tolstoínas para a organização de serviço de salvação da idéia. Cruz e Sousa, porém, anda em esfera muito diferente. De origem Africana . . . sem mescla de sangue branco ou indígena, todas as qualidades de sua raça surgem no poeta em interessante luta com o meio civilizado que é o produto de atividade cerebral de outras raças. A primeira consequência desse encontro é a sensação da "maravilha." (In Magalhães Júnior, *Poesia e vida*, 83)

> (Between *Canções sem metro* and the Catarinense poet's work there exists a great difference determined by the race and temperament of each. Raul Pompéia possesses the acuity of the new generation's psychologists and a spirit profoundly inclined toward suggestive philosophy, so that his writings always appear permeated with what Proudhon called *l'expression de l'avenir*: Tolstoian tendencies toward organization in the service of the idea's salvation. However, Cruz e Sousa moves in a very different sphere. Of African origin . . . with no mix of white or Indian blood, all the qualities of his race surge within the poet in an interesting battle with civilization, which is the product of the cerebral activity of other races. The first consequence of this encounter is the sense of the "marvelous.")

Araripe Júnior elaborates on this assertion as he imagines Cruz e Sousa walking down Rio's fashionable Rua do Ouvidor, dumbstruck by the goods on display in shop windows. The critic also projects onto the poet his anxiety about writing like his (white) contemporaries:

> Nesse momento a raça sente a necessidade de um grande esforço para fugir só ao ritmo natural dos antepassados, mas também sua predileção pelos tons vermelhos e pela passagem rápida das cores vivas, sem ancenúbios, que caracterizam a arte primitiva. Como, porém, evitar essa fatalidade? O poeta lê e busca vertiginosamente, nos livros dos nefelibatas e nas obras indicadas pela escola, o vocabulário, a técnica e as situa-

ções individuais que mais lhe convém adaptar. Uma verdadeira caça à palavra e ao gesto. (In ibid., 84–85)

(At this moment his race feels the need to make a giant effort to flee not only the natural rhythm of his ancestors, but also its predilection for red tones and the quickly moving vivid colors, without nuances, that characterize primitive art. But how to avoid that fatality? The poet reads and searches vertiginously in the cloud-dwellers' books and in works read at school for the vocabulary, technique, and individual situations that are most agreeable for him to adapt. A veritable hunt for the right word and gesture.)[39]

José Veríssimo, who was the country's major literary critic alongside Araripe Júnior, avoided a racial interpretation in his critique and simply dismissed *Missal* as an "'amontoado de palavras . . . [que] não servem para não dizer nada'" (heap of words that serve to say nothing) (ibid., 85).

Cruz e Sousa's response to the disparaging comments about himself and his work was "O emparedado." In it, he writes of pain, suffering, an uphill climb with "todos os empiricismos preconceituosos" (all the prejudicial empiricisms) strapped onto his back, and a slog through the "lama das teorias" (mud of theories) in search of an ideal—a feeling of peace, personal and aesthetic freedom, and mutual understanding, all of which he is denied as a black man and poet. In his words, he was "fatalizado pelo sangue" (condemned by his blood) and forever struggling because of his race, "que a ditadora ciência d'hipóteses negou em absoluto para as funções do Entendimento e, principalmente, do entendimento artístico da palavra escrita" (which the dictatorial science of hypotheses negated in absolute terms from any functions of Understanding and, principally, from artistic understanding of the written word). Cruz e Sousa describes his poetry as his "nefando Crime" (nefarious crime) by which he transgressed as if he were the biblical Cain or a delirious Othello. In manifesto style, he defends and exalts his difference: "Eu não pertenço à velha árvore genealógica das intelectualidades medidas, dos produtos anêmicos dos meios lutulentos" (I do not belong to the old genealogical tree of measured intellectualities, of anemic products from muddy means); he fights for the right to "respirar livre" (breathe freely) and release "toda a onda viva de vibrações e de chamas do Sentimento que contivemos por tanto e tão longe tempo guardada na nossa alma" (all the ardent wave of Geeling's vibrations and flames that we have contained so much and for such a long time kept in our souls).

The poem contains several beautiful stanzas dedicated to Africa, portrayed in one line as a sublime land of epic "solidões maravilhosos" and "esquisita Originalidade" (marvelous solitudes, exquisite Originality) that are deserving of a black Dante or colossal and prodigious sculptures. But the ugly walls built silently around the African race by forces such as "Prejudices, Science, and Criticism, Ignorance and Imbecility" continue to grow upward, stone by stone, toward the stars. This tragic prison-house imagery perhaps explains Cruz e Sousa's repeated references to night and stars in his verse. As critic Heitor Martins has observed, the poet opted for a large, black canvas on which to write his words with stars, writing "white on black" as opposed to the more conventional "black on white." As "O emparedado" makes clear and many of his other poems suggest, Cruz e Sousa experienced racial prejudice and barriers that emancipation and the republic could never erase or dismantle. Fortunately for his readers and those later critics like Raimundo Magalhães Júnior, who proclaimed him Brazil's foremost symbolist poet, Cruz e Sousa was still able to see the stars.

~ THREE ~

Oriental Imaginings and Travel at the Turn of the Twentieth Century

Os japoneses dizem: tempura *(de "tempero"). . . . A palavra é também conhecida em África, de importação portuguesa claramente; eu conheci, em Moçambique, uma negra que se chamava* Tempura.

(The Japanese say: tempura *[from* tempero *(seasoning)]. . . . The word is also known in Africa, clearly imported from Portugal; in Mozambique I met a black woman who was called* Tempura.*)*

WENCESLAU DE MORAES, *O CULTO DO CHÁ*, 1905

Despite the gradual loss of shipping routes and territories, such as Calicut, Bombay, and Malacca, in the seventeenth century, the Portuguese continued to govern Goa, Daman, Diu, East Timor, and Macau. Decorative reminders of the heyday of maritime exploration in the East continued to be produced in the form of *china de encomenda*, Chinese porcelains that were first exported to Portugal in the sixteenth century.[1] The earliest, called Kraaks, after the Portuguese ships (carracks) that transported them, were delicate white-and-blue ceramics with landscape designs; later porcelains added Portuguese coats of arms, the Jesuit "IJS," the astrolabe, and other emblems of Portugal's navigational acumen and territorial reach.[2] Still other locally crafted luxuries brought back to Portugal included crucifixes, statues of Catholic saints, oratories, and writing desks used by the Jesuits in Asia. Finely carved and lacquered Oriental furnishings; Japanese and Chinese silks, screens, and fans; and even more utilitarian items such as mugs and snuffboxes were also exported.[3] The commercial appeal of the blue-and-white porcelains from the Ming Dynasty (1368–1644), Transitional Period (1620–1638), and Qing Dynasty (1644–1911), alongside the desire to modernize Portugal, led the marquis of Pombal to found a chinoiserie factory in Lisbon in 1767. The Real Fábrica de Louça do Rato (Royal Dishware Factory of Rato) was an annex of the Real Fábrica das Sedas (Royal Silks Factory) founded in 1734 to produce silks in imitation of those from Asia. These two factories continued to make chinoiserie and other Far East–inspired goods into the nineteenth century (plates 20 and 21).[4]

The delicate designs, furnishings, and decorative pieces were part of a highly rarified and aestheticized nineteenth-century image of the Orient, contrasting sharply with the equally pervasive image of a wily and barbarous Asia given over to corruption, drugs, and prostitution. This dual image was especially true of China, which Fernão Mendes Pinto described in the sixteenth century as an enlightened society and in many ways superior to the West. The counterimage of a fierce and brutal people was undoubtedly fueled by an incident that took place in Macau in 1849. In a travel memoir titled *Apontamentos d'uma viagem de Lisboa à China e da China a Lisboa* (1852) (Notes of a voyage from Lisbon to China and from China to Lisbon), Carlos José Caldeira recounts the assassination of José Maria Ferreira do Amaral, a naval hero and then governor of Macau, by a group of Chinese. The killing was a result of an 1845 Portuguese decree that declared Macau to be an open port, shortly after the British turned Hong Kong into a free and commercially attractive port city. The Portuguese decree, which terminated a Mandarin-controlled customs operation in Macau, was followed by a series of actions to further entrench and extend Portuguese colonial rule in the area, including the occupation of the island of Taipa to the south, where the Portuguese built a fort and raised the Portuguese flag.[5] Caldeira spares no detail in his description of Amaral's murder near the Porta do Cerco, the barrier gate erected by Jesuits in 1573 to demarcate Macau from surrounding lands:

> Na tarde de 22 d'Agosto de 1849, o governador Amaral saíra a cavalo a passear no campo, como de costume, e nesse dia só ia acompanhado pelo ajudante de ordens Leite: a menos de duzentos passos antes de chegar á Porta do Cerco, um china se lhe aproximou apresentando um papel como de requerimento, e outros saíram de repente detrás de uns pequenos combros de areia que os escondiam, e ao todo sete o atacaram com *taifós* (espadas curtas e rectas que os chinas usam aos pares, manejando uma em cada mão), e foi-lhe fácil de sucumbir um homem, ainda que bastante valente e corajoso, que estava desarmada e só tinha o braço

3.1. *Kraak porcelain (16th century)*

3.2. *Detail, Chinese screen with Portuguese hunters (17th–18th century), replica*

3.3. *Portuguese chinoiserie (18th–19th century)*

esquerdo: derrubaram-no do cavalo, e bem assim o ajudante Leite. Cortaram-lhe a cabeça e a mão, e sem medo ou precipitação as levaram, passando pela Porta do Cerco, onde então havia um posto de guarda chinesa, que a duzentos passos observou pacificamente tudo isto, e dei-xou a passar em sossego os assassinos! (113)

(On the afternoon of August 22, 1849, Governor Amaral left by horse to go into the countryside, as was his custom, and on that day was only accompanied by his adjutant Leite: less than two hundred paces before reaching the Porta do Cerco, a Chinese man approached him with a paper as if it were a formal petition; others suddenly came out from hiding behind some small hillocks of sand, and all seven attacked him with *taifós* (short, straight swords that the Chinese use in pairs, wielding one in each hand), and it was easy to overcome a man, even one quite valiant and courageous, who was unarmed and only had a left arm: they pulled him from his horse as they did the adjutant Leite. They cut off his head and his hand, and without fear or haste, they walked through the Porta do Cerco, where a Chinese guard post, from two hundred paces away, watched all this peacefully and allowed the assassins to pass through calmly!)

Caldeira also reports that, fearing mass invasion by the Chinese, several hundred of whom now occupied the nearby Passaleão fortress, three dozen Portuguese soldiers, commanded by Lieutenant Nicolau Vicente Mesquita, charged and captured the fort the day after Amaral's assassination (114). News of Amaral's brutal killing and the Portuguese success in ousting the Chinese from Passaleão circulated widely in Portugal and England and fed the "yellow peril" fear associated with the mass migration of coolies from Macau and Hong Kong to the West and with a long siege in China known as the Taiping Rebellion (1850–1864). Perhaps this is why, as critic Álvaro Manuel Machado contends, nineteenth-century romantic writers in Portugal, unlike the French and other European authors, were not attracted to the Orient as subject matter, "nem a nível temático geral da evasão do eu em paragens longínquas, nem a nível específico da nossa tradição de um Oriente simbólico da grandeza decadente do país" (*O mito do Oriente*, 78) (neither on a general thematic level about a fleeing "I" to far-off places, nor on a specific level about our tradition of an Orient symbolic of the country's decadent greatness). However, literary interest in the Orient is evident later on, with the Portuguese Generation of 1870, whose critique of the homeland's decline and backwardness raised anew, albeit in somewhat different fashion, the image of the Portuguese in Asia.[6] Among the authors and works most closely associated with this topic is José Maria de Eça de Queirós and his novella *O mandarim* (1880) (*The Mandarin*).

EÇA AND THE ORIENT

Si tu pouvais, par un seul désir, tuer un homme à la Chine et hériter da sa fortune en Europe avec la conviction surnaturelle qu'on n'en saurait jamis rien, consentiras-tu a former ce désir?

(If thou couldst by a mere wish kill a fellow-creature in China, and inherit his fortune in Europe, with the supernatural conviction that the fact would never be known, wouldst thou consent to form such a wish?)

FRANÇOIS-RENÉ CHATEAUBRIAND,
LE GÉNIE DU CHRISTIANISME, 1802

Tuer le mandarin. Commettre une action mauvaise, dans l'esperánce qu'elle ne sera jamais connue.

(To kill the mandarin: To commit an evil act in the hope that it will never be known.)

ÉMILE LITTRÉ, *DICTIONNAIRE*

As the above quotations indicate, the idea of killing a Mandarin for profit and getting away with it was well established by the time Eça de Queirós wrote *O mandarim*, about an amanuensis named Teodoro who, in Faustian fashion, sells his soul to the devil when he knowingly rings a bell that results in the death of a Mandarin whose fortune he inherits.[7] Like many of Eça's fictional works, *O mandarim* is a satire of a decadent, fickle, corrupt, and self-absorbed Portuguese society. Unlike most of Eça's writings, *O mandarim* employs fantastic elements to make its point, including not only the wish-filling demise of a wealthy Chinese but also the Mandarin's occasional returns from the dead, to his killer's considerable dismay. In *O mandarim* Eça is deeply concerned with the contrasting notions of the Orient that were current in his day, oscillating between the valorization of a Far East aesthetic sensibility associated with empire and the vilifica-

3.4. *Eça de Queirós dressed as a Mandarin*

tion of a yellow population regarded as barbarous and a threat to Western civilization. The novel itself is a first-person memoir written in later
life by an ailing Teodoro, who describes his early ambitions and journey
to China to find and make amends to the Mandarin's family. As such, it
evokes sixteenth- and seventh-century texts about travel to the East, perhaps none more so than Fernão Mendes Pinto's own somewhat fanciful
memoir, *Peregrinação*. A scribe in the Ministério do Reino (Ministry of the
Realm), Teodoro is also in the tradition of the many official scriveners who
memorialized their overseas adventures.

Prior to reaping the rewards from his fateful act, Teodoro lives in a Lisbon boardinghouse, where he dreams of fine foods, fine wines, and beautiful women. One night, as he ponders an intriguing proposition about a
bell and a Mandarin found in an old folio, the devil appears. After some
discussion, Teodoro seals his fate and the pact by ringing the bell. Unlike
mariners, soldiers, and others who risked their lives in the *fossado* (obligatory military service) to find new lands and riches for the realm, Teodoro
acquires a Mandarin's fortune while in situ and without risk of physical
harm or prosecution. His newfound wealth opens up a lifestyle akin to that
of Eça's later aristocrat characters, Carlos Eduardo da Maia in *Os Maias*
(1888) (*The Maias* [1965]) and Jacinto de Tormes in *A cidade e as serras*
(1901) (*The City and the Mountains* [1967]). Despite his more humble social class background, Teodoro is now so rich that he is regarded as part of
the nobility. His conspicuous consumption ranges from delicacies served

in fine porcelain dishes and specially tailored clothes on the order of an Indian silk dressing gown, to frequenting a boudoir where attractive young women in Japanese attire fan the delicately scented air around his head (*O mandarim*, 53).

Teodoro's guilt emerges in the form of the Mandarin, who unexpectedly and repeatedly materializes, to his assassin-heir's annoyance. Although Teodoro's frustration leads him to proclaim, "*Preciso matar este morto!*" (60) (*I need to kill that dead fellow!*), his conscience reminds him of the terrible fact that he had not only "*assassinado um velho!*" (60) (*assassinated an old man!*) but also impoverished the Mandarin's family. His anguish is such that he avidly reads up on current events in China. He learns from Jesuit missionary and other travel accounts that uprisings are springing up everywhere there and concludes that he alone is responsible for bringing chaos and ruin to the empire (72). He hires a ship called the *Ceylon* (a reference to the former Portuguese colonial outpost) to take him East to return part of his ill-gotten gains to the Mandarin's family. Teodoro's description of his arrival in China is wonderfully ironic, showing the extent to which the surfeit of Oriental fineries in Lisbon influences his first impression of the foreign land: "[T]oda a paisagem dessa província, que se assemelha à dos vasos de porcelana, d'um tom azulado e vaporoso, com colinazinhas calvas e de longe em longe um arbusto bracejante, me deixou sombreamente indiferente" (79–80). (The province's entire landscape, which resembles the small barren hillocks and occasional budding bushes found on those porcelain vases of a vaporous blue hue, left me somberly indifferent.)

The timing of Teodoro's voyage of so-called amends coincides with a particularly tumultuous period, beginning in the 1860s, when China sought Russian support in controlling Muslim uprisings that threatened political stability, borders, and commerce.[8] By 1870, rebel forces had cut the main line of communication between St. Petersburg and Peking; in 1871, Russian troops entered Peking to defend Russia's consulate and commercial interests.[9] In the novella, Teodoro's arrival in the city is under the protection of the Russian general Camilloff, who has learned of the wealthy Westerner's visit and offers him accommodation in his residence, a palatial home with fragrant gardens, superb food and wine, and other Oriental luxuries, including silk- and satin-walled rooms and a porcelain bathtub in which lime slices and little lilac-scented sponges float. Camilloff's beautiful wife adds to the aesthetic delights of Teodoro's Chinese welcome. The cult of Oriental refinement is complete when Teodoro adopts Mandarin attire and proclaims his total cultural assimilation—which is necessary and fitting for his elaborate plans to honor his deceased benefactor. Eça's amusing description of Teodoro's Mandarin aestheticization as conduit to a Chinese sentience deserves citation:

> Eu trazia uma túnica de brocado azul escuro abotoada ao lado, com o peitilho ricamente bordado de dragões e flores de ouro: por cima um casabeque de seda de um tom azul mais claro, curto, amplo e fofo: as calças de setim cor de avelã descobriam ricas babouches amarelas pospontadas a pérolas, e um pouco da meia picada de estrelinhas negras: e à cinta, numa linda facha franjada de prata, tinha metido um leque de bambu, dos que têm o retrato do filósofo Lá-o-Tsé e são fabricados em Swaton.
>
> E, pelas misteriosas correlações com que o vestuário influencia o carácter, eu já sentia em mim ideias, instintos chineses: —o amor dos ceremoniais meticulosos, o respeito burocrático das fórmulas, um ponto de ceticismo letrado; e também um abjeto terror do Imperador, o ódio ao estrangeiro, o culto dos antepassados, o fanatismo da tradição, o gosto das coisas açucaradas. (94–95)

> (I wore a dark blue tunic that buttoned at the side, the front of which was richly embroidered with dragons and gold flowers; on top of that a lighter blue silk jacket that was short, generously cut, and comfy; from under trousers of hazelnut-colored satin peeked rich yellow slippers backstitched with pearls, and a portion of the stockings were dotted with little black stars; at the waist, in a pretty sheath fringed in silver, was a bamboo fan of the kind that has a picture of the philosopher Lá-o-Tsé and is made in Swaton.
>
> And through the mysterious correlations by which dress influences character, I now felt within me Chinese ideas and instincts:—the love of meticulous ceremonials, the bureaucratic respect for formulas, a pinch of lettered cynicism; in addition to an abject terror of the emperor, a hatred of foreigners, the reverence for ancestors, the fanaticism of tradition, and the pleasure of sugary things.)

His purported acculturation is especially ludicrous considering that Teodoro admits to knowing only two Chinese words: *mandarim* and *chá* (tea), both of which are stereotypic of a rarified view of the East. Camilloff informs him that *mandarim* is actually a Portuguese word derived from the verb *mandar* (to command) and introduced to China by sixteenth-century Portuguese explorers. The Russian adds that while the word *chá* is widely used, knowledge of this single term hardly supports his guest's elaborate plans to find and recompense the Mandarin's family. Teodoro's ignorance of the language is similar to his misinformed understanding of the Chinese uprisings. He imperiously declares, "*Mandamos lá cinquenta homens e varremos a China*" (*Let's send fifty men there and we will clean up China*). It is a ridiculous statement, yet one whose sentiment may actually have been shared by the Portuguese in light of Mesquita's unusual small-force victory over the Chinese in 1849 Macau.

From Peking, Teodoro departs on horseback to the remote land of Ti-Chin-Fu, named after the deceased Mandarin, whose identity is discovered by Camilloff's astrologer-contact. The expedition into the interior is supported by the Russian's Cossack troops and a coolie contingent that transports the large amounts of money and foodstuffs to be distributed to the deceased's family. Upon reaching Tien-Hó, word circulates among the locals that a "foreign devil" has arrived with a treasure, and they attack the entourage, which has stopped overnight at an inn. To save himself, Teodoro scatters all the money among the angry crowd and, despite suffering a head injury, manages to escape. Found unconscious by a Catholic missionary, who takes him to his monastery, Teodoro recovers and enjoys a different kind of aesthetic pleasure associated with an idyllic monastic existence undisturbed by visions of the Mandarin. This particular part of Teodoro's story evokes Fernão Mendes Pinto's account of meeting the Jesuit Francis Xavier in Asia and gaining a measure of peace from his travails by temporarily joining the religious order.

From the monastery, Teodoro writes to Camilloff that he has suffered and sacrificed enough and asks the Russian to send other monies banked in Peking to the Mandarin's family. In Camilloff's reply he attempts to console Teodoro with the news that the villagers who attacked his entourage have been charged by the Chinese government and fined a tax exactly equal to their spoils, an extortion that the general states has greatly gratified the imperial treasury. In a postscript, he informs Teodoro that the astrologer erred in the identity of Ti-Chin-Fu, whose family actually lives in Canton, which was part of the Pearl River trade route that included Macau. Teodoro also learns that the government is giving part of its extortion proceeds to the general to compensate for the loss of his Cossacks in battle and that one aide-de-camp who survived the attack is willing to accompany Teodoro on another expedition to locate the Mandarin's family. Infuriated by the news and incensed by his mistreatment by the "raça bárbara" (163) (barbarous race) whose society he sought to improve, Teodoro heads back to Portugal, at which point the Mandarin's nightly visitations resume.

Teodoro's decision to return to his modest boardinghouse and former lifestyle as a form of penitence to ward off the deceased fails to satisfy the Mandarin. Snubbed by acquaintances who assume he lost his fortune, he decides to resume his life of luxury. Eventually he retreats from high society altogether and spends his days in solitary contemplation. Encountering the devil one evening, he begs him unsuccessfully to undo the Faustian pact and restore the Mandarin to his family. The narrative ends some time later at Teodoro's sickbed, where the dying man advises the reader, *"Nunca mates o Mandarim!"* (181) (*Never kill the Mandarin!*). He appends to this warning a consoling thought: that every Mandarin might be wiped off the earth should his readers succumb to the same temptation and cast their fate with the devil.

In his book *Orientalism* (1978), Edward Said expresses displeasure with a European literary tradition that suborned and vilified the Middle and Far East. Unfortunately, he does not discuss *O mandarim*, which is a striking exception to such literature.[10] It is important to note, however, a distinction between France and England on the one hand and Portugal on the other in the late nineteenth century: whereas the former were reaching the height of their imperial powers in Asia and Africa, the Portuguese were mainly overseeing their few remaining possessions. The Portuguese attempt to annex a large swath of African territory to connect Angola and Mozambique, based on claims of historic sovereignty in the 1885 "rose-colored map," ended disastrously when the British Ultimatum forced Portugal to acquiesce. That humiliating retreat was a national disgrace and fueled the growing republican cause that in 1910 ultimately toppled the centuries-old monarchy.

O mandarim is in the tradition of historiographic works about Portuguese exploration and even of Camões's epic poem, but it is far more critical of colonial occupation. As a member of the Generation of 1870, Eça seems particularly focused on Portugal's failure to produce anything of consequence and its cult of excess in the form of luxury items and refinements. In later works, he poured on his contempt for the self-indulgent aristocracy. With the character of Teodoro he seems to be saying that the average educated Portuguese citizen has no interests or aspirations beyond lassitude, finery, and self-indulgence. In a sense, Teodoro's ill-conceived, arrogant, and disastrous expedition is no less fanciful than his Mandarin visions; it not only mocks the official record of empire but also anticipates by ten years the folly that resulted in the 1890 Ultimatum in Africa. Eça is particularly good at making fun of Portugal's rarefied notions of the East based on commodities such as Chinese porcelains and Mandarin robes made for export, and he is savagely ironic in his description of Teodoro's project to "save" a population that he has secretly plundered. Teodoro's complaints about Chinese barbarism, based on the villagers' attack on his bounty, are especially sardonic given that the Portuguese, like all empire builders, carried out heinous and violent seizures of property belonging to others. This might be said of Teodoro himself, whose dreams of fortune led him to kill a Mandarin.

O mandarim was only one of several works in which Eça wrote about the East. *A correspondência de Fradique Mendes* (1900) is another prime example. Eça's heteronym protagonist, Carlos Fradique Mendes, is a dilettante philosopher who has no special interest in his homeland and prefers to live mostly in France and travel the world. An Orientalist, he dons Chinese silk robes and affects Mandarinlike ways to assuage his need for aesthetic refinements. Among his peeves is any attempt to bring modernity to the Middle and Far East—a move that ruins for him their purity and picturesque appeal. Another example of Eça's Orientalism is his essay "Chineses e japoneses," which was serialized in the Rio-based *Gazeta de Notícias* in December 1894.[11] Ostensibly about the war between China and Japan over Korea (1894–1895), it is in fact a broader critique of Western notions about Asia that he satirized in *O mandarim*, as well as a discussion of political and economic realities in that part of the world. Eça's contact with coolie laborers while he was Portuguese consul in Havana undoubtedly influenced his image of a people that, in many ways, evokes Fernão Mendes Pinto's descriptions about a superior culture. In "Chineses e japoneses" Eça reflects,

[E]sses povos da extrema Ásia, por ora só conhecemos pelos lados exteriores e excessivos do seu exotismo. Com certos traços estranhos de figura e trajo, observados em gravuras, com detalhes de costumes e ceremônias aprendidos nos jornais . . . e sobretudo com o que vemos da sua arte, toda caricatural ou quimérica—é que nós formamos a nossa impressão concisa e definitiva da sociedade chinesa e japonesa. . . . A ambos concebemos uma habilidade hereditária em fabricar porcelana e bordar seda. . . . [P]or trás do rabicho e dos guarda-sóis de papel, e das caturrices, e de todo o exotismo, existem sólidas instituições sociais e domésticas, uma velha e copiosa literatura, uma intensa vida moral, fecundos métodos de trabalho, energias ignoradas, o europeu mediano não o suspeita. (*Obras completas* 2:1258)

(We only now know these people from the Far East based on superficial and excessive facets of their exoticism. From certain strange tracings of figure and dress observed in engravings with details of customs and ceremonies learned from newspapers . . . and especially from what we see of their art, all that is caricatured or chimerical—with which we form our concise and definitive impressions of Chinese and Japanese society. . . . We regard both cultures as having an inherent ability to make porcelain and silk. . . . But behind the pigtail and the paper parasols and the obstinacy and all the exoticism are solid social and domestic institutions, an ancient and copious literature, an intense moral life, fecund work methods, and unrecognized energies that the average European never suspects.)

Eça also discusses Asians' impressions of Europeans, such as the image of the "diabo estrangeiro" (foreign devil), which is precisely how the villagers regarded Teodoro in *O mandarim*. The only facet of European life that the Asians admire, he tells his reader, is machinery, early examples of which include the fast-moving caravels and armaments that the Portuguese introduced to the East in the sixteenth century. His article reflects on the implications for Europe as well as for Brazil of the seemingly inconsequential and distant Sino-Japanese war should Japan defeat the Chinese. For Eça, Japan's successful imitation of European industrialization could lead to the defeat of China in the struggle over Korea (which did happen). If that should occur, he writes, China will adopt the same modernization tactics to protect itself and, in doing so, become "a mais ponderosa nação militar da Terra" (2:1266) (the most powerful military country on Earth). And should that happen, and this is the main point of the article, there would be no stopping an invasion—not of Chinese vandals, which was the image popularly associated with the yellow peril, but rather of a talented, dedicated, and mobile workforce far superior to those of Europe and the Americas, whose arrival would change the economy and culture of those regions.[12] He imagines how Brazil, which had opened its doors to immigrant labor after the abolition of slavery, "será uma China" (will become a China) and, on a jocular note, predicts that half of the *Gazeta*'s pages will be printed in Chinese (2:1270).

Of course Eça's prediction about a transformative Chinese workforce in Brazil did not come to pass. It was ultimately the Japanese who migrated in far greater numbers and assumed a significant presence there. (More recently and for similar economic reasons, Japanese Brazilians began a reverse migration that continues today.) Nonetheless, his reflections about Orientalism anticipate postcolonial commentary about Western fantasies and demeaning stereotypes of the East. His concern about complacence in Europe and the Americas with regard to the Sino-Japanese war was insightful for the times, especially given that less than fifty years later, a second Sino-Japanese conflict erupted into the war in the Pacific.

The richly garbed Mandarin was part of Europe's Oriental imaginary, but there is nothing decorative or artful about Eça's Mandarin, who tenaciously returns from the dead to chip away at Teodoro's complacency and ultimately brings about his downfall. As if parodying the Old Man of Restelo's warning in *Os lusíadas* about the consequences of greed, the dying Teodoro seems hopeful that humanity's inherent avarice will kill off every last Mandarin. Ultimately their demise as a powerful political and economic group did come to pass, but by a civil-servant class introduced after the fall of the Qing Dynasty. To make a long-distance killing today in China, Teodoro would have to ring a stockbroker. As always, the devil is in the details.

PORTUGUESE WRITERS IN ASIA:
WENCESLAU DE MORAES AND CAMILO PESSANHA

Não voltaste. P'ra quê, se a terra do Japão
te pode alimentar melhor a fantasia;
se a tua alma oriental viveu como queria;
se o verdadeiro amor te encheu o coração?

(You did not return. What for, if the land of Japan
were to better nourish your fantasy;
if your Oriental soul lived as it wished;
if true love filled your heart?)

HUGO ROCHA, "A WENCESLAU DE MORAIS," 1940

The year Eça published "Chineses e japoneses" in Rio, his slightly younger contemporary, Wenceslau de Moraes, was living in Macau and writing his major work, *Dai-Nippon: O grande Japão* (1897) (The great Japan), a highly personalized study of Japanese life and culture that also addresses the

Sino-Japanese war. A student of the Escola Naval (Naval School), Moraes (sometimes spelled Morais) was trained as a gunner and sailed to various Portuguese colonies, including Mozambique, which was the subject of several pieces that appeared posthumously in his *Páginas africanas* (1952) (African Pages). From 1887 to 1898, he resided in Macau, where he attained the rank of gunship commander and also taught school. He traveled several times to Japan during this period and participated in talks to resume Luso-Japanese diplomatic and commercial relations. He finally moved to Japan and became Portuguese consul-general in Kobe, an appointment that lasted from 1891 until 1913. A prolific writer, Moraes published five volumes of correspondence from Japan that cover the period 1902 to 1913.[13] In addition to broad studies of Japanese life, he wrote books about specialized topics, including *O culto do chá* (1903) (The cult of tea), a slim volume illustrated by Japanese artist Yoshiaki, and *Serões no Japão* (1926) (Soirées in Japan). He regularly commented on the Portuguese empire in the East and dedicated an entire volume to *Fernão Mendes Pinto no Japão*.[14] Moraes did not read Japanese, and his works like *Dai-Nippon* often refer to locals who instruct him in the manners and legends of Japan.[15]

It is interesting to compare the images of the East drawn by Eça and Moraes, both of whom lived outside Portugal and served in the diplomatic ranks. In his fiction and nonfiction, Eça used the East largely as a foil to ridicule the lassitude and foibles of Portugal's middle and upper classes.[16] As seen in *O mandarim*, the calamitous meeting of East and West is darkly ironic, while "Chineses e japoneses" draws from Eça's experiences with coolie laborers to critique dreamy notions about a distant land and people. Like Teodoro, other of Eça's characters use travel as a balm of sorts for tedious or troubled Portuguese lives. Failing to discover there what they believed they would find, the majority, like Teodoro, return dissatisfied to some degree, or disillusioned. Eça's journalistic warnings about a Chinese invasion might well be perceived as an extension of the yellow peril theme. Laden with ironies that culminate with a Chinese-language *Gazeta*, his observations seem less xenophobic and more in keeping with a desire to engage his readership with the reality of a distant and seemingly internecine war that, like all wars, has global consequences.

Moraes is more in the tradition of the sixteenth-century soldier-scribe who sailed to the East under the Portuguese flag and remained there for the rest of his life. Presumably referring to modern times, critic Paulo Franchetti even describes him as the "cronista do Oriente em português" (*Estudos*, 219) (chronicler of the Orient in Portuguese). Like his predecessor, the chronicler Diogo do Couto, who wrote at the apogee of expansionism,

Wenceslau de Moraes

O CULTO DO CHÁ

BI.028

3.5. *Cover of* O culto do chá

Moraes was unhappy with his homeland. He wrote about these feelings more than once in letters to his friend Sebastião Peres Rodrigues (*Cartas*, 35); his discontent seems as much attributable to his long absence and sense of alienation as to any one particular financial, family, or political matter back home. Nor was he ultimately happy in the decade he spent in Macau, where he lived with his Chinese wife, Atchan, and their two young sons. In fact, when he moved to Japan in 1898, he left his family behind and subsequently had little personal contact with them.[17]

His attitude toward China and Japan is perhaps best expressed in *Dai-Nippon*, his contribution to the quadricentennial of Vasco da Gama's discovery of the route to India. Moraes dedicates the work to the memory of Fernão Mendes Pinto, who he felt had done a good job of portraying Japan at that time. Moraes published the book just prior to moving permanently to Japan. Like Eça, he wrote about Chinese and Japanese societies but with the advantage of witnessing the Japanese defeat of China. However, unlike Eça, who commended the Chinese work ethic despite the feudal conditions in which the people labored, Moraes had little laudatory to say about his adopted homeland, the "monstro misterioso da lenda" (209) (mysterious monster of legend), with its anthill-like populations and abject poverty. He even describes a cholera outbreak in Japan as China's pestilent revenge for having lost the war (200). Quoting a friend, he compares exiting China for Japan with the following analogy: "É sair de uma caverna e entrar num jardim" (12) (It is like leaving a cave and entering a garden).

Unlike Eça's flâneur character Fradique Mendes, who worries that modernity would destroy the picturesque exoticism of the East, Moraes is jubilant about Japan's imitation of Western industry and its manufactured copies of silks and porcelains originally produced in China. When it comes to Japanese art, his exuberance is over the top, and perhaps rightly so, given the delicacy and simplicity of Japanese painting. But one cannot help associating his breathy tributes along the lines of "A influência d'essa arte, como um perfume sutil que se dilue no espaço imenso, alcança Europa" (*Dai-Nippon* 88) (The influence of this art, like a subtle perfume that disperses into the immense space, reaches Europe) with similar paeans expressed by Eça's Jacinto de Tormes, the über-aesthete in *A cidade e as serras* who turns up his nose at Portugal, resides on the Champs-Élysées, and lives a life of art for art's sake. Among the many examples of Moraes's Orientalist enthusiasms in *Dai-Nippon* is his guided tour of a modest house that he treats lavishly in detail as if it were a sacred temple or museum of fine arts.

Among other objets d'art that Moraes praises are Japanese women, especially the geisha. In *Dai-Nippon* he states, "A mulher japonesa define-se como o requinte pueril do feminino. A *guesha* é o requinte pueril da japonesa, o que equivale a dizer que, falar dela, é viajar no éter" (250). (The Japanese woman is defined as the puerile height of the feminine. The geisha is the puerile height of the Japanese woman, which is the same as saying that to speak of her is to journey into the ether.) His two devoted Japanese lovers and literary muses receive even more attention in his tribute to them titled *O-Yoné e Ko-Haru* (1923).[18] However, not every woman in Japan is artful or necessarily superior to those in China. He regards the "half-caste" Eurasian in China as more delightful and graceful than the sometimes "ugly" Japanese "mestiza," whom he describes as the product of a "repulsão de dois sangues diferentes" (*Dai-Nippon*, 196) (hostility between two different bloods). For Moraes, the Chinese Eurasian represents the harmonious coming together of races, with "evolutionary" results, whereas racial mixing in Japan has tragic consequences: "a mestiça é um náufrago da vida" (197) (the mestiza is a castaway in life). His attitude toward Chinese women partakes of nineteenth-century discussions about the benefits of eugenics. Macau was also a colony, and, unlike Japan, intermarriage between Portuguese men and Chinese women had long been prevalent and socially accepted. This was the case with Moraes himself, who fathered two children with his Chinese wife.[19] But as he claims in *Dai-Nippon*, Japanese women are perfection, and as with prized art objects, any additions to the original result in devaluation.

Eça and Moraes wrote about an area now called "languages in contact," although the writers' objectives are different. As we have seen, Teodoro's so-called knowledge of Chinese consists of two words: *mandarim*, a Portuguese neologism for the scholar-official class, and *chá*, a Cantonese term adopted by the Portuguese and subsequently introduced into India and back home. In an article titled "Vestígios da passagem dos portugueses no Japão" (Vestiges of the passage of the Portuguese into Japan), Moraes provides a more explicit lesson in language contact between the Portuguese and Japanese. It should be mentioned here that linguistic transmission was also true of other areas colonized by the Portuguese and largely attributable to Jesuits and other missionaries who introduced Christian concepts and terminology into the local culture.[20] Moraes provides several examples, including "Kirisuto" and "Kirisutan" for "Cristo" (Christ) and *cristão* (Christian), *anima* for "soul," and "Kontasu" for *contas* (rosary). He also lists Portuguese words adopted for everyday objects, such as *koppu* for *copo* (cup) and *shabon* for *sabão* (soap); a few culinary references, including *tempura* from *tempero* (seasoning) and *pan* for *pão* (bread); as well as the word *tabako* from *tabaco* (tobacco), which the Portuguese introduced into Japan. He includes a few examples of spoken Japanese words that entered the Portuguese vocabulary, such as *biôbu* (*biombo* [screen]), *cháwan* (*chávena* [teapot]), and *bonzo* (Buddhist priest). Moraes's reflections on linguistic transmission is an important reminder that language

3.6. *Jesuits in Macau*

travels along with people and commodities and is an important factor in any analysis of diaspora.

Moraes embodied the romanticized image of the adventurer who journeys to an exotic land and remains. (In the 1980s, he was the subject of two films by Portuguese director Paulo Rocha.[21]) But he kept close ties with Portugal through letters with friends and with a much larger audience who read his books about the feminine seductions of Japan. He is in many ways a contradiction: a man who cared little about living in Portugal but who looked to his homeland for community and recognition as a writer, and a writer who oscillated between a lavish and often exaggerated, overblown prose style and detailed, quasipointillist commentary on topics such as the serving of tea. Moraes lived in China with a wife and children but regarded Japan as his true love and one for which he left his family. Although he wore Japanese robes and was versant in Oriental customs, he never went completely native, as suggested by his use of a Portuguese snap-brim hat. He was too attached to Portugal, too invested in the tradition of the soldier-scribe, chronicling for his readers back home the great Japan.

Quase já estou animado a escrever sobre coisas do Oriente. A vida, por aqui, é cheia de impressões novas cada dia, ou eu me finjo que

é, em um delírio artificial de grandezas, que me serviu de coragem
para partir, e ainda me vai servindo para não esmorecer de todo.

(I am almost excited now to write about things of the Orient. Life
around here is filled with new impressions every day, or I pretend to
myself that it is, in an artificial delirium of greatnesses that gave me
courage to leave and that still serves me so as not to lose heart about
everything.)

LETTER FROM CAMILO PESSANHA TO HIS FATHER, MAY 28, 1894

In 1894, the same year Eça's article on the Sino-Japanese war appeared in
Rio, the poet Camilo Pessanha left Portugal for Macau, where he began
teaching alongside Wenceslau de Moraes at the newly established Liceu
de Macau. Like Eça, Pessanha studied at the Universidade de Coimbra,
where he published his first poems and stories and led a somewhat turbulent, bohemian life in the style of the Generation of 1870, whose members
he greatly admired. After finishing his law degree, in 1892, he made plans
to go abroad, initially to Timor, then to Daman in Portuguese India, but
a bout of depression and a move to the Portuguese town Óbidos to work
with his friend, the judge Alberto Osório de Castro, kept plans on hold
until the Macau opening appeared. In Macau, he and Moraes became good
friends and remained so even after Moraes's move to Japan; they also dedicated works to one another. In 1896, Pessanha had a son, João Manuel,
with his Chinese partner, Lei Ngo Long; the boy was baptized a year later
as a child of unknown parentage. Despite his own close family ties, in 1900
Pessanha gave his son up for adoption to a local Chinese family, possibly
related to Kuoc Ngan Ieng, who lived with Pessanha after Lei Ngo Long's
death and remained with him for the rest of his life.[22]

Unlike Moraes, who seemed to flourish in Asia, Pessanha returned
to Portugal for long periods to address chronic health problems that included depression. At the time, opium was a medicinal drug widely available in China; Pessanha became addicted and ultimately ceased trips back
home to stay near his sources in Macau. While Moraes was publishing volumes of prose at an extraordinary rate, Pessanha sent occasional verses to
literary magazines and newspapers in Macau and Lisbon. Because of the
ephemeral nature of newspapers, several of his poems were lost. In 1920,
his slim volume of verse titled *Clepsidra* (Water clock) appeared in Lisbon at the instigation of longtime friends Ana and João de Castro Osório,
who collected his poems and published the book.[23] Compared to Moraes,

Pessanha seems uninterested in making a name as a writer, although his poor health, which was a subject of his many letters, may have been a factor. Ironically, *Clepsidra*, his only published book, earned him almost immediate entry into the Portuguese literary canon, while Moraes received no such distinction. A possible reason is that *Clepsidra* is not about the East but rather about well-wrought Western themes, such as life's transitory nature and the melancholic lyric, cast in a synaesthetic and often hermetic language typical of Symbolist verse. In a short essay, "Macau e a gruta de Camões" (1924) (Macau and the Camões grotto), Pessanha comments on the difference between prose and poetry composed "in exile":

> Ora a inspiração poética é emotividade, educada, desde a infância e com profundas raízes, no húmus do solo natal. É por isso que os grandes poetas são em todos os países os supremos intérpretes do sentimento étnico. Toda a poesia é, em certo sentido, bucolismo; e bucolismo e regionalismo são tendências do espírito inseparaveis. Notáveis prosadores (basta lembrar, dentre os contemporâneos, Lafcádio [*sic*] Hearn, Wenceslau de Morais e Pierre Loti) têm celebrado condignamente os encantos do países exóticos. Poeta, nenhum. Os poucos que vagueiam e se definham por longínquas regiões, se acaso escrevem em verso, é sempre para cantar a pátria ausente para se enternecerem (os portugueses) antes as ruínas da antiga grandeza da pátria e, sobretudo, dar desafogo à irremediável tristeza que os punge. E se na reduzida obra poética colonial desses escritores—Tomás Ribeiro, Alberto Osório de Castro, Fernando Leal . . . se encontram dispersos alguns traços fulgurantes de exotismo, é só para tornar mais pungente . . . a impressão geral de tristeza—da irremessível tristeza de todos os exílios. (In *China*, 61)

(Now then, poetic inspiration from infancy is emotive, educated, and deeply rooted in the humus of native soil. For this reason the great poets of every country are the supreme interpreters of ethnic sentiment. All poetry is, in a certain sense, bucolic; and the bucolic and regional are inseparable tendencies of the spirit. Notable prose writers (sufficient to recall, among contemporaries, Lafcadio Hearn, Wenceslau de Morais, and Pierre Loti) have celebrated with distinction the delights of exotic lands. As for poets, none. The few who wander and pine away for distant lands, if by chance they write verse, always sing of their absent homeland and turn tender (the Portuguese) before the ruins of the country's former greatness and, especially, to give respite to the irremediable sadness that afflicts them. And if in the reduced colonial poetry of those writers—Tomás Ribeiro, Alberto Osório de Castro, Fernando Leal . . . are scattered some resplendent traces of exoticism, it is simply to turn poignant . . . the general impression of sadness—the unfailing sadness of all exiles.)[24]

Pessanha wrote about China in his essays and spoke about it in public lectures. His most extensive and provocative commentary is "Introdução a um estudo sobre a civilização chinesa," a lengthy introduction to *Esboço crítico da civilização chinesa* (1912) (Critical outline of Chinese civilization) by his physician-friend António Filipe de Morais Palha, who wrote disparagingly about Chinese character, habits, and culture. Pessanha agrees with his friend's condemnation of Chinese brutality and misery. As a jurist in Macau, Pessanha writes vividly in this introduction about the horrors of a corrupt legal system and "execution grounds" where decapitated heads are displayed for a price and share space with a ceramics factory and a children's playground ("Introdução," 28). His observations here and elsewhere in the first part of the essay are in keeping with those of Palha and other Western images of China as a barbaric land—not unlike the one portrayed by Teodoro in *O mandarim*—and one from which Wenceslau de Moraes fled in 1898.

However, there are interesting twists and reversals in Pessanha's introduction, one of which evokes Michel de Montaigne's 1580 defense of Brazilian Indians' ritualistic anthropophagy as more humane than European torture-killing. For Pessanha, the ancient Chinese penal code is far superior to the "sanguíneo livro V das nossas *Ordenações* e sincrónica legislação criminal dos outros Estados europeus" (42) (bloodthirsty book 5 of our *Ordinances* and synchronic criminal legislation of the other European states). Where his opinions diverge most prominently from those of his friend Palha and where we find him in agreement with Eça are in his observations about the industriousness of the Chinese. His list of their accomplishments is long but gives special attention to their language and artistic skills. In particular he commends their

> prodigiosa capacidade receptiva das inteligências, que lhes torna possível aprenderem sem fadiga, em poucos anos da adolescência, a sua inverosímil língua escrita, que a grande maioria da população não apenas possui como rudimentar instrumento de utilidade, mas aprecia sob os complexos e transcendentes aspectos da beleza literária das composições e da beleza plástica das grafias artísticas;—[e] a riqueza da imaginação criadora e delicadeza de gosto dos artifices, e o alto nível médio

do senso estético da população, tão espontâneo que pode chamar-se
instintivo—equilibrado, sóbrio, pitoresco e enternecidamente panteísta.
(45)

(minds' prodigious receptive capability that makes it possible for them
to learn untiringly, and within a few years of adolescence, their improb-
able written language that the majority of the population not merely
knows as a basic and useful tool, but appreciates for the complex and
transcendent aspects of the literary beauty of composition and the visual
beauty of artistic design; [and] the richness of a creative imagination
and delicacy of taste in artisanship, alongside the population's high average level of aesthetic sense, so spontaneous that it can be called instinc-
tive—balanced, sober, picturesque, and tenderly pantheistic.)

Pessanha almost seems to channel Eça in his assessment of the Chinese and their wondrous ability to imitate Western advances and the possibility of becoming a global force that would impact Europe both politically and economically (44). But whereas Eça was writing in 1894 about a
possible Chinese labor invasion as a result of the ongoing Sino-Japanese
war, Pessanha scoffs at any notion of an "amarelo perigoso" (dangerous
yellow-skinned person), stating that no European who lived in Asia ever
took that idea seriously.[25] For Pessanha, the labor most to be admired was
on display in the "formidáveis acervos de géneros e artefactos" (41) (for-
midable archives of provisions and artifacts)—those little shops that sold
dried fish, vegetables, scalded rats, and dog meat alongside others selling
fine silks, embroideries, porcelains, and ivory carvings.

Like Wenceslau de Moraes, Pessanha was a connoisseur of Oriental
art, and his large personal collection included paintings, calligraphies,
brocades, vases, bronzes, sculptures, and ceramics from the Ming, Qing,
and earlier Song Dynasties. Some of these objects were the same kinds of
decorative pieces that found their way to Portugal beginning in the early
sixteenth century and that over the centuries helped shape, along with
accounts by earlier and later writers such as Moraes, Portugal's Oriental
imaginary.

However, not everyone valued Chinese artworks as much as Pessanha
did. In 1914, when he believed he might die, he gave one hundred items
from his collection to the Portuguese government for the Museu de Arte
Nacional in Lisbon. As critic Daniel Pires describes in *Camilo Pessanha:
Prosador e tradutor* (1992) (Camilo Pessanha: Prose writer and translator),
the shipment of art still had not arrived by July 1916—a great frustration

3.7. *Macau street sign*

3.8. *Camilo Pessanha*

for the still living and breathing poet, who complained to friends about such ill treatment by a country that had occupied Macau for over four hundred years (20). When the shipment finally arrived, the museum director, José de Figueiredo, failed to appreciate the collection's value as part of the country's patrimony and deposited it in a warehouse, where it remained for several years. In December 1924, the question of the collection's whereabouts came to widespread public attention in an article published in the *Diário de Lisboa* titled "Dez anos descorridos . . . Onde está a preciosa coleção de arte chinesa oferecida por Camilo Pessanha ao governo português?" (22) (Ten years later . . . where is the precious collection of Chinese art gifted by Camilo Pessanha to the Portuguese government?).

Despite the museum director's affront, in 1926, just prior to his actual demise, Pessanha donated another large portion of his collection to the Portuguese government, with the proviso that it be housed in Coimbra, in the Museu Nacional de Machado de Castro, along with the pieces first donated in 1914. Pires notes that the poet's second bequest also experienced shipping delays, until 1928, because it was diverted to Seville for a Portuguese-sponsored exhibit there. The shipment finally arrived in Portugal in 1930, but minus six pieces, Pires notes (22), which apparently were desirable enough to steal. Ultimately, most of Pessanha's collection was acquired by the Fundação Oriente in Lisbon, where it remains for exhibitions and scholarly research on Pessanha, Chinese art, and the Portuguese presence in Macau.

PLATE 1. *Vasco da Gama, in* Livro de Lisuarte de Abreu *(ca. 1565)*

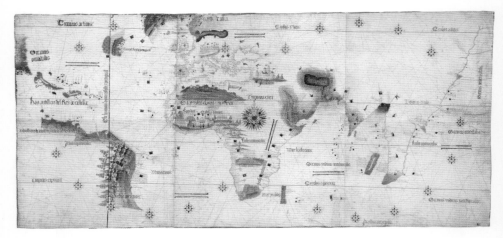

PLATE 2. *Cantino planisphere (1502)*

PLATE 3. *The state of India, in the Lopo Homem-Reinéis map,* Atlas Miller *(1519)*

PLATE 4. *Benin saltcellar with Portuguese figures (15th–16th century)*

PLATE 5. *Frontispiece,* Leitura nova *series, Livro 2 de Reis (16th century)*

PLATE 6. *Portuguese woman on a litter in Goa (mid-16th century)*

PLATE 7. *Indo-Portuguese writing cabinet (17th century)*

PLATE 8. *Kraak porcelain bottle with Jesuit emblem (16th century)*

PLATE 9. *Detail, Namban screen*

PLATE 10. *Detail, Namban screen*

PLATE 11. *Namban stirrups with Portuguese figures (16th century)*

PLATE 12. Atlas de Lázaro Luís *(1563)*

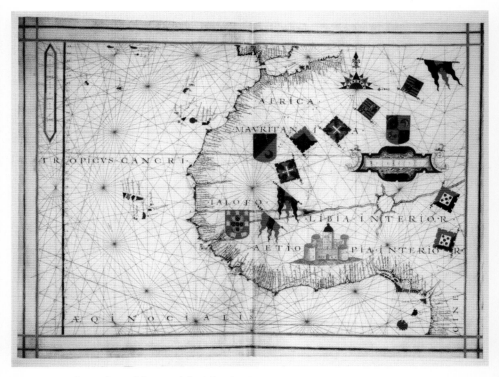

PLATE 13. Atlas Universal *(ca. 1565), by Sebastião Lopes*

PLATE 14. Chafariz d'el Rei *(late 16th century), anonymous*

PLATE 15. Adoração dos Magos *(ca. 1505), by Grão Vasco (Vasco Fernandes)*

PLATE 16. Adoração dos Reis Magos *(16th century), by Jorge Afonso*

PLATE 17. Batalha dos guararapes *(1758)*

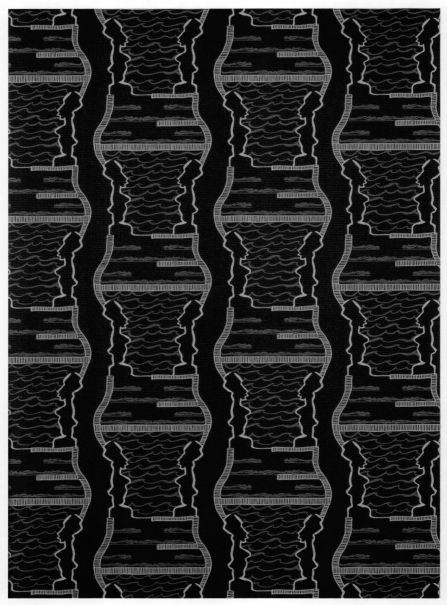

PLATE 18. Tumbeiro *(2008) (Middle Passage), by Goya Lopes. Courtesy of Goya Lopes.*

PLATE 19. Tráfico *(2008) (Slave trade), by Goya Lopes. Courtesy of Goya Lopes.*

PLATE 20. *Qing Dynasty plate with Dom Pedro de Lancastre coat of arms (ca. 1715–1720)*

PLATE 21. *Portuguese chinoiserie tiled panel (1750–1760)*

PLATE 22. *A despedida* *(1858)* *(The Farewell), by António José Patrício*

PLATE 23. *Macau entryway, Jardim do Ultramar*

PLATE 24. *Ventura in the Calouste Gulbenkian Museum*

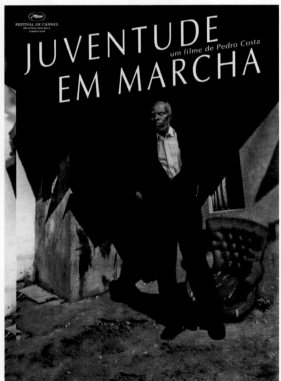

PLATE 25. *The chair outside Bete's home in Fontaínhas*

Into the Wilderness

THE RACE TO AFRICA AND
THE PROMISE OF BRAZIL

As viagens n'África produzem sempre um romance, e algumas vezes também um livro de ciência.

(Travels in Africa always result in a novel and sometimes a book of science as well.)

ALEXANDRE DE SERPA PINTO, *COMO EU ATRAVESSEI A ÁFRICA*, 1881

Historian Malyn Newitt has written extensively about Portugal's relaxed interest in the African colonies of Mozambique and Angola until the mid-nineteenth century. Brazil was by far the main focus of imperial attention and colonization, especially after gold and then diamonds were discovered in the late seventeenth and early eighteenth centuries and one hundred years later, in 1807, when the royal court and thousands of Portuguese fled to Rio to escape the Napoleonic invasion (*Portugal in Africa*). Historian João Paulo Borges Coelho has argued that with the exception of a few interior trade routes that supported commercial pursuits in slave trafficking, ivory, and gold, the crown knew little about Mozambique and Angola beyond the narrow coastal strips with their small fortifications and trading centers ("African Troops," 131). That situation changed after Brazilian independence in 1822, when Portugal looked increasingly to its African holdings to secure new revenue, shore up coastal towns, explore the interior, and claim new lands. According to historian Manuel Villaverde Cabral, the mid-nineteenth-century agricultural crisis in northern Portugal, created by new, restrictive landholding legislation and the mechanization of farm labor, resulted in the departure of approximately fifty thousand Portuguese, out of a population of around four million, between the years 1866 and 1888 (*Portugal na alvorada do século XIX*, 30–34). The abolition of slavery in Brazil in 1888 opened new employment opportunities for Portuguese and other Europeans, who emigrated there to work in the urban centers and the interior.

Brazilian poet José Basílio da Gama's neoclassical tribute to the Angolan captain Quitubia on behalf of the Portuguese describes one of the many "guerras pretas" (black wars) by which the Portuguese empire largely retained its holdings in Mozambique and Angola. African leaders loyal to Portugal served the monarchy in battles against other tribal chiefs; their armies proved far more effective than troops from Portugal who, despite better training and weaponry, struggled with disease and harsh climate conditions in combat areas along the Zambezi River and in northern Mozambique. Like Quitubia, the African-born warriors received commendations, titles, and gifts from Portugal for their many victories won in the name of the crown.[1]

Like Portugal's reaction to early French and Dutch occupations of Brazil in the sixteenth and seventeenth centuries, the medical missionary David Livingston's transcontinental explorations from Luanda, Angola, to Quelimane, Mozambique, between 1854 and 1855 — not to mention encroachments by South African Boers — spurred the Portuguese monarchy to further explore and populate its African territories. For centuries, maritime discoveries and coastal conquests from the sea were characteristic of the Portuguese approach to empire. Explorations into the interior were less common and normally carried out by individuals or small teams from Portugal who employed locals for their knowledge of the area and as supply carriers. One such person was Major Alexandre de Serpa Pinto, who accompanied a combat mission into the Zambezi region in 1869 to chart the area's topography and water sources.

In 1877, Serpa Pinto joined Hermenegildo Capelo and Roberto Ivens, two naval officers and explorers, in a government-supported scientific expedition into the Angolan interior. While readying their land exploration, Serpa Pinto learned that Henry Morton Stanley was in the Cabinda region to the north and needed assistance to return to Luanda. Serpa Pinto made arrangements to meet up with the famous Welsh explorer and brought Stanley back to Luanda, where he stayed for a period as Serpa Pinto's houseguest.[2] Later, a split between the Capelo-Ivens team and Serpa Pinto occurred as the latter was exploring terrain just east of Bié, in central Angola.

According to his account in *Como eu atravessei África*, his two-volume memoir of the journey published in Portuguese and English in 1881,[3] Serpa

4.1. *Studio portrait of Ivens, Stanley, Capelo, and Serpa Pinto with Africans in Luanda (1877)*

Pinto was surprised to learn of his colleagues' decision to break with him, which placed his small party in jeopardy:

> Abri pressuroso as cartas: eram duas oficiais e uma particular, assinadas por Capelo e Ivens. Diziam-me que tinham resolvido seguir sós. . . .
>
> Só o pouco ou nenhum conhecimento do sertão africano que então tinham os meus companheiros podia desculpar um tal proceder. Eu achava-me num país hostil e, se até ali tinha sido respeitado, fora só porque o gentio me julgava a vanguarda de uma grande comitiva capitaneada por eles e o receio de represálias tinha até então sustido a rapacidade dos indígenas. . . .
>
> Que seria de mim logo que se soubesse que toda a minha força consistia em 10 homens? (1:99)

> (I opened the letters in all haste. Two of them were official and one was private, all signed by Capello [*sic*] and Ivens. They informed me that they had resolved to go on alone. . . .
>
> It was only their imperfect knowledge of the interior of Africa which could excuse my friends in acting in so strange a manner. I was at that time in a hostile country, and if I had been respected hitherto it was only

because the people round me looked upon me and my little band as the vanguard of a considerable troop under command of my friends in my rear, and a fear of reprisals had, up to that moment, restrained the natural rapacity of the natives. . . .

What would my fate be if it were known that my entire force consisted of ten men? (1:92–93)

Serpa Pinto managed to reach Bié, where he decided to continue his cross-continental journey; when disease, difficult climate conditions and terrain, and loss of supplies made his goal of the Mozambican coast untenable, he headed south along the Zambezi, through the Transvaal, until finally reaching Durban, South Africa, in 1879. In the meantime, Capelo and Ivens remained in Angola and explored its vast interior until 1880.

Vital to Portuguese interests at the time, and a major factor in the nation's "scramble for Africa" alongside England and other European countries, was the Sociedade de Geografia de Lisboa (Geographical Society of Lisbon), founded in 1875 to support Portuguese explorations, especially in Africa. The different approaches to Africa taken by Serpa Pinto and the Capelo and Ivens team reflected a fundamental difference of opinion within the society with regard to exploration of the continent. Most society members were enthused by Serpa Pinto's desire to explore not only Angola and Mozambique but also the territory between the two regions. Others agreed that Capelo and Ivens's focus on lands already under Portuguese sovereignty was preferable.[4] The European and British race to Africa ultimately made a Portuguese transcontinental crossing imperative. In 1884, four years after their Angolan excursion and with backing from the Ministry of the Navy, the society, and the newly established Comissão de Cartografia (1883–1936) (Cartographic Commission), Capelo and Ivens successfully carried out the transcontinental mission, which gave impetus to Portugal's "mapa cor-de-rosa" (rose-colored map), its claim to lands that connected Angola and Mozambique.[5]

What made Serpa Pinto a hero and household name in Portugal as well as in Brazil was his memoir's description of his determination to cross Africa. *Como atravessei a África* is rich in observations on topography, climate, waterways, flora, and fauna; its detailed and illustrated cultural and ethnographic information is reminiscent of the best works by early Portuguese chroniclers and soldier-scribes. The main difference between early sixteenth-century historiography and Serpa Pinto's account is that by the mid-nineteenth century, territories under Portuguese control in Africa and elsewhere were largely populated by mixed-race societies, members of which (as in the "guerras pretas") constituted the local military.[6] On his trek through Africa, Serpa Pinto regularly encountered African soldiers, merchants, traders, and farmers who had Portuguese names. Several of his bearers are described as mixed-race; some were loyal to him, others not.

Serpa Pinto recounts commerce's ability to bring Portuguese customs and habits into the remotest of areas, where Africans in European dress were common.[7] However, he was surprised at seeing an African chieftain wearing a Portuguese ensign's uniform, an outfit he later learned was once owned by his own former military school classmate. His epic journey into the wilderness occasionally brought him into contact with other Portuguese, including the explorer José de Anchieta, whom he called the first zoological specialist in Africa. Serpa Pinto regularly denounces the exiled Portuguese criminal-profiteer class turned native whose slave trafficking and other grave offenses contributed to Portugal's notoriety on the continent: "José Alves, Coimbras e outros, esses nem ao menos são portugueses de nascença; não se parecem com portugueses na cor, são indígenas, sem instrução, verdadeiros selvagens, de calças e chapéus" (2:57). (José Alves, Coimbras and others of the same class may be Portuguese by birth, but have little of the Portuguese in heart; they are men without education or manners, mere savages in European clothes [2:67].[8]) Like the French intellectual Michel de Montaigne, who in his essay "On Cannibals" (1580) defends the anthropophagic rituals of Brazilian Indians over the heinous acts performed by Europeans at war, Serpa Pinto regards African cannibals as civilized in comparison to the cunning and treacherous Portuguese criminal class (2:67 [2:57]).

In addition to his narrative, the two-volume memoir contains 133 engravings and fifteen maps based on Serpa Pinto's drawings of people, lands, plants, and wildlife. He credits a chemist referred to simply as Monteiro with three illustrations in volume 1 that are detailed, photograph-based wood or possibly metal engravings of Mundombe people from the Bié region in Angola. It is interesting to consider the function of such images alongside texts, a type of presentation that can be traced back to illustrated medieval and Renaissance manuscripts. Woodcuts, engravings, and other pictorials are a mainstay of the literature of discovery and exploration, although they were often made by artists who never left the homeland and based their illustrations on the written word. Oftentimes artists got it completely wrong. This was the case with an edition of the German Hans Staden's account, *Warhaftige Historia* (1557), of his captivity among the Tupinambá in Brazil. Instead of images of Indians and village life that appear in the official 1557 Marburg edition, the likely pirated Frankfurt edition of that same year contains woodcuts of sultans, elephants, and camels—as if there were no differences among exotic lands and peoples outside Europe.[9]

Serpa Pinto's illustrations are rich in detail and provide a picture book of the many different peoples and habitats he encountered on his African journey. Like all illustrations in the various periods of Portuguese exploration, these document the colonial enterprise and capture faces and places that more often than not became acquisitions of the empire. The three Monteiro images in volume 1 are especially intriguing because they are so lifelike compared to hand-drawn illustrations. These early photographic examples consist of group shots of Africans who are posed in their finery and look directly at the camera, and they give a sense of the important role that photography was to play in future discoveries, explorations, and conquests.[10] The illustrations in Serpa Pinto's memoir inspired works like Portuguese artist Miguel Ângelo Lupi's painting *Os pretos de Serpa Pinto* (1881, The blacks of Serpa Pinto), which was first exhibited posthumously in 1883.

Monteiro's photographs also appear in Capelo and Ivens's account of the 1877–1880 expedition that initially included Serpa Pinto. Prior to publishing their two-volume *De Benguella às terras de Iaca* (1881)(*From Benguella to the Territory of Yacca* [1881]), they read Serpa Pinto's newly released book and quickly added a prefatory rebuttal of their former colleague's claim that they had abandoned him. According to Capelo and Ivens, their decision to part ways with Serpa Pinto was by mutual agreement. While Serpa Pinto decided to try to cross the continent, Capelo and Ivens felt obliged to follow the Geographical Society's strict instructions about the areas to be explored (the Cuango, Zambezi, Cunene, and Cuanza River regions) and considered it especially important to update and complete existing maps on areas under Portuguese control. They readily admitted that the government would not have objected to their crossing the continent as Serpa Pinto tried to do, a feat that would have brought them considerable fame; they ultimately accomplished the continental crossing in an 1884–1885 expedition. But Capelo and Ivens were quick to point out that their initial African trek required covering more miles and enduring greater hardships than a coast-to-coast crossing from Benguela in Angola to Sofala in Mozambique.

Capelo and Ivens's account is as fascinating to read as Serpa Pinto's travelogue. Not surprisingly, their respective works cover many of the same topics, such as information on flora and fauna, commentaries about river routes and trade with local inhabitants, and often amusing anecdotes about individuals and incidents they encountered along the way. Capelo

Fig. 3.—MUNDOMBE MEN. (From a photograph by Monteiro.)

4.2. *Mundombe men photographed by Monteiro*

4.3. Os pretos de Serpa Pinto *(ca. 1881), by Miguel Ângelo Lupi*

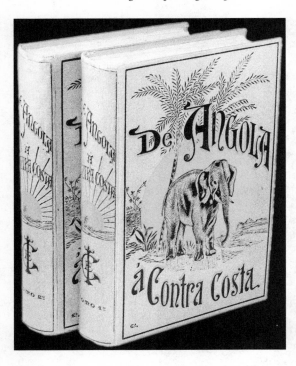

4.4. *Cover of Capelo and Ivens's transcontinental travelogue (1886)*

and Ivens were also keen to fill a gap in expeditionary literature about how to prepare an African caravan. Their book is in many ways a primer on the subject. Among the many topics they address is how to convince locals to sign on to an expedition into the interior whose purpose was scientific study and not the more lucrative trade industry.

Although Capelo and Ivens were acclaimed for their later cross-continental scientific expedition, a year prior to the release of their two-volume *De Angola à contra-costa* (1886) (From Angola to the coast of Mozambique) about that journey, the physician Manuel Ferreira Ribeiro published his *Homenagem aos heróis que precederam Brito Capello e Roberto Ivens na exploração da África austral: 1484 a 1877* (1885) (Homage to the heroes who preceded Brito Capelo and Roberto Ivens in the exploration of Eastern Africa: 1484 to 1877). In this work Ribeiro provides an overview of Portuguese expeditions into the African interior for the purposes of trade. These included two commissioned by Angola's governor and captain-general, António Saldanha da Gama, in the early 1800s, the second of which reached Mozambique shortly after the first (105). But the impetus to explore and claim the lands between Angola and Mozambique comes later in the century.[11] Writing in 1877 in *A província de S. Tomé*, Ribeiro, a specialist in tropical diseases and acclimation in the overseas territories who worked for the naval ministry, was among those who most forcefully urged the nation to carry out the transcontinental colonizing mission:

> Recordarei os nossos brilhantes feitos do século XV e XVII, para nos servirem de exemplo. Não será menor a glória que nos espera se não desanimarmos, se tornarmos as palavras em obras, se cuidarmos enfim de colonizar de raiz e a preceito a província de Angola e a zona trópico-equatorial que se estende d'ali à outra costa, a África portuguesa, onde podemos criar um império maior do que o do Oriente. (In *Homenagem*, 122)

> (I shall recall our brilliant deeds from the fifteenth to the seventeenth century to serve us as example. The glory that awaits us shall be even greater if we do not lose hope, if we change words into deeds, if finally we take care to colonize from the source and with rigor the province of Angola and the tropical-equatorial zone that extends from there to the opposite coast, Portuguese Africa, where we can create an empire even greater than that of the Orient.)

Ribeiro's urgings to claim a greater part of Africa continued into the next decade, and *Homenagem* is his testament to Portugal's ability to build on its territories there. He ends his book with a rallying cry for the cause and a description of the shameful consequences of failing to carry out the colonizing mission:

> Não se diga que não podemos, seria recusar a nós mesmos a aptidão colonizadora. E o país onde se tiverem por milagre os grandes prodígios do progresso, onde se explicar a imprevidência pela fatalidade e onde se atribuir ao impossível o que apenas é resultado da ignorância, não tem em si condições de vitalidade, não tem força para progredir e estará fatalmente condenado a ser absorvido, a desaparecer—a servir de exemplo do modo *como se perdem as nações*. (128)

> (Don't say that we cannot, it would be denying to ourselves our aptitude as colonizers. And the country where the great wonders of progress should be considered as miracles, where one explains improvidence because of fate and where one attributes to the impossible what is merely

the result of ignorance, the country that lacks within itself the vitality and the strength to progress, will be fatally condemned to be absorbed, to disappear—and will serve as example of *how nations are lost.*)

CARLOS FRADIQUE MENDES, WORLD TRAVELER EXTRAORDINAIRE

E com estes elementos alegres que nós procuramos restaurar o nosso império de África!

(And it's with these slaphappy elements that we seek to restore our African empire!)

JOSÉ MARIA EÇA DE QUEIRÓS, *A CORRESPONDÊNCIA DE FRADIQUE MENDES*, 1900

The above epigraph appears in a letter written by Carlos Fradique Mendes, the fictional nineteenth-century world traveler who is the central protagonist in Eça de Queirós's posthumously published satiric volume, *A correspondência de Fradique Mendes* (1900) (*The Correspondence of Fradique Mendes* [2011]).[12] In this letter, addressed to his godmother, Madame Jouarre, from his residence in Paris, Fradique complains about the collapse of a recently constructed building on his Portuguese estate in Sintra and the cost of the architectural debacle. Furious with the builder, who he notes is also a senator who pens "melancholic" fiscal reports for the newspaper, Fradique uses the incident to deride "slaphappy elements" in power in Portugal who propose to restore the African territories but whose incompetence will cost the nation a fortune.[13] He summarizes his feelings about his homeland by complaining that "tudo tende à ruína num país de ruínas" (75) (everything tends toward ruin in a country of ruins). His critique comes at the same time as explorations by Serpa Pinto, Capelo, Ivens, and others who were mapping the African territories to stimulate greater colonization and commerce. Eça notes in his introduction that Fradique "died" in 1888, two years prior to the British Ultimatum; had Eça allowed him to survive beyond that date, he likely would have taken satisfaction in, if not total credit for, predicting the humiliating rose-colored-map fiasco.[14]

Eça's Fradique is an überdandy and aesthete, but unlike his real-life contemporary Oscar Wilde, he is also a self-indulgent and somewhat feckless dilettante. Like Eça's ultrarefined Jacinto de Tormes, the protagonist in his satiric, posthumously published *A cidade e as serras* (1901), Fradique suffers from excessive contemplation and chronic ennui. However, unlike Jacinto, who fears leaving the modern comforts of his Parisian home, Fradique relieves his boredom by traveling from his homes in Paris and Sintra to distant lands. He is a connoisseur of Asian customs; his vast knowledge of the region and people makes Eça, his supposedly acolyte biographer and the author of the volume's prefatory "Memórias e notas" (Memories and notes), nearly swoon: "Com quanta profundidade e miudez conhecia o Oriente este patrício admirável!" (33). (This admirable patrician knew the Orient in such depth and detail!) Indeed, Fradique has many of the traits of the nineteenth-century Orientalist; he wears a Mandarin robe at home, where he displays imported ceramics and other Asian objets d'art. One of the most humorous scenes in the book describes his dilemma of getting an Egyptian mummy past a Lisbon customs agent who has no idea what it is or how to tax it. Eça's mock hagiographic introduction includes praise for Fradique from his various acquaintances in Portugal's Generation of 1870, including historian Oliveira Martins, poet Antero de Quental, and essayist Ramalho Ortigão, who gushes over Fradique as "o mais completo, mais acabado produto da civilização" (39) (the most complete and finished product of civilization). A dissenting voice in the generation is the "ascetic" character J. Teixeira de Azevedo (purportedly based on writer-diplomat Jaime Batalha Reis), who refers to Fradique and those of his ilk as "bocados do *Larousse* diluídos com água de colônia" (40) (little bits of *Larousse* diluted with cologne water). Eça notes in the preface that despite Fradique's awe-inspiring displays of cultural capital, his only publication is a slim volume of his early poetry in an art-for-art's-sake style titled *Lapidárias* (Lapidaries). For this reason, Eça contends, Fradique cannot be considered an author.

A self-proclaimed *touriste*, Fradique is no mere traveler: he perfectly fits the profile of the nineteenth-century grand tour connoisseur whose main interests are classical history and the art of "primitive" cultures. In keeping with his Old World sensibility, he prefers the picturesque "velho Portugal" (old Portugal) over modern, "Frenchified" Lisbon, just as he prefers the "linguagem tão bronca e pobre [do povo sem] a influência do lamartinismo ou das sebentas de direito público" (55) (the [Portuguese] folks' coarse and impoverished language free of Lamartine or greasy public law inflections). He is a purist who appreciates foreign customs and landscapes as long as they are unspoiled by modern cultural contamination. In one letter he complains that "as duas grandes artes orientais ... a dança e a poesia, iam em misérrima decadência" (36) (the two great Oriental arts . . . dance and poetry were in the most miserable decline). Colonization and the grand tour as well as other forms of travel associated with empire were themselves responsible for cultural transformations of colonized people. By visiting another culture, Fradique changes it.

Like Asia, Africa is a recurring image in *A correspondência de Fradique Mendes*. Eça's playful reminiscences refer to Fradique's various trips to the African continent, and he gives special attention to an encounter in Egypt, where Fradique has become passionate about *babismo*, a new religious movement that temporarily relieves him from boredom and depressing thoughts about the banality of existence. Originality, Fradique writes to Carlos Mayer, a well-known Lisbon aesthete,[15] requires a two-year meditative residency in the primitive and tranquil wilds of the Hottentots (whose first European contacts were the Portuguese) or Patagonians (43). Fradique's letters refer briefly to his African travels and a few incidents that include an encounter with an African chieftain who communicates with God by whispering devotional messages to slaves whom he quickly dispatches to heaven. At one point in the introduction to the correspondence, Eça recalls asking Fradique why, with all his firsthand knowledge, he does not write a book about Africa. Fradique dismisses the suggestion, claiming that he has nothing new to report, that his impressions will do nothing to alter national opinion, and that the Portuguese language has yet to be able to convey anything beyond the most modest of intellectual insights.

As *A correspondência de Fradique Mendes* makes abundantly clear, writing a book on Africa, or doing anything useful, is anathema to Fradique's enjoyment of leisure, travel, artistic contemplation, and studied refinement. He is a parody of world-weary historical figures such as Carlos Mayer and the Lisbon bohemian (and Eça's friend) Carlos Parede, as well as a tongue-in-cheek characterization of a "man of letters" whose life's work consists of a few artful poems, personal correspondence, and philosophical conversations that Eça and his generation self-mockingly adulate. At the same time, there are differences between Fradique and his supposed admirers of the period. While he prefers "old Portugal" and the classics over modern French influences, the Generation of 1870 initially criticized the country's pre-industrial character and looked to France as inspiration for progress. Despite this basic difference, however, ultimately both Eça and his heteronymic character became disillusioned with Portugal and were happier living abroad, meanwhile corresponding regularly with friends (and readers) back home.[16]

The fictional Fradique is a touristic flâneur whose visits to Asia and Africa are stimulants for his tastes in art and sensual pleasure; his creator,

Eça, who was in fact widely traveled, never visited Asia or Africa. But in 1997, a little over one hundred years after *A correspondência de Fradique Mendes* appeared, the Angolan writer José Eduardo Agualusa resurrected Fradique with the publication of a "secret" cache of letters in which the famous nineteenth-century traveler writes in detail about the African adventures alluded to in Eça's work. Supposedly written between his arrival in Luanda in 1868 and his death in 1888, a few of the twenty-five letters are addressed to his godmother, Madame Jouarre, with whom he corresponds regularly in Eça's volume. Fradique also writes to Ana Olímpia, his Angolan lover, a widow and former slave who, we discover, is the mother of his child, and to his friend and future biographer, Eça. These letters, plus a final one from Ana to Eça years after Fradique's death, constitute Agualusa's novel *Nação Crioula: A correspondência secreta de Fradique Mendes* (1997) (*Creole* [2002]).

Unlike Eça's text, *Nação Crioula* has no prefatory material to introduce Fradique's secret correspondence, probably because Fradique was now a well-known fictional character. In another sense, Fradique's letters needed no introduction; they speak for themselves about adventures in the South Atlantic, while Agualusa, the true author of the volume, speaks indirectly from the African periphery about the Portuguese empire in Africa and the practice of miscegenation and slavery. A few years after *Nação Crioula* appeared, Agualusa commented on the challenges of this kind of writing from the margins to the center about Africa:

> African writers are in a curious position: Our readers are not in our own countries but in Europe. We write for foreigners, and it changes the way we write. We, as African authors, are more like translators—always trying to translate our reality for the foreign reader. I see it as a challenge more than an obstacle, however—a challenge that forces us to find literary solutions for our fiction.[17]

What better way to describe the mid- to late nineteenth-century African experience for twentieth- and twenty-first century Portuguese readers than to adopt the guise of Fradique, one of Portugal's foremost travel commentators, and devise a project based on "extant" letters by him that were kept in Africa and withheld from Eça until too late for inclusion in his *Correspondência*? By using Eça's title with the addition of the word "secret" for his novel, Agualusa constructs a literary provenance of sorts for these new letters, which are only now available to readers in Portugal.

Agualusa's Fradique shares with Eça's character several traits, perhaps none more important in this case than his capacity to adapt to non-European cultures. In other words, he is far from a conventional *touriste*. As Eça describes him: "Fradique não se limitava, como esses [*touristes*], a exames exteriores e impessoais, à maneira de quem numa cidade do Oriente, retendo as noções e os gostos de europeu, estuda apenas o aéreo relevo dos monumentos e a roupagem das multidões. Fradique . . . transformava-se em 'cidadão das cidades que visitava'" (45). (Fradique did not limit himself, as these [*touristes*], to superficial and impersonal examinations, on the order of one who in a city in the Orient retains European notions and tastes and studies merely the surface relief of monuments and attire of the multitudes. Fradique . . . transformed himself into a "citizen of the cities he visited.")[18] This art of adaption goes hand in hand with what Eça describes as Fradique's "poder de *definir*" (power of *defining*): "Possuindo um espírito que *via* com a máxima exactidão, possuindo um verbo que *traduzia* com a máxima concisão—ele podia assim dar resumos absolutamente profundos e perfeitos" (47). (Possessing a spirit *to see* with the utmost exactitude, possessing the word *to translate* with maximum concision, he could thus provide totally profound and perfect summations.)

Agualusa uses Eça's description of Fradique's chameleonlike character and translation expertise to develop a Fradique whose language and style differ from Eça's cosmopolitan aesthete. Instead, he translates Fradique into a character whose style conveys a sense of Africanness for a predominantly Portuguese readership. This Fradique also employs the language of romantic heterosexual love when he writes to Ana about his *saudades* whenever he returns to Europe.[19] In opting to give Fradique a different way of speaking, Agualusa ensures that *Nação Crioula* maintains a certain independence from the source text (Beebee, "Triangulated Transtextuality," 201). That independence was made possible by the idea of a secret that had yet to be disclosed about Fradique's African travels and that this cache of letters finally reveals.

What are some of the characteristics that distinguish Fradique's voice in *Nação Crioula*? First of all, his style is more accessible, bordering at times on the colloquial as opposed to the more literary voice of Eça's protagonist, whose philosophical musings and occasional emotional outbursts have a dry humor and savage irony. In contrast, Agualusa's character is more given to direct exposition and storytelling with simple plot lines, intrigue, heroic and villainous figures, and strange occurrences that border on the fantastic. This Fradique even writes to Eça on one occasion that he might be accused, like Fernão Mendes Pinto (whose name echoes his own), of greatly exaggerating his adventures.

Agualusa's Fradique is less removed and secure, less the grand tourist associated with fine hotels, restaurants, and museums. He is more like a novitiate traveler who speaks the language of this new land but depends heavily on others and feels that he has "deixado para trás o próprio mundo" (11) (left the real world behind [3]).[20] His arrival in Africa is a case in point: unlike fellow passengers from Luanda who wade from the boat to shore, he makes a ridiculous entrance as two Angolan sailors carry him across the water and unceremoniously dump him, humiliated and wet, on the beach. Like Serpa Pinto, he also discusses the deported Portuguese criminal class that, through shady dealings, is part of Luanda's social and political elite and views Angola as not only its home but also its rightful domain.

Fradique's attitude toward his exiled kinsmen is less explicitly disparaging than Serpa Pinto's and more complicated. For example, Fradique becomes the houseguest of Arcénio Pompílio Pompeu de Carpo, who has made a fortune in illegal slave trafficking.[21] Agualusa based this character on a historical figure of the same name, born in Madeira and exiled to Africa, who was a successful slave trader. His birth name was Santos, which he decided to change to the more aristocratic-sounding Pompílio Pompeu de Carpo, of which Agualusa takes full advantage for its ridiculousness. When Fradique questions his host about his illegal trafficking, Arcénio defends his business by arguing that it is a patriotic act in defiance of the British embargo and the petty politicians back in Portugal who always kowtow to England's demands. Arcénio further claims that shipping slaves is his way of contributing to the growth of Brazil and staving off the inevitable "whitening" that will occur with increased migration from Europe once slavery is abolished. Although opposed to slavery and slave trafficking, Agualusa's Fradique is sympathetic with Arcénio's critique of Portugal's weak-kneed, subservient position vis-à-vis Britain and quotes him in his letter: "os Portugueses de hoje são tão pequenos que até cabem em Portugal!"(14) (there is so little substance to the Portuguese people today, you could even fit them all into Portugal! [6]). Fradique follows Arcénio's words with an observation that has its own degree of irony: "Portugueses como antigamente, da velha cepa de Cabral, Camões e Fernão Mendes Pinto só restam dois, querida madrinha, ele [Arcénio], e este seu afilhado" (14). (And as for the Portuguese of yesteryear, from the old stock of Cabral, Camões and Fernão Mendes Pinto, there are, I think, only two left, my dear godmother—he and I [7].)

Like Eça's work, *Nação Crioula* emphasizes Fradique's adaptability; after only two months in Luanda, he proudly writes to his godmother that he is "quase africano" (25) (almost African [17]). Not only does he adapt to his new surroundings, he also falls in love with Ana, with whom he has a child.[22] Notice that in this respect he is quite different from a character like Brazilian novelist José de Alencar's Martim (*Iracema*, 1865), who falls in love with the Indian maiden Iracema, with whom he has a son. Martim is the quintessential epic-heroic Portuguese colonizer who roams the Brazilian wilderness and valiantly battles his enemies. Fradique may adapt and procreate, but he is far from a heroic figure. Arcénio's son and his comrades even leave Fradique behind when they rescue Ana, who has been widowed and sold into slavery by her rapacious brother-in-law, Jesuíno. They also arrange for Fradique and Ana to flee Luanda for Brazil on the *Nação Crioula*, presumably the last slave ship to sail from Africa to Brazil and a symbol of Portugal's transatlantic enterprise founded on slavery and racial mixing.

In Brazil and far removed from the rigors and dangers in Africa, Fradique buys an island plantation, infuriates fellow landowners by freeing his slaves, and travels to Paris to promote the abolitionist cause, which becomes a means to escape the tedium that plagued Eça's character whenever he was in one place for too long. After a few trips back to Brazil and Portugal, he returns permanently to Paris, where he dies from pleurisy. Like Fernão Mendes Pinto, whose writing called attention to the Portuguese in Asia, Fradique's various adventures, encounters, and voyages in *Nação Crioula* give a sense of the centrality of the African colonies to the formation and consolidation of the Portuguese empire and the present-day Lusophone population. In fact, Agualusa gives Ana, a former African princess and slave, the last word.

In her lengthy letter addressed to Eça, she recounts the period from Fradique's first arrival in Angola in 1868 to their dramatic flight to Brazil in 1876, where, shortly thereafter, Sophia is born to an unsuspecting, astonished, but pleased Fradique, who is back in Europe. Since his death, Ana has returned with Sophia to Luanda, where she marries a former suitor, a "filho do país" (of mixed Portuguese and African descent), and heads a thriving business. Her ostensible reason for writing is to send Fradique's correspondences that she had denied Eça some years earlier when he requested them for his book. But her letter also suggests that Agualusa wanted an African and a woman who was doubly colonized to assume the role of biographer-explicator associated with Eça's original work. The August 1900 date on her missive, the same month and year of Eça's death, indicates that the packet of letters did not reach him in time for publication in his *Correspondência*. As a result, Fradique's various transatlantic adventures, including his romance with a former slave and the birth of their child, remained a secret until a cache of letters from Luanda suddenly appeared more than a century later.

Ultimately, although Eça never went to Africa except for a trip to Cairo, his novel traveled there. In time it was adapted and transformed by an African writer who sent it back to Portugal. We might say that a kind of textual travel changed the implication of a canonical work and deepened its cultural ironies.

BRAZIL BOUND

Tudo selva, selva por toda a parte, fechando o horizonte na primeira curva do monstro líquido.

(It was all jungle— which everywhere shut out the horizon at the first curve of this monstrous river.)

JOSÉ MARIA FERREIRA DE CASTRO, *A SELVA*, 1930
(*JUNGLE* [1935])

The Crown encouraged Portuguese emigration to Africa by first eliminating passport fees in 1896 and then, in 1907, abolishing the need for passports to travel to territories in the remaining empire (R. Pires, *Portugal*, 38). But from around 1850 onward, and especially after World War II, Brazil was the preferred destination for Portuguese migrants (30). Between 1886 and the early post–World War II period, an estimated one and a quarter million Portuguese, mostly from rural areas, left to work in Brazil. It is estimated that more than 40 percent of those who left for Brazil at the end of the nineteenth century returned to Portugal, and more than a few did so with considerable savings and even fortunes (31). Wealthy returnees were sometimes viewed with suspicion or less than favorably as "Brazilians," as Eça de Queirós points out in his novels about old-money aristocrats and their encounters with members of this nouveau riche. Portugal's own economic well-being relied substantially on emigrant remittances from Brazil and investments by such returnees. However, not everyone succeeded financially. Newspaper promotional ads and stories as well as word of mouth about fast and easy wealth were far from the reality for most who traveled to Brazil.

Two of the earliest and most important novels on this subject are *Emigrantes* (1928) and *A selva* (1930) by José Maria Ferreira de Castro, who migrated to Brazil as an impoverished youth and spent eight years there, two of them in the Amazon jungle. Although considerably older, the farmer Manuel da Bouça in *Emigrantes*, like Ferreira de Castro himself, leaves and returns to Portugal after years of toil without the fortune that the "palavra mágica, o Brasil" (2:298) (magic word, *Brazil*) evoked at the time.[23] In straightforward and wrenching detail, we learn of Manuel's anxious departure from his family, his journey across the Atlantic, and his years of servitude, first on a São Paulo coffee plantation and later as a shop assistant in the capital. Seeking solace from a compatriot who has just returned to Brazil for a second time, Manuel learns that "o mal é a gente sair a primeira vez" (2:398) (the mistake is to leave home the first time). As the years pass, the rural homeland that offered Manuel nothing but hardship and disappointment becomes in his mind an idealized place, a *locus amoenus* (plate 22).[24]

But emigration also changes Manuel, beginning with his initial Atlantic crossing and his contact with an ethnically diverse community onboard ship—what critic Keith Hollinshead has described, using Homi Bhabha's terminology, as "halfway populations" who share their anxieties and ambivalence about leaving their homelands.[25] In Brazil, Manuel eventually leaves his rural peasant status to join the São Paulo proletariat. Once in the city, he becomes involved with trade unionists and even a revolution. After nearly a decade in Brazil, he manages to buy a return ticket, but only by committing a theft. Ironically, the joy and relief at leaving Brazil fade into solemnity as he realizes that this foreign land has become his home: "A sua alegria desvanecera-a. . . . Agora que ia abandoná-la, a terra do exílio ligava-se-lhe por uma suave melancolia, como por uma saudade que ele vira a sofrer—uma saudade da terra e de quem nela vivia" (2:491). (His happiness had vanished. . . . Now that he was about to depart, he realized that the land of exile was binding him with a gentle melancholy, like a longing he would come to suffer for the land and the people who lived there.)

Reverse migration also has its complications. Ashamed of his penurious circumstances, Manuel pretends to be a "Brazilian" of means to his family and friends back home, where he learns to his dismay that a few who stayed put have fared far better. Despondent at his poor prospects and, most importantly, without the comradeship and support of the migrant community back in Brazil, he decides to leave "home" again. However, unlike his initial departure, which the entire village turned out to celebrate, he slips away, careful not to be seen, and takes a bus to join the anonymous ranks of the Lisbon lumpen proletariat.

Emigrantes was an important work for several reasons: It introduced a new kind of writing in Portugal whose publication interestingly coincided with José Américo de Almeida's *A bagaceira* (1928), another, albeit different, portrait of migration that is widely regarded as the precursor of the social-realist novel in Brazil. Although the beginning of social realism, or neorealism, in Portugal is generally associated with the late 1930s and writers such as José Ribeiro and Alves Redol, there seems little doubt that Ferreira de Castro's novel opened the way for more socially committed literature about the rural and working classes. Literary historians António José Saraiva and Óscar Lopes observe that *Emigrantes* was the first Portuguese novel to describe the desperation and indignities of the Portuguese migrant experience (1041), in contrast to earlier works that either simply referred to migration or concentrated on wealthy returnees. The novel also deals with the historically conflictive relations between Portuguese and Brazilians and gives a sense of the melting-pot community in Brazil following emancipation.

Two years after the publication of *Emigrantes*, Ferreira de Castro published the novel *A selva*, which drew more directly from his migrant experience in the Amazon. Widely translated, for years it was one of the most popular works of Portuguese literature within and outside the country; it remains unsurpassed in its poetic descriptions of the rainforest as both a place of extraordinary beauty and a "green hell," a *locus horrendus*.

A selva's protagonist is a young Portuguese named Alberto who has fled Portugal for Belém do Pará in the Amazon. Unlike Manuel da Bonça, whose flight was economically driven, Alberto is a university student and monarchist whose participation in a 1918 revolt against the republican government at Monsanto has forced him into exile. Unemployed and living off his uncle, who migrated to Brazil years earlier during the height of the rubber boom, he reluctantly signs on to a rubber plantation deep in the Amazon ironically called Paraíso (Paradise). Because of his education, Alberto hopes for decent employment and expects first-class food and accommodations aboard the *Justo Chermont*, bound for the plantation upriver. Instead, he finds himself relegated to the squalid and overpopulated lower deck alongside impoverished Northeasterners who have signed on as rubber tappers. Unlike Fradique Mendes aboard the slave ship *Nação Crioula*, Alberto has no special authority or privileges; unlike Manuel, who found fellowship within the halfway population onboard ship, Alberto remains aloof and an outsider. He neither identifies with the dark-skinned Northeasterners nor receives acceptance by the largely white managerial and landowning class, who refer to him as the "estrangeiro" (foreigner).

Marooned in Paraíso, Alberto is assigned to an isolated tapper station far removed from the plantation's big house and river station; there he comes under the tutelage of the Northeastern tapper Firmino. The story of their relationship has certain affinities with Daniel Defoe's *Robinson Crusoe* (1719). As we know, Crusoe, who owns a plantation in Brazil and traffics in slaves, is stranded on an island in the Atlantic. Fearful but armed, he rescues a prisoner from a cannibal tribe and names him Friday. Following the ostensibly civilizing mission and dictates of the time, Crusoe instructs Friday in the Gospel, teaches him English, and transforms the so-called barbarian into a faithful servant. In an interesting twist in *A selva*, Firmino owns the gun and instructs Alberto in the culture of the Amazon. He teaches him basic survival tactics that include how to hunt, fish, and avoid headhunting Indians.[26] In their jungle isolation, a friendship evolves between the tapper and his pupil. Yet from the very beginning, and despite his training and ownership of a firearm, Firmino accedes to Alberto as his superior because he is white. He addresses him as *senhor* (sir) and assumes, like Friday, the attitude of the loyal servant, in keeping with the deep-rooted tradition of master and slave that characterized plantation society long after emancipation.

Sometime later, Alberto is rescued from the jungle by the offer of a clerical job in the big house, which he accepts, albeit with a measure of guilt for abandoning his devoted companion. But once he enters the plantation household, whose environment and manners are familiar, Firmino is of no real use to Alberto. At the same time, Firmino's loyalty never wavers; he even consoles Alberto although his departure places Firmino at greater risk in the jungle. Later on, Firmino seeks Alberto's help to escape the jungle, but Alberto puts him off to protect the bookkeeper, Mr. Guerreiro, who is left temporarily in charge and with whom Alberto has now bonded. A despondent Firmino reluctantly accepts Alberto's reasoning, although his own life is in far greater need of protection. Finally, Firmino and four other tappers manage to flee with Alberto's help in getting a boat, but they are caught, brought back in restraints like fugitive slaves, and whipped at the order of the plantation owner, who has now returned.

Tiago, an elderly and crippled former slave who lives on the plantation, reacts to their heinous treatment by setting fire to the big house and killing the owner. He is the least powerful figure in the novel and often the butt of cruel jokes because of his limp; but he jeopardizes his own freedom to protest any action against the law that freed the slaves: "Negro é livre! O homem é livre!" (1:300) ("The black man is free! Man is free!" [338]). In the tradition of the *Bildüngsroman* and the neorealist novel that it anticipates in Portugal, *A selva* ends with Alberto's political awakening to class

4.5. *Cover of* A selva

struggle and refutation of his earlier monarchical beliefs. With money sent by his mother, and in light of the recent political amnesty in Portugal, he decides to return home and complete his studies. But quite different from his earlier views about social class, he also decides to dedicate himself to fighting for social justice and equality.

Although certain actions in the novel, especially Alberto's last-minute conversion, are melodramatic and often predictable, Ferreira de Castro's powerful description of the rainforest as both setting and protagonist of mythical proportions is unmatched in literature. There are many long passages devoted to the jungle and the rivers that read like epic poetry. At one point, Ferreira de Castro writes spellbindingly of the heavy rains and floodwater that transform the jungle into a fantasy underwater world:

> O rio começara a encher. Era um dilúvio anual que vinha do Peru, da Bolívia, dos contrafortes dos Andes, veios que borbulhavam, blocos de gelo que se derretiam, escoando-se na terra alta, regougando nas cachoeiras e destoçando, de passagem, tudo quanto se lhes opunha. Dir-se-ia que o Pacífico galopara a cordilheira e viera esparramar-se, em fúria cilópica, do lado de cá. Minava, abria, contorcia-se nas enseadas, engrossava com as chuvas e ia sempre, sem descanso, a caminho dos pontos baixos. . . . A terra encharcava, então. O manto aluvial, descendente do bíblico, invadia lentamente, soturnamente, a selva arrepiada. . . . Hoje, um palmo; um metro, amanhã; um quilômetro depois e, por fim, léguas sem conta — toda a gleba traspassadinha, como se a selva não fosse mais do que floresta submarina, trazida, por artes mágicas, à superfície de nunca visto oceano. (1:193)

> (The river was beginning to rise. It was an annual deluge that came from Peru, Bolivia, and from the watersheds of the Andres: a bubbling torrent with blocks of ice which melted and decanted themselves through the high ground, roaring over waterfalls and destroying everything that came in its way. It would seem as if the Pacific Ocean had overstepped the mountains to arrive with cyclopean fury and spread itself out on the eastern side of the *cordilheira*, that vast Andean range. . . . The earth became completely soaked. The deluge of rain, worthy descendant of its biblical ancestor, slowly but relentlessly invaded the terrified jungle. . . . Today one foot; a yard tomorrow; a kilometer later: and finally throughout countless miles, covering the whole earth, turning as it were the whole jungle into a submarine forest that had been raised by magic art to the surface of an uncharted ocean.) (171–172)

A selva is about a form of travel radically different from Fradique Mendes's *dépaysement*, which involves leaving the homeland voluntarily to experience the exotic. Forced to migrate, Alberto struggles to adapt to the exigent life in the Amazon, as do Northeasterners like Firmino, the difference being that this strange new world is, ironically, part of their homeland. In *A selva* Ferreira de Castro also describes the arrival of Japanese laborers in the Amazon in perhaps their first major appearance in literature in Portuguese. Their foreignness mystifies the Northeasterners, one of whom believes them to be Indians. While Alberto explains who the new arrivals are, the narration provides additional background about the work ethic and success of Japanese farmers in São Paulo that have led to an initiative to attract Japanese farmers to the Amazon.[27] The novel contrasts the Japanese, whose migration is permanent, with the Northeasterners, who work in the jungle in order to return home. At the same time, the novel poses the question of whether even a group as skilled and committed as the Japanese would succeed in taming the Amazon and rebuilding its economy as the demand for rubber declined.

That question had already been answered by the time Ferreira de Castro's novel appeared. The Japanese who relocated to the Amazon between the mid-1920s and World War II remained in Brazil, but disease and other hardships drove most of them to São Paulo, where they joined an established community whose first members arrived in 1908.[28] A second rubber boom during World War II involved the forced migration of Northeasterners whose relocation was financed by the United States through the Brazilian government. It has been estimated that 54,000 Northeasterners, known as "soldados da borracha" (rubber soldiers), mainly from Ceará, were inducted into the war effort and that of these, less than 15 percent survived the Amazon to return home.[29] A novel on that subject has yet to be written.

Brazil continued to attract Portuguese workers as well as political exiles in the years after World War II. Following the publication of *A selva*, relatively few authors wrote about the Portuguese in Brazil in any substantial way.[30] Perhaps this is not surprising given Ferreira de Castro's authoritative, epic treatment of the topic. In the spirit of Serpa Pinto's and Capelo and Ivens's works, *A selva* also introduced readers to a largely unknown part of the Portuguese-speaking world through descriptions of indigenous inhabitants and majestic flora and fauna that harked back to the earliest historiographies about new lands. Although the empire was well into its decline, and the Portuguese who sailed were now seeking jobs and not new worlds, *A selva* showed that there were still adventures to be had and frontiers to be explored.

~ FIVE ~

The Casa dos Estudantes
do Império and Mensagem

*Cada vez mais as nossas colónias estão integradas no pensamento
da Metrópole, e é bom reforçar o elo que reúne o escol do Ultramar
ao do Continente.*

*(Our colonies are increasingly integrated into the Metropole's way of
thinking, and it is good to reinforce the link that joins the brightest
from the Overseas with those from the Continent.)*

FRANCISCO VIEIRA MACHADO, MINISTER
OF THE COLONIES, 1944

Portuguese emigration to Brazil continued to be strong in the years after World War II. The many thousands of workers who left for Brazil included a small number of mathematicians, scientists, writers, and members of the military who sought political asylum from António de Oliveira Salazar's right-wing Estado Novo dictatorship (1933–1974).[1] Meanwhile, the growth of the Angolan and Mozambican economies in the 1950s resulted in a brief, sharp increase in what had been a relatively modest migration from Portugal to the African colonies. In comparison to the great majority of those who traveled to Brazil, these emigrants were often better educated and recruited by businesses and the private sector for their skills; regardless of education, those who ventured to Africa had higher social and economic expectations as incoming members of the colonial elite (R. Pires, *Portugal*, 38).[2]

So far I have largely focused on literary and artistic works inspired by different types of travel from Portugal to the overseas empire and its former colony, Brazil. A few of these works also deal with the return home of Portuguese migrants and, as we saw in Ferreira de Castro's *Emigrantes*, the shifting perception of homeland resulting from years spent abroad and a sense of fellowship and belonging within tight-knit migrant communities. In the present chapter I examine a relatively small population of young, largely male adults who left their homes in the colonies to reside, some temporarily and others more permanently, in the metropole, or imperial "homeland." As Eça's Fradique Mendes notes in one correspondence, even leisure travel abroad involves a degree of adaptation. In this particular instance, students who initially arrived in Portugal were mostly children of Portuguese settlers in Africa who spoke Portuguese at home and were familiar with certain customs. Other, later arrivals to Portugal included black Africans who went to schools with majority white and mixed-race students in the colonies, where they learned Portuguese and the values of an empire that sought to "civilize" them and other indigenous (black) inhabitants.[3] From the outset, the idea of homeland was a more complicated affair, especially for blacks, because Portugal, and not Africa, with its own rich heritage of languages and cultures, was the example and focus.

Historically, Portugal was the destination for students from the colonies who had the training and resources to further their educations. Even after the establishment of law schools in Recife and São Paulo in 1827, five years after Brazilian independence, many from the former colony still preferred to study at the Universidade de Coimbra, one of Europe's oldest and most revered universities. Unlike the situation in Brazil, institutions of higher education did not exist in the African colonies until 1962, when the Portuguese government finally opened two universities, one in Mozambique and the other in Angola. For that reason, students from Africa, India, Macau, and Timor went to Coimbra and, increasingly, to the Universidade de Lisboa, whose doors opened in 1911. Both the Universidade de Lisboa and the Universidade do Porto were founded that year by the republican government (1910–1926). Established in 1559, the Jesuit Universidade do Espírito Santo had been closed since 1759 by the marquis of Pombal. It reopened in 1973 as the Instituto Universitário de Évora and six years later became the Universidade de Évora.

The history of what became known as the Casa dos Estudantes do Império (CEI) (House of Students from the Empire) in Lisbon began in late 1943, when a group of university students from Angola proposed the founding of a cultural center that would provide a space for meetings, mutual support, and social and cultural events.[4] As historian Cláudia Castelo has noted, and as reported in the January 1944 issue of the government's *Boletim Geral das Colónias* (General bulletin of the colonies),

5.1. *The building that housed the Casa dos Estudantes do Império on the Avenida Duque d'Ávila in Lisbon (2014)*

their proposal had the support of Marcelo Caetano, a law professor at the Universidade de Lisboa and head of the Mocidade Portuguesa, the youth movement of the Estado Novo (Castelo, "Casa dos Estudantes," 28).[5] The creation of a house for Angolan students generated interest by others from the colonies, and in due course, houses appeared for students from Macau, Cape Verde, India, and Mozambique.[6] Castelo and others have commented that government concerns gradually rose over the difficulty of monitoring and controlling the activities of these various student groups and venues. The issue of separate houses and communities also conflicted with the regime's propaganda about an indistinguishable collective called the *ultramar* (overseas), whose best and brightest would come under the tutelage of professors in Portugal and, as Minister of the Colonies Francisco Vieira Machado contended in 1944, become leaders in the colonial enterprise in their homelands. To ensure that nothing would deter its various objectives and interests, the government consolidated the houses into a single entity called the Casa dos Estudantes do Império. Founded in June 1944, the CEI in Lisbon began operating in October 1944. After a brief presence on the Rua Praia da Vitória, the CEI relocated to a building on the Avenida Duque d'Ávila, where it remained until its closure.[7]

There is little question that the government promoted an umbrella-style social and cultural center as important to the students' continued adaptation and thus key to its efforts to prepare them as future colonial leaders. What the administration did not necessarily or fully anticipate was that such an assembly might also facilitate discussion and dissemination of ideas other than the government's "one and indivisible" Lusotropicalist propaganda.[8] Carlos Ervedosa, president of the CEI General Assembly in the 1950s, wrote in his memoir, *Era nos tempos das acácias floridas* (1990) (When the acacias were in bloom): "A CEI era uma associação politica-mente neutra por força estatutária, mas de esquerda por força da acção política dos seus dirigentes. Multiracial na sua composição étnica e nos ideias de sociedade" (in Faria, *Casa dos Estudantes*, 51). (The CEI was a politically neutral association because of its statutes, but it was left-wing because of its leaders' political action. Multiracial in its ethnic composi-tion and ideas about society.) From its inception, the CEI's administrative structure consisted of sectional leaders to represent its different constitu-

5.2. *Students in the Casa dos Estudantes do Império*

encies from Africa, India, and Asia.[9] In other words, the CEI reproduced for its governing body the very separateness rejected by the regime in terms of the *ultramar*. The general membership included university students born and/or raised in the provinces as well as those who had moved to Portugal prior to university study. A set of statutes published in a January 1952 circular specified that Portuguese nationals needed a minimum of five years' residency in any of the colonies to be eligible for membership.[10]

Between its inception in 1944 and its closure in 1965 by the secret police, PIDE (Polícia Internacional e de Defesa do Estado), the CEI in Lisbon solicited and promoted literary production of all kinds, examples of which appeared regularly in *Mensagem* (Message), an in-house circular whose first issue appeared in July 1948.[11] The CEI and its various activities, among them *Mensagem* as well as the Coimbra CEI, were subsidized by the Ministério do Ultramar (Overseas Ministry). A special issue of *Mensagem* dedicated to Angola received income from businesses such as the Companhia de Diamantes de Angola (Angolan Diamond Company) and the Companhia de Açucar de Angola (Angolan Sugar Company) that bought advertising space in the circular. Other revenues derived from ticket sales for CEI-sponsored sporting events, dances, and carnivals and from the on-site canteen as well as a largely volunteer-staffed and low-cost medical clinic and a small cluster of rooms that were rented to students. An early and central figure in the CEI and a *Mensagem* editor for several years, Tomás Medeiros from São Tomé discussed with me the importance of these rooms for black Africans who had difficulty finding places to rent in Lisbon. He described how they would knock on doors with vacancy signs only to be told by owners that the rooms had just been let.[12]

Mensagem's significance as the vehicle that launched some of Africa's most important writers, not to mention several of the leaders in the struggles for independence, cannot be overestimated. Its publication history spans a sixteen-year period and consists of distinct phases. Between July 1948 and January 1952, thirteen issues appeared along with two special supplements, one dedicated to Angola (*Mensagem Angolana*) and a second devoted to Mozambican poetry.[13] A more elaborate version of *Mensagem*, with artwork and subtitled *Boletim mensal da Casa dos Estudantes do Império* (Bulletin: Monthly organ of the Casa dos Estudantes do Império), appeared between 1959 and 1964. This was also the period when the CEI supported the publication of numerous individually authored booklets of poetry and prose by, among others, Agostinho Neto, who became Angola's first president, and Mozambican poet José Craveirinha, recipient of the CEI's Alexandre Dáskalos Prize in 1962. It also produced several anthologies to introduce writers from Angola, Mozambique, and São Tomé and Príncipe to readers in Portugal.[14]

The five-year period between 1952 and 1957 saw a government take-over of the CEI's administration because of increased anticolonialist activities associated with its membership and works—including *Mensagem*. The takeover in May 1952 coincided with the publication of the CEI-sponsored volume titled *Godido e outros contos de João Dias* (Godido and other stories by João Dias), whose tales of conflict between colonizer and colonized undoubtedly contributed to the regime's displeasure. For the next five years, no CEI circulars or other publications appeared, with the exception of a small anthology titled *Poesia negra de expressão portuguesa* (1953) (Black poetry in Portuguese). After a period of negotiations, the government returned control to the students in 1957, albeit with provisos that included a ban on the original administrative design of separate country sections and leaders that, as mentioned above, was anathema to nation-state propaganda. From 1957 to 1959, the CEI returned to publishing a "bulletin," but without the *Mensagem* title.[15] The bulletin is clearly a continuation of the original circular, with poems and other creative writing featured alongside fiscal reports and other announcements.[16] By 1959, on the cusp of *Mensagem*'s official return, the bulletin was composed almost exclusively of literary works.

MENSAGEM, THE CIRCULAR (1948–1952)

Portugal, meu país de que me ufano,
Cabeça dum Império dilatado,
Pátria querida, cativante eirado
Donde a Europa se lança sobre o oceano!

(Portugal, my country of which I am proud,
Head of a vast Empire,
Beloved country, captivating esplanade from
Which Europe rushes into the ocean!)

UNKNOWN, "VOZ DE ANGOLA" (SONETO DO COLONO),
OCTOBER 1948

(Voice from Angola [The colonist's sonnet])

Cuidado com o branco
Que anda por lá ...
Não sejas roubado
Cuidado, cuidado!

(Careful with the white man
Who goes about there ...
Don't be robbed
Take care, take care!)

ALEXANDRE DÁSKALOS, "O QUE É S. TOMÉ"
(THIS IS S. TOMÉ), OCTOBER 1948

In its initial phase, *Mensagem* published poetry, short stories, and essays on topics such as art, culture, women's rights, and history, as well as critical reviews and lists of books acquired for the CEI's library collection.[17] The verses cited above are examples from a 1948 special issue on Angola (Ferreira and Amarílis) of the divergent points of view and attitudes that characterize the circular's first phase. The anonymous "Voz de Angola" (Voice from Angola) is modeled in part on Fernando Pessoa's "O dos castelos" (Of the castles), the famous hymn to Portugal that opens his epic poem also titled *Mensagem* (1934). Pessoa describes Portugal as the sphinx-like face of Europe that gazes across the ocean to the "futuro do passado" (future of the past) and to the country's imminent resurgence as a spiritual empire based on its early overseas conquests. The initial lines of "Voz de Angola" also evoke Brazilian Afonso Celso's popular pedagogical treatise *Por que me ufano de meu país* (1900) (Why I am proud of my country), which, not without its critics, offered moral and civic lessons to bolster the idea of unity within the vast and diverse Brazilian nation. As with Pessoa's poem, the focus of "Voz de Angola" is the spirit, more specifically "a Lusa fé" (7) (the Luso faith) that forged an empire and continued to guide the colonial enterprise despite "horas negras" (black hours) and "cruéis revezes" (cruel reverses).[18] In the poem, the faithful colonist beseeches Portugal to treat Angola lovingly, as a mother would her child. This is paternalistic condescension at best, but the plea describes a nation-state that was not necessarily warm or humane in its internal relations.

Alexandre Dáskalos (1924–1961) was a different kind of voice from Angola whose poems were among the earliest examples of protest literature in *Mensagem*. In fact, his call for student solidarity in a poem titled "Companheiros" (Comrades) appears with "Voz de Angola" in the same 1948 special issue on Angola.[19] In "O que é S. Tomé," appearing in the October to December 1948 issue, he gives voice to a plantation worker victimized by a landowning system that treats "nossa terra" (our land) as if it were its own. The question of who owns the land is a major motif; another is an un-named worker's assimilation, with repeated references to his shaved head; his use of the white man's shirt, shorts, and cap; and his speech, which is now different from "a língua da minha gente" (6) (the language of my people). Fearful of the white man's treachery, he ultimately finds himself stripped not only of his money but also of his identity: "Onde está o meu dinheiro / Onde está o meu calção / Meu calção e meu boné / O meu din-heiro arranjado / Nas roças de S. Tomé?" (6). (Where's my money / Where are my shorts / My shorts and my cap / My money earned / In the fields of S. Tomé?) The poem concludes with the single word "AIUÉ," a sound of suffering. By capitalizing the word, Dáskalos gives the worker's cry a spe-cial added force, transforming his private grief into public protest.

Although very few women CEI members appear in *Mensagem*, the Angolan Alda Lara (1930–1962) was among its earliest and most impor-tant contributors. In fact, a talk that she delivered to incoming members, entitled "Os colonizadores do século XX" (The twentieth-century colo-nizers), was the first essay to appear in the July 1948 inaugural issue. Of Portuguese descent and born in Angola, Lara attended high school in Lis-bon and later studied medicine at the university there and in Coimbra.

Lara's essay is a good example of the nostalgia and romanticism as-sociated with images of homeland that, in this case, derived from her lengthy absence from Angola. Her essay's initial focus is the heroics of late nineteenth-century Portuguese who migrated to Angola, where they settled in a majestic but daunting environment that ultimately became "sua verdadeira terra" (4) (their true homeland). She emphasizes that, un-like the Portuguese in Brazil and elsewhere, those who went to Africa re-mained—despite economic gains that enabled them to return to Portugal. Those gains, she adds, were used to build schools for their children who, like herself, ultimately left home to further their education. They are the future of Angola, or "new colonizers" to whom her essay is addressed.

Lara contends that their most important responsibility as students is to return to Angola to build "o escol da civilização africana" (9) (the best of African civilization) and provide future generations access to a univer-sity education at home. Her reference to *escol*, and in fact her essay in large part, are in keeping with Francisco Vieira Machado's comment about the provinces' "best and brightest," who would return home to support the colonial agenda. Lara has little to say in her essay about the majority black population, although at one point she refers to "indolent" and "stupid" fieldworkers who rob and desert white landowners (4).[20] Notably, her description of black-white worker relations is the exact opposite of the image of white corruption and black suffering in Alexandre Dáskalos's poem about São Tomé.

Lara's essay departs somewhat from Estado Novo propaganda in its emphasis on Portuguese women whom Angolans might marry while studying in Portugal. Lara is insistent that her male colleagues realistically prepare these women for the different and more rigorous life in Angola so that they may effectively participate in the civilizing mission as teachers, artists, missionaries, or housewives. Interestingly, although Lara returned to Angola accompanied by her Mozambican husband, Orlando de Albuquerque, she does not regard the few university-educated Angolan women, like herself, to be anywhere near as crucial to the future of Angola as Portuguese women. In her words, educated Angolan women would always abide by the will of their spouses. She also discounts women back home in Angola who have abandoned their studies for other interests. Nothing more is said about this significant population, but Lara makes clear that the future of Angola rests not with them but with Portuguese middle-class women whose educational backgrounds make them more suitable and better helpmates in the civilizing cause. Although dispiriting, Lara's position on women's subordinate role is not unusual for the time, especially given her strict Catholic upbringing. Her comments also speak to the reality of a period when few Angolan women were well educated, let alone university-trained professionals.[21]

Lara's poems in *Mensagem* elaborate on the essay's theme of returning home. Her poem "Regresso" (Return), also appearing in the 1948 inaugural issue, evokes Brazilian Gonçalves Dias's "Canção do exílio" (1843) in its theme of longing for the homeland, *saudade*, and its nativist-style comparisons that privilege the pastoral Angola over the "insane struggle" of urban Portugal. Both poets praise their respective countries' natural wonders: Dias writes about Brazilian palm trees and the incomparable song of the *sabiá* (thrush), while Lara describes the colorful Angolan landscape with its swaying palms and smell of humus rising from a scalding African earth. She longs for the stillness of African nights with the sound of *batuques* in the distance over the strident, convulsive Lisbon streets with their "clamoring fishwives" (18).

Published in the February to April 1949 issue, Lara's poem "Rumo" (Bearing) reintroduces the theme of return but with a somewhat different emphasis. She dedicates the work to João Dias (1926–1949), a black Mozambican university student who died in Lisbon from tuberculosis. Dias had written several short stories while in Portugal, among them "Godido," about a boy whose servant mother protects him from his white landowner father in Africa by sending him to the city.[22] In "Rumo," Lara writes of blacks and whites united as *companheiros* and equals in their return to build a better Angola—an image radically different from Dias's description of the wretchedness of black lives under colonial rule.[23] "Godido" is also about the city, or "terra dos brancos" (white man's land), that offers little hope for the ill-equipped and frightened boy from the interior. While "Rumo" celebrates an equality associated with the urban university environment, "Godido" suggests that the city, whether in Angola or Portugal, is an intimidating and unfriendly place for those who are not white.

Using the pen name Vera Micaia, the black Mozambican poet Noémia de Sousa (1926–2002) writes about this fear in her poem likewise titled "Godido," which is dedicated to Dias and appears in *Mensagem*'s July 1951 special issue on Mozambican poetry.[24] While Dias's story ends before Godido actually sets foot in the city, Micaia's "Godido" describes a black female migrant's memories as a newcomer to the alien and hostile urban world that "[e]smagou com os pneus de seu luxo, / sem caridade / meus pés cortados nos trilhos do sertão" (35) (crushed with the tires of its luxury, / without caring, / my feet cut on the trails of the backlands). Similar to Dias's tale, the mother protects her daughter from the unfriendly surroundings, and the memory of her once comforting presence contrasts with what remains "a cidade cruel" (36) (the cruel city). Micaia's "Godido" seems more inspired by the author João Dias than by his fictional character. Like Micaia, he arrived in Portugal from Mozambique and became irremediably "desorientado e perdido" (36) (disoriented and lost) in the white city. The poem is both a eulogy for her "irmão negro" (36) (black brother) and a song of exile, albeit different from those of Gonçalves Dias and Alda Lara in its denunciation of "civilization" and racial prejudice.[25]

Mensagem's May to December 1949 issue showcased Cape Verdean poetry and prose by, among others, Amílcar Cabral (1926–1973), future founder of the PAIGC (Partido Africano para a Independência de Guiné e Cabo Verde) (African Party for the Independence of Guinea and Cape Verde), and Alda do Espírito Santo (1926–2010), who became one of Cape Verde's leading poets. Cabral contributed two works, the first of which was a short essay based on the memoir by his father, Juvenal Cabral, titled *Reflexões e memórias* (1947) (Reflections and memories). Quoting the book's description of the 1904 "monstro" (monster) drought that assailed the archipelago and its people, Amílcar Cabral focuses on the recurring cycle

5.3. *Amílcar Cabral, by João Pedro Cochofel*

of droughts whose defeat, in his words, requires a united effort by Portuguese and Cape Verdeans for the welfare of both Portugal and the greater cause of the *ultramar português* (9). Anyone familiar with the early writings of Cabral recognizes that this pronouncement was in keeping with his father's position, which was to denounce ills such as drought and racial discrimination in Cape Verde but not the Portuguese colonial presence.

Cabral's second contribution, in the May to December 1949 issue, the poem "Rosa negra" (Black rose), celebrates a young woman's beauty and vitality. It also predicts her future of postpartum suffering in terms of "varizes nas pernas e dores no corpo" (11) (varicose veins in [her] legs and body aches), when she will no longer be recognizable as the lovely and vital Rosa. What begins as a chauvinistic view of female beauty and seductiveness hijacked by motherhood is partly salvaged in the final stanza, which introduces a different reading of what the future, *amanhã* (tomorrow), holds. The use of the politically charged "tomorrow" suggests that a better life awaits Rosa and, by extension, her children and the country.[26]

A different attitude toward black women in Africa can be found in Alda do Espírito Santo's article titled "Luares de África" (African moonlight). Santo condemns the double colonization of black women, who represent "a[s] última[s] entre os negros que já são últimos na concepção vulgar dos demais povos de categoria civilizada" (12–13) (the lowest among blacks, who are already regarded as the lowest in commonplace notions held by the other people from the civilized category).

What distinguishes Santo from others writing for *Mensagem* at this time is her broader, continental view of black African female exploitation at the hands of both white and black men. Especially provocative is her denunciation of rich men who travel to Africa, seek the comfort of women whom they impregnate, and then abandon them to their fate.[27] She repeatedly defines African women's treatment in terms of slavery and demands the better life to which Cabral alludes in "Rosa negra." Santo's essay is explicit about what the future should offer women, including basic human rights and access to education. The article ends with a rallying cry for their just recognition and solidarity: "Mulheres negras de toda a África, vós não sois a escrava. Sois a esperança de África . . . sois a própria África" (14). (Black women from all of Africa, you are not slaves. You are the hope of Africa . . . you are Africa.) For Santo, black women are the shining lights (*luares*) of the continent, and her essay suggests an emergent African nationalism.

Mensagem's last two circulars, dated January to July 1951 and January 1952, feature segments from "A literatura negra e os seus problemas" (Black literature and its problems), one of the most influential early essays on black literature by Angolan poet Mário Pinto de Andrade (1928–1990).[28] As a co-founder with fellow writers Francisco José Tenreiro (1921–1963) and Noémia de Sousa of the Centro dos Estudos Africanos (Center for African Studies) in Lisbon in 1951, he was already a noted spokesperson on the problems of Africa.[29] His three-part essay was written in response to a lecture by Tomé Agostinho das Neves on black literature that appeared in the December 23, 1950, issue of *O brado africano* (The African roar).

5.4. *Mário Pinto de Andrade in Paris. Courtesy of the Fundação Mário Soares/ Arquivo Mário Pinto de Andrade.*

Andrade begins his piece by citing Neves's admission to his audience that his talk should not be construed as a scholarly presentation because he neither specialized in black literature nor reviewed requisite sources for his comments.[30]

From that revelation, Andrade segues into a critique of several points in the talk, including Neves's assertion that with few exceptions, black poets did not write about their innermost feelings as blacks. He also criticizes Neves's failure to distinguish between poems superficially about Africa and black poetry. Most importantly, however, Neves's lecture provided a platform for Andrade's own informed commentary about black literature, which he classifies in terms of an "essentially black" (5) oral tradition and written forms. He poses two areas of study for the latter: the degree to which they reflect a partial or total assimilation of European values and the actual content and language in which they are written.

In the essay's second part, January 1952, Andrade writes about distinctions between black literature from Africa and from the Americas. Andrade's knowledge of black literature is extensive; he references US spirituals as just one example of a powerful oral literature about black feelings. He briefly discusses important early writers in the United States, such as Phyllis Wheatley and George Moses Horton, and is especially drawn to writings by the contemporary figures Claude McKay and Langston Hughes of the Harlem Renaissance. For Andrade, the negritude movement produced the kind of activist poetry to which African literature should aspire, and he considered Cuban Nicolás Guillén the premier "black poet." He concludes this part of the essay by citing lines from Guillén's celebrated "Llamada," a poetic call to rally against a system that fostered racial tensions and class divisions. Andrade's own call, whose third and final segment was scheduled for the follow-up issue of *Mensagem*, was cut short by the government's displeasure with CEI political activism, resulting in a takeover of the house that lasted the next five years. Publication of the circular was suspended, and silence replaced its many voices of dissent.[31]

THE *BOLETIM*, 1957–1959

Eles nem são amigos do Rei
E a entrada lá é limitada,
Por isso é que eu não fujo
duma vez, pra Pasárgada

(They aren't even friends of the King
And entry there is limited,
For that reason I do not flee
at once for Pasárgada)

RUI KNOPFLI, "TERRA DE MANUEL BANDEIRA," APRIL 1958

Negotiations in 1957 between CEI student members and the government's administrative commission resulted in the return of the house to student control. The transition was a difficult period for members, who had been kept in the dark about fiscal and other pressing matters that were now their responsibility to manage. In fact, the first two bulletins issued, in November 1957 and January 1958, were exclusively informational, dealing with the many administrative challenges ahead. The second issue also discussed the new student administration's intention to raise the status of the bulletin to that of literary review. The title *Mensagem* did not appear on the cover during this transitional period, but the word was used several times in a lead article titled "Como se faz um boletim" (How one makes a bulletin) in the February 1958 issue, with obvious reference to the original publication: "Daqui em diante começará a sua mensagem e a sua propagação. . . . O Boletim nasceu, transmitiu a Mensagem da CEI" (12). (From here on [the bulletin] will begin its message and its dissemination. . . . The Bulletin is born, and the CEI's Message has been sent.)

Given the circumstances, the bulletin was far less militant than its circular predecessor, whose contributors included many who were active in the political opposition. What further distinguished the bulletin is the larger space given to prose works, especially the essay and short story; as a result, issues were considerably longer than the circulars, averaging thirty to thirty-five pages. There was also an interesting shift in representation from the initial predominance of Angolans to a greater mix of voices from other territories, with a significant increase in Cape Verdean compositions by poet-essayists Aguinaldo Fonseca (1922–2014) and Gabriel Mariano (1928–2002). Possibly as a result of Mário Pinto de Andrade's celebration of African oral traditions and languages, the bulletin featured African proverbs, stories based on African fables, and poetry and prose featuring Quimbundu and Cape Verdean Creole. Two prime examples are Andrade's poem "Muimbu ua Sabalu" in Quimbundu with its Portuguese translation, "Canção de Sabalu" (Salabu's song), and the poem "Maxibim Poçon" in both Portuguese and Creole, by São Tomé's Tomás Medeiros (1931–).

Among newer prose items to appear in the bulletin were fictitious conversations between two members identified simply as Sócio Jota (Member J) and Sócio Agá (Member H), who discuss day-to-day matters of the house. Signed by Africano Paiva, one of several pen names adopted by the prolific Angolan writer Francisco Fernando da Costa Andrade (1936–2009), the conversations between J and H are often ironic commentaries about students' reluctance to write for the bulletin or attend meetings.

In one particularly amusing exchange, the two characters portray fellow members' critiques of their *Mensagem* conversations as lowbrow. Despite their humorous approach, J and H were likely piqued by the criticism, and they do not appear again in the bulletin.

Although the bulletin was generally moderate in its politics, authors did not shy away from writing about controversial topics, such as slavery, white oppression, illiteracy, and hunger. Among the best examples of a more nuanced protest style is Mozambican poet Rui Knopfli's (1936–1997) "Terra de Manuel Bandeira," which is based on the Brazilian Manuel Bandeira's famous 1930 poem "Vou-me embora pra Pasárgada" (I'm going to Pasárgada).[32] For Bandeira, Pasárgada represents an imagined utopian realm of comfort and solace from the trials of everyday living—a place to which the poet has special entree as an "amigo do Rei" (friend of the king). Knopfli begins his poem by indicating that he, too, had wished to flee to Pasárgada, but on reflection, he realizes that everything in his provincial town holds him fast, including a loving wife and children, close friends, and traces and memories of those departed. The playful opposition that Knopfli creates between his verses and Bandeira's gives way to a forceful political commentary in the final stanza. Unlike Bandeira, he says, none of them are "friends of the king," a reference to the distance between the seat of imperial power and the colonies. Even more provocative is the follow-up proclamation that "entry [into Pasárgada] is limited" (27)—an image rife with racial implications. "Terra de Manuel Bandeira" comes full circle in the final two lines as the poet declares that for these reasons he does not flee at once to Pasárgada.

Among the many short essays to appear in the bulletin, three deserve particular attention. Two of them represent the greater Cape Verdean presence in the publication, and the third provides a sense of the challenges facing the CEI as it entered its third and final phase, marked by *Mensagem*'s official return.

In *Boletim* of April 1958, Aguinaldo Fonseca published "O cabover-deano visto por um caboverdeano" (The Cape Verdean viewed by a Cape Verdean), an excerpt from his longer piece titled "Apontamentos sobre o homem caboverdeano" (Notes on the Cape Verdean man). Fonseca is strongly critical of what he describes as the innate complacency of Cape Verdeans, which he attributes to "o cruzmento do lirismo exacerbado da raça lusitana com o recolhimento medroso do escravo negro" (24) (the crossing of an exacerbated lyricism of the Lusitanian race with the fearful withdrawal of the black slave). There is nothing optimistic in his assessment of his people except for his hope that they will recognize their complacency and act before it is too late. His comment might be construed as a call for his compatriots to embrace PAIGC, the new independence movement founded in 1956 by former CEI member Amílcar Cabral, who was a close friend of Fonseca's.[33]

Gabriel Mariano's essay "O mestiço na formação de Cabo Verde" (The mestizo in the formation of Cape Verde) forms an interesting companion piece and response to Fonseca's. Taking issue with Gilberto Freyre, who credits the Portuguese with creating Cape Verde as part of the Lusophone empire, Mariano recognizes Africans as foundational to the island's racial homogeneity, rich cultural heritage, and Creole language. He also describes important differences between Cape Verde and other colonies that make the island unique. Most significant is the absence of the traditional island plantation economy and the social and racial hierarchies associated with it. Because of its erratic climate and frequent droughts, Cape Verde developed an economy based on small farms, with emphasis on diversified crop raising as opposed to the monoculture characteristic of other African colonies as well as Brazil. According to Mariano, that small-farm economy allowed for greater social mobility for blacks and mulattoes and access to basic education. He also discusses the value placed on literacy, the island's active literary culture, and the significant and growing *mestiço* presence in Cape Verdean language arts.

Fonseca's and Mariano's articles exemplify the differences of opinion even within the CEI's smaller communities. Fonseca's somber psychological assessment of his compatriots is also reflected in poems such as "Identidade" (Identity) (March 1958), in which he wistfully declares, "Chora em mim a saudade daquilo que não fui" (The longing of what I was not weeps within me). However, as in his essay, he leaves open the possibility of change: "Canta em mim a alegria daquilo que serei" (21). (The joy of what I will be sings within me.) For Mariano, the Cape Verdean economy fostered the formation of a Creole society to which Portuguese settlers there were forced to adapt (6–7). From Fonseca's perspective, the fusion of black and white resulted in a timid and self-indulgent race; for Mariano, the strong African presence in the racial mix led to the emergence of a vibrant Creole language and culture.

The last article in the February 1959 issue was titled "Tribuna dos sócios: Ponto de vista de Edmundo Rocha" (Members' tribunal: Point of view by Edmundo Rocha). The Angolan Rocha (1931–) was studying medicine in Lisbon and was part of what he later called the Nova Vaga (New Wave), a CEI contingent that he later characterized as supporting independence and a "progressive nationalist" (as opposed to a strictly Marxist) agenda for the colonies (*Mensagem: Número especial*, ed. Borges et al., 104). The main objective of the essay was to discuss the various challenges confronting the CEI, although Rocha first describes the impact of the five-year government takeover of the CEI, whose membership fell from several hundred to around one hundred students. The tight rein held over the house at the time prevented overt political activism, and the CEI took on the ironic name Pensão do Arco do Cego, a reference to its reduced function as a simple residence in the neighborhood called Blindman's Arch. Rocha describes his own self-imposed exile from the house and his later return to support those who worked to restore the CEI to its original functions and statutes.

But the return to student control brought with it challenges that Rocha generally enumerates as lack of interest in CEI activities and an unsatisfactory economic situation. To address the first item, Rocha urges the CEI directorship to recognize and take advantage of the heterogeneity of its constituency to build interest and consensus. At the same time, he calls on all members to offer themselves for elected positions and to volunteer at least one hour per week to make the house a success. The second item refers to the *sede* (CEI headquarters), for which there are no funds. Rocha also registers concerns about the relationship between the Lisbon and Coimbra houses and the importance of ensuring the success of the proposed house in Oporto. The third, with obvious connection to the second item, is the general lack of finances that, from Rocha's point of view, required the newly elected administration to adopt austerity measures and adhere to a tight budget.

Despite these various problems, the bulletin published between 1957 and 1959 showed a clear commitment to restoring CEI's literary-cultural agenda. It was also a different publication that, out of political necessity, found a new, more measured, but no less effective voice to articulate concerns that the earlier generation addressed in far more militant terms. That was perhaps the CEI's most important achievement of the period and, as a result, *Mensagem* was officially reborn.

MENSAGEM 1959–1964, THE FINAL YEARS

Na terra dos trópicos . . .
(Coca-cola bem gelada)
e cansaços áfricos contra as duras paredes de vidro
da cidade maquilhada e sem alma.

(In the land of the tropics . . .
[Coca-Cola good and cold]
and African fatigue up against the hard glass walls
of a dolled-up city without a soul.)
JOSÉ CRAVEIRINHA, "3A ODE AO INVERNO," NOVEMBER 1962

Desde janeiro de 1963 que o Ministério do Ultramar não nos
entrega os subsídios concedidos pelos orçamentos das Províncias
Ultramarinas.

(Ever since January 1963, the Overseas Ministry has failed to hand
over to us the subsidies earmarked in the budgets for the Overseas
Provinces.)

EDITORIAL, "ATENTADO CONTRA A CEI," *MENSAGEM*, JUNE 1963

In April 1959, the title *Mensagem* reappeared on the bulletin's cover, along with an announcement of its monthly publication. But various factors prevented *Mensagem* from appearing on a regular basis during this last phase. These included the beginning of the colonial wars in 1961, which resulted in no issues for a year; a brief return to a governmental takeover of the CEI; and the Overseas Ministry's decision to withhold all CEI funds beginning in 1963. Notwithstanding those and other factors, the many bulletins that did appear were exceptionally well produced, and a few approached one hundred pages in length. They were largely devoted to literature and featured talented former and new house members as well as writers in the war-torn provinces and other parts of Africa and Europe. Contributors included Angola's Luandino Vieira (1935–),[34] Agostinho Neto, and Viriato da Cruz; the Mozambican José Craveirinha; and the new author "l. Bernardo," also from Mozambique. That was the signature of Luís Bernardo Honwana (1942–), who became a political prisoner in 1964 and ultimately one of the most recognized names in African literature in Portuguese.

Between the April 1959 issue, which featured poems by the Cape Verdeans Aguinaldo Fonseca, Gabriel Mariano, and Ovídio Martins (1928–1999); an essay on Angolan novelist Castro Soromenho by Fernando Mourão; and works by Agostinho Neto, and the January 1960 issue, the CEI underwent another change in administration that brought New Wave members to the fore under the presidency of Goan César Monteiro (1939–2003). More than six hundred strong, the CEI membership was also changing incrementally and racially, with greater numbers of black Africans ar-riving to study in Portugal. This increase in community members is borne out by the directorship report of an estimated two hundred meals being served daily by the cantina and by the dormitory's 100 percent occupancy.

At the same time, the new administration called attention to govern-ment cutbacks in support funds; it also urged students to pay their housing bills and support the CEI's new initiative to increase its visibility through-out Lisbon. Of particular interest in the January 1960 issue is a seven-part questionnaire, reproduced from the Angolan journal *Cultura*, seeking stu-dent feedback on plans by the Portuguese government to build a university in Angola (24). Designed for the CEI community, the first question asks students to identify specific problems encountered during their residency in Portugal. That question undoubtedly led to valuable feedback and dis-cussion; in 1962, the bulletin reported that university campuses in Angola were already operating in Luanda, Sá de Bandeira, and Nova Lisboa. Obvi-ously, the government was trying to reach an accommodation with the *es-col* of Angolans and others who sought access to higher education at home. Opening the campuses was also part of a strategy to prove fellowship and trust between the *ultramar* and the metropole—a strategy too little and too late to appease demands for independence or counter actions that ulti-mately led to more than a decade of armed struggle. In November 1962, an essay appeared on the mental health problems suffered by overseas stu-dents and was explicit about their causes (38–43).

Although *Mensagem* did not appear during 1961 and 1962, the CEI was far from inactive.[35] One of the most publicized events took place in Febru-ary 1961, when one hundred African students from the various CEIs fled to Paris in response to the call by the Movimento Popular de Liberação de Angola (MPLA) for help in fighting the wars for independence that had broken out there and in other parts of the African *ultramar*.[36] The students were also concerned about being drafted by the Portuguese government to fight against their compatriots back home. Edmundo Rocha and Graça Távares (1926–?), CEI members who were also part of the Movimento dos Estudantes Angolanos (MEA) (Movement of Angolan Students), were chosen by the MEA to arrange the students' escape with the backing of the Lisbon-based Movimento Anti-Colonialista (MAC) (Anti-Colonialist Movement). According to Rocha, logistical and financial support for this massive operation came from various outside sources, including the World Council of Protestant Churches; the Paris-based organization CIMADE, which housed refugees from Eastern Europe and other war-torn areas;

and an African student organization in West Germany, as well as two CIA operatives (*Mensagem: Número especial*, ed. Borges et al., 109).[37]

What became known as the "fuga dos cem" (flight of the one hundred) involved students from all the African colonies.[38] From their asylum in Paris, the majority, including São Tomé's Tomás Medeiros, went to Ghana and from there traveled to France, the United States, the Soviet Union, and Eastern Bloc countries. Others went to Switzerland to join Jonas Savimbi and his organization. A few joined the liberation cause, which included the FNLA (Frente Nacional pela Liberação de Angola [National Front for the Liberation of Angola]); medical students like Rocha supported the Angolan liberation movement in nearby Leopoldville in the Congo. After a couple of years, they were expelled from there and went to Algeria.[39]

Despite reduced funding and ultimately no subsidies from 1960 through 1964, the CEI published twenty booklets of poetry and prose by members and other contributors and five country-specific anthologies, four of poetry and one of short stories. Among the authors to appear in print were former members Agostinho Neto and Viriato da Cruz, who were leading the MPLA struggle outside Angola, and Alexandre Dáskalos, who died in 1961 and for whom a literary prize was named by the CEI. Works by current members included the poetry of Costa Andrade and Aguinaldo Fonseca and essays on Angolan literature and negritude by Carlos Ervedosa and Alfredo Margarido, respectively. In addition, Margarido authored a collection of popular poetry from Nova Lisboa (Angola). The CEI also published works by two of its major outside contributors: José Craveirinha's *Chigubo* (1964), his first published volume of poetry, and Luandino Vieira's *A cidade e a infância* (1961) (The city and childhood), a collection of stories based on his impoverished youth in Luanda.[40]

There is a notable lack of women's voices in the last years of *Mensagem*, although CEI member Noémia Gabriela Tavira (1937–?) attempted to rally women to contribute in her February 1960 essay "Que fiz eu da minha vida?" (What did I do with my life?), which was to be the first in a series called "Presença Feminina" (Female presence). Alda Lara's death in Angola in January 1962 brought renewed attention to her works. An issue published later that year reprinted two of her poems, as well as a long tribute by Alfredo Margarido, who describes hers as poetry of exile with longings for the Angola of her childhood. Noémia de Sousa and Alda do Espírito Santo each had one poem appear, in August 1962 and June 1963, respectively. Sousa's "Se me quiseres conhecer" (If you wish to know me) combines personal reflection with protest, as can be seen in these lines: "Torturada e magnífica, / altiva e mística, /África da cabeça aos pés / —ah, essa sou eu! (47) (Tortured and magnificent, / proud and mystic, / Africa from head to toe / —ah, that is who I am!). Santo provides an ironic contrast between a people's hunger and struggle against the background of a quasi-idyllic island setting. A "new authors" section proudly featured the first published works of the Angolan poet who signed herself Maria do Céu. There is no further mention of her poetry in *Mensagem*. Another new writer to appear in this section is the Angolan Artur C. Pestana (1941–), who later changed his name and became the internationally renowned Pepetela.[41]

The last issues of *Mensagem* were graphically more interesting, with occasional attractive cover-art designs. Using the pen name Angolano de Andrade, the poet Costa Andrade created one of the first covers, which depicts two naked figures in outline against the backdrop of a modern city. The juxtaposition of their nakedness against the square solidity of apartment buildings conveys the human figures' vulnerability. They are portrayed in the act of hauling something heavy; the ropes with which they pull bind them together and look like slave chains. A later cover used for various issues is by the artist Noémia Delgado (1933–), who became a filmmaker and was married to poet Alexandre O'Neill. The image is striking in its simplicity: an African in traditional ceremonial dress holds the symbolic war lance in his right hand, while his left hand holds a modern sign with the battle cry "Mensagem."

Among other images to appear is the illustration titled *Família* (Family), a *linóleo* by Luandino Vieira.[42] The drawing's spare, interlocking curved lines portray the closeness of the father, mother, and child figures. The unsigned cover of the last issue of *Mensagem* resembles a photographic negative in which dark and light images are reversed. The scene is stark: three spare palm trees on a level plane or coastline with a small telephone pole in the distance. It could be anywhere, but it suggests an African landscape whose sun is so brilliant that its entire spherical shape appears emblazoned on the palm fronds.

According to historian Fernando Rosas, the flight of the one hundred in 1961 resulted in a PIDE attempt to close the CEI ("A CEI no contexto," 19). That did not happen, although, as mentioned above, there was a short-term return to government control of the CEI administration in the first months of 1961. Rosas also describes the greater PIDE interventions after the mass student escape; these included searching the CEI offices, arresting certain members, and harassing others (20). As Rosas and Cláudia Castelo have noted, by 1963 student numbers from the provinces were already considerably diminished as a result of the war. The PIDE's much-

5.5. Mensagem *cover art,* Família, *by Luandino Vieira. Courtesy of Luandino Vieira.*

belated discovery of links between the CEI and the student arm of the Portuguese Communist Party during its dismantling of the latter in 1964 resulted in government authorization to close the house and to prevent further activities by its members. In September 1965, the PIDE entered the CEI premises, took possession of its storehouse of documents, and shut down its operations (ibid., 20). *Mensagem* had already been silenced for more than a year by that time. However, its legacy as a venue for young authors during its more than two decades of existence would prove to be considerable, as demonstrated by the many important books written by former CEI members in the years that followed.[43]

SIX

A Lusotropicalist Tourist and Soldiers, East Indians, and Cape Verdeans on the Move

In December 1937, just one month after the installation of Getúlio Vargas's Estado Novo dictatorship (1937–1945), Humberto Mauro's period film *O descobrimento do Brasil* (The discovery of Brazil) was released and became one of the first major propaganda efforts of the new regime. Based on Pero Vaz de Caminha's famous letter of 1500, the film has been interpreted as less a celebration of Brazil's "discovery" by the seafaring Portuguese than an allegorical glorification of the Estado Novo's arrival and the beginning of a new era for the Brazilian people, represented by the docile, wonderstruck Indians who receive benevolent attention and gifts.[1] The movie was not a unique instance of using history to forward a national agenda on screen, but it was an expertly timed, government-sponsored release that identified a momentous historical voyage and encounter with a new political course at home.

Salazar's Estado Novo dictatorship (1933–1974) was intensely aware of the potential of film to forward Portugal's nationalistic agenda, which, in the post–World War II period, came under increased international scrutiny for refusing to withdraw from Africa and Asia. Long a standard-bearer of the Portuguese empire and a "great man" figure closely associated with Salazar himself, Luís Vaz de Camões also became the subject of a much-publicized film in 1946 by José Leitão de Barros, whose cinema and other projects in literature and folk culture supported the dictatorship's agenda.[2] Despite its generous budget, *Camões* had modest returns, although it was the first Portuguese film to compete at the Cannes Film Festival. António Ferro, Salazar's director of the Secretariado da Propaganda National (Office of National Propaganda) and a major supporter of literature and the arts, overstated the film's reception at Cannes: "[S]e não ganhou em Cannes o prémio que merecia, apesar das palmas que interromperam a sua exibição, foi apenas porque nesse concurso e nesse momento, o nacionalismo elevado, puro, não estava na moda" (in Ramos, *Dicionário*, 67). (If it didn't win the prize it deserved at Cannes, despite repeated rounds of applause during its exhibition, that was merely because, at this competition and at that particular moment, a lofty nationalism in the purest sense was unfashionable.)

In 1951, proponents of the Portuguese Estado Novo attempted to assuage the growing international demand for Portugal to withdraw from

6.1. *Allegory of the arrival of the Brazilian Estado Novo*

6.2. *Post–World War II nationalism and the Portuguese Estado Novo*

the colonies by inviting the celebrated anthropologist Gilberto Freyre to travel to Portugal and the overseas territories—this in the belief that, based on his previous writings, he would report in favor of Portugal's continued colonial presence.[3] Freyre's arguments in *Casa grande e senzala* (1933) (*The Masters and the Slaves* [1946]) and *Sobrados e mocambos* (1936) (*Mansions and the Shanties* [1945]) about the sexual "excess" of the Portuguese and the importance of widespread miscegenation in colonial Brazil were not supported by ideologues in the Salazar government. Neither was Freyre's argument that racial mixing in Brazil derived from centuries of Portuguese-Arab relations in the Iberian Peninsula, resulting in what the anthropologist Miguel Vale de Almeida has described as Freyre's notion of a "bicontinental nature" that allowed colonizers to "live well with the excesses of the tropical milieu" (*Earth-Colored Sea*, 47). However, Freyre's image of familial relationships between Portuguese settlers and African slaves in the Brazilian plantation society, along with his observations about the economic, social, and cultural benefits and advances that derived from such benevolent contact, strongly appealed to the regime's defenders. Freyre's arguments and the even more specific Lusotropicalist ideas espoused in his book *O mundo que o português criou* (1940) (The world that the Portuguese created) were perceived by the dictatorship as a means to argue in the world court for the maintenance of a racially mixed cultural formation, or "way of being Portuguese in the world," that distinguished Portugal and its territories from the racial and cultural segregation characteristic of modern European colonization in general.[4]

From his first book on Brazil, Freyre asserted that no other modern nation equaled, let alone exceeded, the Portuguese in the degree and extent of their racial mixing with Indians and blacks (*Casa grande*, 10)—and that idea could easily be extended to the colonies in Africa and Asia. The concept of Lusotropicalism also supported Portugal's postwar image of its continuing supposed civilizing mission in the "provinces" (a euphemism adopted by the dictatorship to avoid the increasingly problematic term *colonies*). Freyre's characterization of benign master-slave relations dovetailed nicely with the regime's portrayal of a Portugal united harmoniously with its provinces in the forging of a nation-state, and his work was cited by Portuguese officials at the United Nations in defense of its territories. As historian Cláudia Castelo notes, by the mid-1950s Portuguese academic and scientific communities had embraced Lusotropicalist theory despite the praxis of racism that could be seen everywhere in the territories ("Uma incursão," 12).[5]

Portugal's minister of the overseas, Manuel Sarmento Rodrigues, issued the invitation to Freyre for a one-year tour at government expense. During what was ultimately a seven-month expedition (August 1951–February 1952) and in the style of earlier chroniclers of empire, Freyre kept a diary of his travels through Portugal and Lusophone territories in Africa and India. (Apparently Freyre did not feel compelled to visit Macau, and Sarmento Rodrigues managed to dissuade him from traveling to a turbulent Timor.[6]) The diary was immediately published in Portugal in 1952 and a year later in Brazil as *Aventura e rotina* (Adventure and routine), a title that indicates opposing forces inherent in the travel experience.[7] From the beginning, Freyre assures the reader of his ability to write freely and without prejudice about Portugal's continuing colonization of territories, stating that the government's invitation was both "non-official" (24) and "apolitical" (32). His claim strains credibility given the historical context and obvious political rationale for the invitation. What is equally interesting is that Freyre dedicates a little over half the book to his travels in Portugal, where he meets Salazar, is feted by old friends, and becomes a special guest at gala events sponsored by government officials and the upper class. These include a luncheon hosted by the former minister of the overseas, the banking executive Francisco Vieira Machado, at his summer residence, a former castle, in the Algarve.

Freyre's descriptions of Salazar praise the dictator's intellect, moral bearing, and astuteness. Yet when discussing Salazar alongside others in the pantheon of "os maiores portugueses de todos os tempos" (35) (the greatest Portuguese of all times), he indicates his slight preference for the philosopher, and Freyre's close friend, António Sérgio, a firm opponent of the dictatorship. Freyre criticizes customs officials for their bruising treatment in pursuit of communists and contraband. He also disliked censorship and argues that a free press could not possibly undo Salazar's prestige or threaten the foundations of the Estado Novo.

The closest Freyre gets to the colonies in the book's first two hundred

6.3. *Carving of Africans, Jardim do Ultramar*

pages is a visit to the Jardim do Ultramar (Overseas Garden) in Belém, outside Lisbon, and a brief meeting with Angolan students from the Casa dos Estudante do Império (plate 23). In the garden, Freyre is impressed by the architecture, statuary, and tiles with images from various parts of the empire. He especially admires the array of African and Asian plants that have adapted to Portuguese soil. For Freyre, those colorful hybrid species are symptomatic of the "unidade na diversidade" (358) (unity in diversity) that was foundational to his assessment of race and culture in Brazil. As for the students, he notes in passing the Angolans' differing opinions about the Portuguese presence back home. Nothing more is said about this topic until the end of the book, when he recalls a gathering at the CEI in Lisbon and his favorable impressions of Macanese members and their expressions of a Luso-Chinese-style *saudade* for their homeland (460).

The theme of Lusotropicalism is everywhere present in *Aventura e rotina*. Freyre credits the writings of the deceased António Sardinha, a cofounder of Lusitanian Integralism, with the fundamental recognition of

> o português não apenas como um europeu mas o criador de um sistema extraeuropeu de vida e de cultura, corajosamente assimilador da África negra e não apenas da morena ou árabe. Assimilador de índio

6.4. *Tile panel with Indian musician, Jardim do Ultramar*

no Oriente e de ameríndios no Brasil. Lusotropical, é como hoje creio que se deve caraterizar tal sistema, que dá à cultura lusíada condições excepcionais de sobrevivência na África, na América e no Oriente. Num mundo que já não é uma expansão imperial do Ocidente em terras consideradas de populações todas bárbaras e de culturas todas inferiores à europeia, mas um começo de síntese do Ocidente com o Oriente, da Europea com os trópicos. (114–115)

(the Portuguese not simply as European but as the creator of an extra-European system of life and culture, courageously assimilating black Africa and not just brown or Arab Africa. [The Portuguese were] assimilators of the Indian in the Orient and of Amerindians in Brazil. Lusotropical is how today I believe one should characterize such a system that gives Lusitanian culture exceptional survival conditions in Africa, in America, and in the Orient. The world is no longer about Western imperial expansion into lands thought to be populated exclusively by

barbarians and cultures inferior to that of the European but rather is at
the beginning of a synthesis of the West with the East, of Europe with
the tropics.)

This is a type of statement the Portuguese government was pleased to see,
promoting the idea of a friendly, Hegelian synthesis achieved after the
period of expansion and conquest. Freyre's tribute to the far-right-wing
Sardinha, whom he knew only through letters but regarded as a friend,
also provided a nice counterbalance to his frequent adulation of the so-
cialist António Sérgio.

Freyre's overseas explorations begin in Portuguese Guinea (later
called Guinea-Bissau), where he comments on how the Portuguese investment in health, basic education, and housing has improved the lives of the
population there. Although slavery was a taboo topic under the dictatorship, Freyre also touches upon its long history. He does not deny its ugly
reality, but he regularly intones the mantra of the unique Portuguese style
of "escravidão adoçada pela miscigenação" (378) (slavery sweetened by
miscegenation). He further rhapsodizes, "Daí a naturalidade com que o
preto assimilado—ou apenas em começo de assimilação—diz-se, em terra
portuguesa, português. . . . E sendo português, não se revolta tanto contra
Portugal como o preto das colônias inglesas contra o inglês, ou do Congo
Belga contras os belgas" (378). (Thus the naturalness with which the as-
similated black—or the one who is just beginning to assimilate—refers
to himself, in Portuguese lands, as Portuguese. And being Portuguese, he
does not react as much against Portugal as a black from the British colonies reacts against the British, or from the Belgian Congo against the Bel-
gians.) Freyre is frequently critical of the French, British, and Belgian approaches to commerce and colonization in Africa and more than once
urges the Portuguese to avoid their example in order to remain naturally
gifted colonizers.

Freyre occasionally advocates greater intervention by Brazil in West
Africa, especially in the treatment and prevention of malaria, and he often
refers in his diary to the familial and cultural proximity between Brazil and
the colonies, noting at one point that people and landscapes in Africa often
bring to mind the illustrations of urban and rural Brazil by the nineteenth-
century German artist Johan Moritz Rugendas. He also comments that
soccer in Guinea, influenced by Cape Verdean players, is more Brazilian
in style than Portuguese, and that Cape Verdeans are far more attuned to
Brazilian than Portuguese poetry.[8]

Much like Freyre's earlier writings, the diary has an intimate, engaging prose style. In the tradition of earlier chronicles like those of Fernão Mendes Pinto, whom he cites and whose chronicle *Peregrinação* he greatly admires, Freyre devotes considerable space to flora, fauna, and architecture. At one point he refers to Lisbon as an "Orientalized" city because of its architectural and other public-art reminders of empire.[9] In India, he is repeatedly struck by the architectural similarities between Goa and Brazil, with their common Portuguese heritage and cross-fertilizations:

> Aqui [em Goa] se encontram as varandas de casa, hoje tão da arquitetura doméstica do Brasil; o copiar ou o telheiro em frente à casa, que aqui se estendeu não só às igrejas como aos próprios cemitérios cristãos, protegidos contra as chuvas; a canja, que, no Brasil, é ainda mais prato "nacional" que em Portugal; mangueiras mães das mangueiras hoje tão do Brasil como se fossem americanas e não indianas; coqueiros dos chamados da Bahia mas na verdade da Índia. Em compensação, a Índia portuguesa recebeu do Brasil, pela mão do português o cajueiro, a mandioca, o tabaco, o mamoeiro, a rede. (299–300)

> (Here [in Goa] can be found verandas on houses that today are characteristic of Brazilian architecture; porches, often open and tiled-covered in front of houses, that were also added to churches and Christian cemeteries here to protect them from the rains; chicken soup that, in Brazil, is even more of a "national" dish than in Portugal; enormous mango trees from trees so closely associated today with Brazil as if they were American and not Indian; and coconut trees of the kind thought to be Bahian but that are actually from India. In compensation, Portuguese India received from Brazil and the Portuguese the cashew, manioc, tobacco, papaya, and the hammock.)

Perhaps because of his sense of a strong Brazil-Goa connection, Freyre complains of the restriction against Indians under Portuguese rule (and, more broadly, whites born in the Overseas) serving as government officials, a criticism that harked back to Brazilian newspaperman Hipólito da Costa's attacks from London against the exclusion of Brazilians in the royal government prior to Brazilian independence. Freyre is also critical of the racial bias in Goa's purported anticaste films, which feature exclusively light-skinned actors as heroic figures, and he pursues the issue of racial prejudice in comments on tensions between Indians and Mozambican soldiers stationed in Goa, a topic that Goan author Laxmanrao Sardessi treats in his short story "O barco da África" (The ship from Africa).[10] Far and away Freyre's most surprising statement is that Portuguese India should be a free and independent territory (303–304)—an opinion at complete odds with Salazar and seemingly in accord with Indian Prime Minister Jawaharial Nehru's call for the colony's independence.[11] Later in the book, however, Freyre modifies his position, adding that a liberated Portuguese India must not mean annexation by the Indian Union, which would place its Portuguese heritage at risk (408).

When asked by an Angolan "separatist" if it were not time for his country, like Brazil in 1822, to gain its independence, Freyre adopts a different tack; no, he states, it is not the time, but it is the moment for Brazil to reconnect with Portugal and for Portugal to have closer ties with Brazil in forging a transnational or Lusotropical culture (456). The idea of greater communication for the purposes of commercial and cultural exchange between Brazil, Portugal, and the Overseas is repeatedly stressed. But when he visits Dundo and the headquarters of the long-established, internationally owned Companhia de Diamantes de Angola, or Diamang, diamond mine, his arguments for using a greater Luso-Brazilian exchange to form a less racist approach to employer-employee relations there becomes a flashpoint for its founder and president, Ernesto Vilhena.

Freyre writes that Dundo is one of many places that he would like to study more closely in order to see behind what official hosts allowed him to view. He was interested in visiting a worker's home but permitted only to view exteriors, which he critiques for the zinc coverings that increase the heat in already infernal interiors. He commends the quality health care for workers and their families, although he wonders if the reason for the modern services might not be to protect whites from diseases contracted by blacks. He draws a sharp contrast between the intimacy of Luso-Brazilian and African slave relations and the eugenics of white-black relations at Dundo. He notes the separate maternity wards and churches for whites and blacks and the many comforts afforded to white personnel. His description of black workers under scrutiny in the heavily secured *central*, where machines and workers separated gems from ordinary rocks, brings to mind the Italian Carlos Julião's eighteenth-century watercolors of Minas Gerais, one of which depicts Portuguese officials strip-searching an African diamond miner. Freyre does, however, have favorable comments about the Angolan company's efforts to record and preserve indigenous music and its on-site ethnographic museum.

What Freyre may or may not have known at the time was that the up-to-date health care at Diamang constituted a central showpiece in the Estado Novo's international propaganda imagery of its beneficial presence

6.5. *Gilberto Freyre with worker in Angola*

in Africa. In a 2004 essay on Diamang and health conditions, "A saúde e a Companhia de Diamantes de Angola," historian Jorge Varanda describes the impressive ratio of doctors to workers and the many hospitals and clinics built to serve not only the worker but also populations well beyond the company's territorial domain. But this wide-ranging assistance, he argues, was also the means by which Diamang gained greater power, and access to a larger workforce. Ultimately, better health care meant more productive laborers and greater economic gains—in addition to a ready supply of healthy worker-candidates in the outlying areas.

Perhaps Freyre was unhappy that the company car was late to take him on the long trek to Dundo or because the Diamang headquarters, with its antiseptic atmosphere and antitropical-style gardens and architecture that reminded him of Palo Alto, California, disappointed him. Freyre also expresses uneasiness with the heavy police presence, which he found personally unsettling, making him unsure if he was viewed as a welcomed guest or a thief. He refers to his Diamang host, the company engineer Rolando Suceno, as a throwback to the days of the Inquisition, with his "olhos duros que lembram os do brasileiro almirante Pena Boto: raros em brasileiro ou português" (395) (hard eyes that recall those of Brazilian admiral Pena

Boto: rare in either a Brazilian or Portuguese).[12] Under Suceno, he writes, the strict discipline discouraged individuality and inhibited privacy. He attributes the regimen to Diamang president Ernesto Vilhena, whom he mockingly characterizes as a collector of saintly statuary back in Lisbon.[13]

This and similar comments by Freyre were among the issues addressed in a two-page "critique of a critique" by Vilhena that appeared in the July 16, 1954, issue of Lisbon's major newspaper, the *Diário de Notícias*. In many ways Vilhena's attack on Freyre took the burden off the government to reply to the Brazilian's more problematic arguments about Portugal and the Overseas. In his newspaper rebuttal, Vilhena objects to Freyre's generalizations about Portugal and the Overseas, his confused prose style dotted with "difficult words" such as *miscigenação* (miscegenation) and *escravocrata* (slave-owning), his scatological obsessions, and his attempt to avoid offending either the political right or the left. Although he agrees that Freyre's use of the Lusotropicalist conceit as a way to understand the Overseas is appropriate, he also worries about it: "[O] que está errada é o fazer dentro dele, da 'miscigenação,' da mestiçagem, digamos, a condição forçada da ação portuguesa em África e o remédio para todos os males, presentes e futuros" (4). (What is wrong is the idea that "miscegenation," or racial mixing, let us say, is the forced condition of the Portuguese action in Africa as well as the remedy for any present and future ills.)

After this initial broadside, Vilhena narrows his focus to Freyre's quick, superficial tour of Angola. He quotes him extensively, sometimes derisively, correcting or refuting his observations about discrimination, deprivations, and untoward discipline by the diamond enterprise. Vilhena argues that Freyre rejects categorically, despite his meager knowledge of the African context, whatever does not fit his vision of a Lusotropicalism based on the fundamental necessity of a racially integrated society. Vilhena defends the architecture that Freyre loathes, describing it as Diamang's Californian-style "detropicalization," and contending that this approach is essential to the tropics' *humanização* (humanization) and the welfare of "*nossa*" (*our* [his emphasis]) Africa—that "caldeamento, muito nosso, muito *sui generis* (6) (fusion, very much ours, very much *sui generis*).

Liberal and left-wing readers were also unhappy with Freyre's assessments of the provinces. As Cláudia Castelo and others have noted, the Angolan writer, former CEI member, and political activist Mário Pinto de Andrade, who had fled Lisbon for Paris and was writing for *Presènce Africaine* in the mid-1950s, challenged claims of a harmonious racial mixing. Discrimination, subjugation, and economic exploitation of people of color, he noted, were factors in all forms of colonization, including Freyre's purportedly milder Portuguese version.[14] In 1956, Cape Verdean writer Baltasar Lopes, who had written earlier about similarities between the Portuguese colonization of Cape Verde and Brazil, greatly admired Freyre and expected him to praise the archipelago's mixed-race cultural identity. But Freyre deemed the Cape Verde mix as well as the Creole language to be too African to figure into his ideal of a synthesis between European and African peoples that he called the Lusotropical civilization complex. Lopes went on local radio to debate the Brazilian's dismal pronouncements about the islands, especially Freyre's problems with the Creole language, which Freyre thought was inappropriate as a literary vehicle.[15] For other Africans like Amílcar Cabral, leader of the liberation movement in Cape Verde and Guinea, "Portuguese multi-racialism [was] a myth" (*The Facts*, 5). Cabral critiqued Lusotropicalism's confused biologism and utopian predictions of African colonies filled with "happy natives" (in Medina, "Gilberto Freyre contestado," 54). At its most pernicious, Lusotropicalism was an idea given shape by the dictatorship for its own imperialistic ends and used repeatedly to contest international demands for relinquishing the colonies.[16]

INDIA AND THE ERODING NATION-STATE, 1961

Minha terra tem mangueiras,
Onde canta o muruoni;
. . .
Não permita Deus que eu morra
Sem que eu veja o seu farol,
Suas arequeiras belas,
Seu tão doce pôr-do-sol;
Sem ver as meigas donzelas
De pitambor, noto e chole.

(My land has mango trees
Where the Indian thrush sings;
. . .
May God grant that I might live
To see its lighthouse,
Its beautiful palms,
And its sunset so sweet;

To see the gentle maidens
With yellow silk, jewels and chole.)

PEDRO ANTÓNIO DE SOUSA, "GOA," 1882

In the late 1950s, Portugal's defense ministry began issuing guides for the thousands of young men who were sent from Portugal and the provinces to carry out their compulsory military service.[17] Reissued annually and entitled *Rumo*, the pamphlets provided the soldiers with basic information about the people and lands where they would be stationed. Their main objective was to emphasize each soldier's obligation to ensure Portugal's continued territorial control. A good example is the booklet *Rumo à Índia* (1956), which states, "É vosso dever garantir, a todo o custo, a manutenção da nosssa soberania em Goa, Damão e Diu, e assegurar, na mais completa solidariedade, com os portugueses daqueles territórios, a defesa da paz, na Índia Portuguesa" (It is your duty to guarantee, at all cost, the maintenance of our sovereignty in Goa, Daman, and Diu and to ensure, in total solidarity with the Portuguese from those territories, the peaceful defense of Portuguese India).[18] The pamphlet also informed soldiers from Portugal that they should recognize Mozambican and Angolan troops in India as Portuguese and as military comrades.

Rumo à Índia was the first in the series of informational booklets to appear. The collection as a whole seems created to portray a peaceful military occupation and friendly co-existence among soldiers and inhabitants, in line with the dictatorship's Lusotropicalist rhetoric about a "one and indivisible" nation-state. But in his novel *O signo da ira* (1961) (The sign of wrath), Goan author Orlando da Costa, who was a member of the Casa dos Estudantes do Império, describes a very different relationship between a remote peasant community in the Goan interior and Portuguese soldiers who carry out training maneuvers in the area. Because neither group speaks the other's language, suspicions abound on both sides and violent encounters often occur.[19] Natél, a young peasant girl, wonders how the soldiers can be so bad if they look so much like the "white saints" in the local Catholic church. Even the Catholic priest, who is Indian and bilingual, cannot protect his village parishioners, and most of his attempts at resolution, reconciliation, and salvation end badly. Da Costa's novel was banned shortly after publication by the Salazar dictatorship.

Among the novel's many storylines is a black-market scheme to sell gasoline stolen by a soldier and hidden in a local tavern run by an Indian barkeep named Rumão. Another plot involves a love triangle of sorts between Natél, the peasant farmer Bostian, and a nameless Portuguese soldier who falls in love with Natél from a distance and whose interest, from afar, she returns. The tavern owner Rumão is killed by his partner in crime, who sets the tavern on fire when the scheme to sell gasoline is discovered by the military commander. When Natél's Portuguese admirer is accused of the crime, Natél defends him, claiming she was with him elsewhere at the time; in doing so, she sacrifices her honor and the possibility of future happiness with Bostian. Costa's novel is an unusual, explicit indictment not only of the Portuguese military presence in Goa but also of the Church's failure to serve and protect the poor inhabitants.[20]

As tensions grew between Portugal and the Indian Union, Goa and other parts of Portuguese India saw a military buildup and an order from Salazar to stand firm no matter the cost: "Não prevejo a possibilidade de tréguas, nem prisioneiros portugueses, como não haverá navios rendidos, pois sinto que apenas pode haver soldados e marinheiros vitoriosos ou mortos" (I don't foresee the possibility of a truce or Portuguese prisoners, nor will there be ships surrendered, for I feel that there can only be soldiers and sailors who are either victorious or dead).[21] On December 17, 1961, an estimated 4,500 soldiers in garrisons in and around Goa, Daman, and Diu came under attack by a vastly larger and better-equipped Indian military.[22] At the end of a short campaign, and with lives lost on both sides, the Portuguese were taken prisoner and held for five months in camps, where, to the surprise of their captors, Goan citizens often visited with food and supplies (Moço, "Prisioneiros," 77). In retaliation for the attack and defeat, Salazar ordered the imprisonment of all non-Portuguese Indians residing in Portugal and its remaining provinces. Historian Diogo Moço notes,

> Cinco indianos foram presos em Lisboa e internados no forte de Caxias. No Ultramar, foram presos 56 em Macau, sete em São Tomé e Príncipe, e um em Angola. Em Moçambique, província onde existia uma importante colónia de indianos, 2274 indivíduos foram internados em campos de concentração localizados em Lourenço Marques, Zambézia, e Gaza. Foram-lhes ainda congelados os bens e as casas comerciais que possuíam encerradas. (56)

> (Five Indians were arrested in Luanda and imprisoned in the Caxias fort. Elsewhere in the Overseas, 56 were arrested in Macau, seven in São Tomé and Príncipe, and one in Angola. In Mozambique, which had an important Indian colony, 2274 individuals were interned in prison

camps in Lourenço Marques, Zambezi, and Gaza. Further, their assets were frozen and their businesses were closed.)

After months of difficult negotiations and many delays, the soldiers were shipped back to Portugal in the company of some two hundred family members and acquaintances who were in India at the time. Portuguese citizenship was issued to all those remaining in the former province. Several hundred Goans opted to leave for a country they regarded as a homeland and whose language they spoke, over adaptation to the "foreign" Indian Union. Among the migrants who left just prior to the takeover was a young writer who, once in Lisbon, changed her name from Teresa da Piedade de Baptista Almeida to Vimala Devi. In a bittersweet poem, "Recordação de Goa" (Remembrance of Goa), which appeared the year of the takeover, she describes India as still part of her sentient world, although in a gauzy, quasi-ghostly form because of its distance and loss:

> Dentro de mim,
> O perfume mais suave
> É a tua recordação . . .
>
> Ao contemplar Súria,
> Tua imagem descubro
> Numa breve meditação . . .
>
> Hoje, as tuas canções
> Perdem-se na noite
> Como sonhos
>
> (Within me
> Is the gentlest perfume
> Of your memory . . .
>
> As I contemplate Súria,
> Your image I discover
> In a brief meditation . . .
>
> Today, your songs
> Are lost in the night
> Like dreams)[23]

According to Diogo Moço, the loss of the Indian provinces brought a vague sense of despair, or "India syndrome," to Portugal ("Prisioneiros," 177). In his memoir, *A última crónica da Índia* (1997) (The last chronicle from India), Pedro Pinheiro, a former prisoner of war from the camp in Goa, describes the various ways the dictatorship thwarted any public attempts to welcome the returning soldiers. A radio announcement said that the soldiers were to disembark in Lisbon at 10:30 in the morning, when in fact their ship was scheduled to arrive more than three hours earlier. Pinheiro writes of his frustration and despair over the lack of a proper homecoming:

> Quando a *Pátria* se quedou no meio do Tejo, a emoção pressentida não era mais do que uma imensa desilusão toda ela mágoa, cansaço e uma incomensurável raiva muito a custo dominada. . . . O silêncio que acompanhava o desembarque era impressionante. . . . Desgraçadamente, ao pisar de novo o chão do meu país reparei que estava entre dois cordões de soldados armados, da escada do barco às caminoetas militares que mais à frente esperavam por nós. Como na Índia, no aeroporto da Dabolim, quando deixei de ser um prisioneiro. (308, 309, 310)

> (When the [ship] *Pátria* stopped in the middle of the Tagus, the emotion felt was nothing more than a huge feeling of disillusionment—anguish, fatigue, and an incommensurable rage that was hard to control. . . . The silence that accompanied our debarking was impressive. . . . Upon stepping once again on native soil, I noticed in disgrace that I was being filed between two cordons of armed soldiers that ran from the ship's stairway to the military trucks that waited for us ahead. Just like in India, in the Dabolim airport, when I stopped being a prisoner.)

Pinheiro contrasts this subdued and secretive arrival with centuries of military homecomings from India that were greeted by a rejoicing population. He also describes how the supposedly disgraced troops were taken to the main barracks and made to strip off the clothes given to them on ship. In frustration and defiance, he took from a sack his threadbare prisoner's uniform and put it back on. He adds, "Deixou de se falar na Índia. Foi esquecida, tornou-se um assunto tabu" (322). (People stopped talking about India. It was forgotten; it became a taboo subject.) From that point on, he says, the dictatorship mostly brought troops returning to Lisbon from Africa by airplane in order to keep the reality of the war from public view. Pinheiro is critical of the public's easy manipulability: "[O] 'bom povo português'—facilmente persuasível perante meia dúzia de manobras de diversão, depressa pôs de parte o aviso que a Índia tinha sido. Nos seus festejados brandos costumes esquecia os irmãos, os amigos, os conhecidos que em África sofriam e morriam naquilo que durante 13 anos foi a vergonha deste país" (321). (The "good Portuguese people"—easily persuaded by a half-dozen sleights of hand, quickly forgot the warning that India had been. Despite their celebrated gentle customs, they forgot their brothers, friends, and acquaintances who were suffering and dying in Africa in what for thirteen years was this country's shame.)

THE CAPE VERDEAN DIASPORA ON SCREEN

Estas terras de Cabo Verde parecem ter estado adormecidas, no meio do mar, desde a noite dos tempos, à espera de poderem ser Portugal.

(These Cape Verdean lands seem to have been asleep since the beginning of time and in the middle of the sea, just waiting to become Portugal.)

ADRIANO MOREIRA, MINISTER OF THE OVERSEAS, 1962

As the rank and file and officers, occasionally accompanied by wives and even families, left Portugal for combat duty in the early 1960s, and as economic incentives continued to lure Portuguese to Angola, Brazil, the United States, and different parts of Europe, the labor force in Lisbon grew smaller. Among the many projects being constructed at the time was the Fundação Calouste Gulbenkian, whose oil-rich patron, Calouste Sarkis Gulbenkian, an immigrant himself, born in Armenia, left a large endowment for erecting a museum-foundation to house his world-class art collection. Anthropologist Luís Batalha has written that although workers from Portugal's economically depressed interior filled some of the demand for cheap labor, better-paying jobs outside Portugal had sapped their numbers ("Cape Verdeans," 62). In response to the growing demand, and as a result of depressed conditions in Cape Verde, a mostly male, dark-skinned, poorly educated, and unskilled workforce began arriving in Lisbon from the archipelago. Hired largely for heavy construction work, the workers initially lived in makeshift housing on work sites or in rooms in impoverished, low-rent areas. They also built shantytown communities, where a sense of freedom, fellowship, and cultural identity began to emerge (66).

In the mid-1990s, as first and second generations of workers from the 1960s and 1970s were growing up in these poor neighborhoods, Portuguese director Pedro Costa made *Casa de lava* (1994) (House of lava, released as *Down to Earth*), his first in a series of remarkable films about the Cape Verdean diaspora. *Casa de lava* is set primarily in the archipelago and concerns the forced reverse migration of an injured and comatose construction worker named Leão (Issach de Bankolé). Having fallen from a tall building while on the job in Lisbon, he is taken back to his island home of Fogo (Fire) by Mariana (Inês Medeiros), a Portuguese nurse who also brings medical supplies to treat the local population. There, in Leão's volcanic birthplace, she hopes to locate family or friends to care for him.

Casa de lava is a beautifully made wide-screen movie that has a subtle yet sharp political edge. Featuring a cast of largely nonprofessional locals and color scenes shot in natural light, the film offers a new kind of social realism, characterized by a poetic, otherworldly atmosphere, an experimental sound track, and performances that are notable for their lack of affect. The island, whose pulsing, red-hot volcanic core resembles a surgically exposed beating heart, offers majestic views of high ocean cliffs and sweeping plains. But the natural beauty also has a tough, unforgiving side, suggested by pounding surf, miles of hot-ash road, and an inky-black, rocky terrain fit only for goats.

The film has very little plot in the traditional sense. What we come to know about the people and the place is gradually revealed through Mariana, an unhappy oracle of sorts who roams the island, administers vaccines, and warns the men about the dangers of migrating to Portugal, where they will end up in "a rat hole or a hospital." As suggested by the film's early glimpses of the bleak Lisbon hospital where Mariana works and initially cares for Leão, her life is gray, antiseptic, and generally miserable. The short, red dress she wears on the island suggests an erotic vitality that comes alive—like the bubbling red lava—in a poor yet colorful place rich in music, family ties, and communal warmth. Mariana feels sexual desire perhaps for the first time.[24] Walking the streets and hillsides, opening and closing doors, and riffling through bureau drawers, she searches for clues to the island's secrets. Linguistic and other kinds of barriers, both visible and invisible, are everywhere present, and while the Cape Verdeans accept her medical attention, they ignore her urgings to stay put and not give up.

Unlike Gilberto Freyre, who expressed reservations about the Creole language, Costa celebrates the local speech. Virtually everyone in the film uses it, including the somnambulant Edite (Edith Scob), a middle-aged Frenchwoman who, twenty years earlier, followed her husband-activist when he was sentenced by the dictatorship to the "campo da morte lenta" (camp of slow death), the Tarrafal concentration camp in Cape Verde, with other African dissidents. Now, long after his death in the prison, she spends her days chatting in Creole with local women as they wash clothes and drinking and dancing with Amália, a friend and former Tarrafal cook who had helped her and her husband.[25] Edite also spends a lot of time drinking alone and falling into stupors in a house she shares with her mostly silent yet vigilant adult son.

Costa has frequently talked about his admiration for the Hollywood director Jacques Tourneur, a poetic realist who worked on B horror films and westerns. There are obvious connections between Tourneur's now cult classic *I Walked with a Zombie* (1943) and *Casa de lava*. Both are about young white nurses who leave a modern world to take care of comatose patients in distant island communities marked by colonialism. The difference between Cape Verde and Haiti, the setting of the Tourneur films, is that the former's population, derived from the mixing of Portuguese colonists and African slaves, strongly identifies with the colonizing nation and looks to it as the way to a better life.[26] Black slaves in Haiti did not experience racial mixing as practiced in Cape Verde, and they had nowhere to go under colonial rule. They often sought solace in religious practices, including the trancelike states associated with voodoo, the "zombie curse" in Tourneur's film. In *Casa de lava*, Cape Verde suffers from the gross injustices and neglect caused by centuries of colonial rule plus the recent economic incentives from Portugal that draw husbands to leave wives and children behind. An icon of life there is the island of São Vicente's statue of a mother and child waving goodbye. The pervasive sense of separation is also conveyed in the film by songs of the elderly violinist Bassoé (Raul Andrade); these are *mornas*, a music indigenous to Cape Verde with lyrics that speak of island departures and *saudades* for loved ones and homeland.

After a few days, a semiconscious Leão staggers to his feet and falls onto the ground outside the small, modest island hospital where he is a patient. The incident harks back to his fall in Lisbon where, in an apparent reverie possibly linked to thoughts of his homeland, he tumbles headlong to the ground. But this time is different. With his head pressed to the volcanic terrain, he utters, "My land," as if in relief. Later, on regaining full consciousness, he sits unhappily in his hospital bed and angrily asks Mariana why she brought him back, to which she replies, "You were alone

6.6. *Leão and Mariana*, Casa de lava

there." This is also true of her own situation in Lisbon. In Fogo, she finds
a temporary home and haven of sorts in treating, and being recognized as
part of, the island community. Almost everyone has a shifting, uncertain
home. At a neighborhood party to celebrate Leão's dual return—from Lisbon and from the dead—Leão reveals his kinship with Bassoé, who now
plans to leave Fogo with his other sons, who are played in the film by the
actor's real-life sons. Leão tries to play Bassoé's violin, but the only sounds
he manages to produce are out of tune and wildly off the beat. Later that
night, to his chagrin, he collapses while performing a fast-beat local dance
with Mariana.

The film has a telluric quality that conveys the magnetic and erotic nature of the island's fundament: Mariana stretches out on the beach at night
in a sensual moment of calm; later, she and Edite's son (Pedro Hestnes)
make love on the shore. Shortly after leaving the neighborhood celebration, Mariana and Leão sit on the volcanic rock, where they talk, embrace,
and slowly roll toward the ground off screen. But that night a young couple
in love, Tina (Sandra do Canto Brandão) and Tano (Cristano Andrade
Alves), are discovered lying outside the local hospital, apparent victims
of a tainted vaccine. Tano's tendency toward violence during the film is
one of the few signs of a rage that most islanders hold in check. Dispens-

ing vaccines along with palliatives, Mariana has become the unsuspecting means for the two troubled lovers and recent parents to stay together even if it means death.

Casa da lava does not disclose what ultimately happens to Leão, but love and tragedy have marked Mariana, who after many days changes her red dress for more subdued attire. Bassoé and his sons are on their way to Lisbon, helped by Edite with funds from her widow's pension. As she walks with the departing men, others cry out, "When will my time come?"—reminding her of her promise to help them also leave. The supposedly fortunate men heading to Lisbon are taking mementos with them. They will send back remittances to support their families, and the families left behind send occasional missives from the archipelago to Portugal. As Costa shows in his later film, *Juventude em marcha* (2006) (Youth on the move, released as *Colossal Youth*), in time the remembered faces of loved ones fade, with only letters as keepsakes of the past.

Prior to returning to Portugal from filming in Cape Verde, island residents asked Costa if he would carry letters back to family members and friends in Lisbon. Their requests brought him into contact with the Cape Verdean community in Lisbon that became the subject of his trilogy about the impoverished neighborhood Fontaínhas, the films *Ossos* (1997) (Bones), *Quarto da Vanda* (2000) (*In Vanda's Room*), and *Juventude em marcha*, in which letters play an important role.

Juventude em marcha dialogues with *Casa de lava* in its treatment of migration and family. The visually beautiful *Juventude em marcha* was shot with no crew and only a portable digital camera; the characters' names are based on those of the actors, just as their stories in the film derive from their personal histories in Fontaínhas. The film shows the long-term effects of diaspora, as represented by Ventura, a retired construction worker who came along with others in the 1960s and 1970s to help build a new Lisbon.[27] Nowadays he roams back and forth between the ruins of the labyrinthine Fontaínhas, the shantytown home for many migrants that is being razed by the government, and Casal da Boba, a newly constructed high-rise community to which he and other Fontaínhas residents are being relocated. His wanderings also involve movements back and forth in time. We see his present-day conversations with Vanda and her construction-worker husband, Xana, who have already been relocated to Casal de Boba, but we also see moments from Ventura's past life in Fontaínhas, where he initially lived with fellow laborers. This ebb and flow, in which past and present seamlessly merge, suggests Ventura's continuing migration within a foreign land and his deepening sense of alienation, displacement, and loss.

Ventura's life resembles in some ways the lives of Leão and Bassoé in *Casa de lava*. Like Leão, he has fallen while on a construction site, but because he was wearing a hard hat, he was less severely injured. Like the elderly Bassoé, he has a roaming lifestyle, a quiet and regal bearing, the role of father to many children (who may or not be his own), and a silent yet commanding presence. In scenes of his past life, we see him and Lento, a fellow worker, living in a Fontaínhas shack; he wears a large bandage around his head, listens to Cape Verdean music on an old record player, and writes poetic letters to his wife in Cape Verde. What these and other flashbacks convey is the looming sense of past and lost Ventura experiences as he confronts the imminent move from Fontaínhas to a place farther removed from the city.

Like the molten lava beneath Fogo's black volcanic rock, reds and bright pink and rose colors appear here and there in *Juventude em marcha* and suggest the warm, vital heart that beats within Fontaínhas. The darkened, aged walls inside houses bear markings that inhabitants read like shapes in the clouds: a hen, a lion, a man with a tail, and a cop with a hat. Sharing a quiet moment with Ventura, his daughter Bete mourns the irreplaceable loss of those marks. Casal de Boba's sanitized environment will not have old walls, she remarks: "When they give us those white rooms, we'll stop seeing these things." Perhaps not surprisingly, Bete is the last to leave Fontaínhas. Outside her home, a once plush chair of rose-colored upholstery and indeterminate vintage greets visitors and passersby. Like the shell that was once Fontaínhas, its demise is signaled in a scene where, now missing its two front legs, it slumps toward the ground. There is something venerable and even majestic about the chair's ruined yet still brightly colorful presence—a vestige that stands as a lame sentinel to the shantytown and a reminder of the place a community built and called home for decades.

The chair has its doppelgänger in the form of a seventeenth-century rose-colored sofa by Goeblin on display in the Calouste Gulbenkian Museum, an institution that Ventura helped build and now visits as part of his journey around the city. Dressed in his black suit and white shirt, he casually leans against a museum wall between Rubens and Van Dyke portraits of men who are also dressed in black and white. Like Gulbenkian, whose life-size statue stands on the grounds outside the museum alongside a falcon (which Ventura humorously calls a "penguin"), the two white men in the paintings are able to strike formal poses for portraits and statues. This is the social class for whom men like Ventura, casually elegant and striking his own disinterested pose, have worked to build monuments to status and wealth. Despite his own investment in the museum's creation, Ventura is now barely tolerated there. A young Cape Verdean guard calls him away from the wall with the portraits and uses his handkerchief to wipe the floor of traces where Ventura stood. Cut to the beautiful deep-pink and tapestry-covered Goeblin sofa displayed on a low platform. Then cut to a shot of Ventura seated in a relaxed pose on the sofa, one arm causally stretched along its back, not unlike his easy stance by the rose-colored chair outside Bete's door (plates 24 and 25). A sofa, like a chair, is made not for display but for sitting. This is especially true of a sofa in a place that, even if wiped clean by others, bears in some deep-rooted, visceral way the mark of Ventura's existence.

Ventura leaves traces behind while other Cape Verdeans are employed to remove those traces—the young museum guard, who leads Ventura quietly out the back door to avoid his being seen; the men who go about razing Fontaínhas; and the civil servant Andrés Semedo (António Semedo), formerly a Tarrafal prisoner and now housing agent, who gives Ventura a tour of what will be his new Casal da Boba home. When Ventura leaves a partial handprint on one of the apartment's pristine white walls, Semedo, like the Gulbenkian guard, uses his handkerchief to rub at the spot. But the new residents continue to reaffirm their existence, as attested by the stairwell in Vanda's building, where fresh marks begin to appear on the wall. On a second tour with Ventura of a larger and equally sterile apartment, Semedo states unequivocally, "This move is important for our future." But the scene is full of ironies: locks fail to work, and doors close on their own as if by a resident ghost. In response to Semedo's briefing about housing rules and regulations and the possibilities of furniture arrangements in the small living room space, Ventura points to the ceiling and states with dignified disdain, "It's full of spiders."

There are also moments in *Juventude em marcha* that show the response of migrants like Ventura to the 1974 revolution. While thousands of Portuguese place red carnations in soldiers' rifle barrels to celebrate their liberation, Ventura and Lento dim the kerosene lamp and barricade themselves in Ventura's shack, fearful they will be mistreated or killed by the revolutionary forces. The film has an equally powerful scene illustrating the meaning of African independence for Ventura and his Cape Verdean comrades. Back in his shack and with a bandaged head, Ventura pulls out his old red-covered phonograph and plays a recording of Cape Verdeans singing the praises of their July 5, 1975, independence and of the revolutionary leader Amílcar Cabral, who was assassinated in 1973. The verses refer to the "road to happiness" and "freedom" for the people. But the solemn scene shows there is nothing happy or liberating about Ventura and Lento's place in the new order of things. As the song continues, Lento uses a pen to gouge deep marks into the small table where the phonograph sits. Unlike Ventura, he appears indifferent to the song's lyrics, and his movements cause the needle to skip. The distorted music suggests the often unharmonious aspects of liberation and portends the struggles that beset Cape Verde in the years following independence, including the 1980 coup in Guinea-Bissau that strained relations between the two countries and ended Amílcar Cabral's long-held dream for their political union.

References to a better life and future happiness are repeatedly challenged by the film's portraits of the different Cape Verdean youth (Ventura's "children") who presumably are on the march. Vanda is a recovering drug addict, now on methadone, who struggles to find work and provide care for her daughter. Paulo has a lame leg from bullet wounds and runs a scam that induces charitable women to give him food, money, and clothing. He himself is scammed when his friend goes to those same women for donations to help bury a supposedly deceased Paulo. Another "son," Nhurro, is at first thought to be dead. In a later scene Ventura encounters him and asks if he is now "clean." Nhurro replies, "But really clean, no one can claim that. Clean means three meals a day, no more stealing or parking cars, having a decent job, knowing all the tricks." Being "clean" may be the most the younger generation from Fontaínhas can hope for.

As *Juventude em marcha* weaves back and forth in time, there are constant reminders of migration's adverse effects on loved ones back home. Absence and loss are most poignantly conveyed by the love letter Ventura recites that becomes a leitmotif. Beginning with the Creole salutation "My love," Ventura repeats the lines of the same love letter (based on a 1944 love letter from French surrealist Robert Desnoes to his wife, Youki) that Mariana finds in Edite's house in *Casa de lava* and that Edite's son translates for her from Creole to Portuguese. It is a sad letter about the migrant's hard workdays and desire to give his love "100,000 cigarettes, a dozen snazzy dresses, a car and the house of lava that [she] so longed for" (in Costa and Chaves, *Fora/Out!*, 126). The letter itself is a precious gift, but it and others go unanswered. Just as the widowed Edite squirreled away her letter, Ventura stuffs his pockets with papers—possibly letters written but never sent or old letters safeguarded over the years. They are the only items he salvages from the bits and pieces left of his thirty years of "pick ax and cement"—a life now rendered nearly invisible, not unlike the people themselves who built Fontaínhas and called it home.

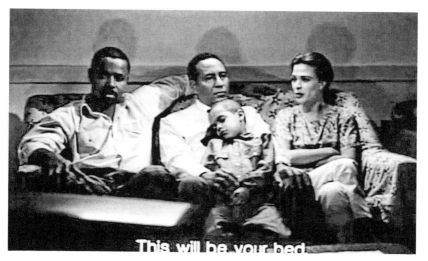

6.7. *Mané in Lisbon*

Portuguese director Fernando Vendrell made *Fintar o destino* (1998) (*Dribbling Fate*). Although the film is largely about Cape Verdeans who stay in the archipelago, one of them, the middle-age protagonist, Mané (Carlos Germano) — a Mindelo barkeep, part-time soccer coach, and star goalie in his youth — continues to dream about Lisbon and what life might have been had he followed his friend Américo (Horácio Santos) to Portugal to play for the Benfica team. His feelings of a chance lost become increasingly painful as the Portuguese Cup approaches. He looks to Kalu (Paulo Miranda), a talented young player whom he trains, to fulfill his dream.

In the social-realist tradition, *Fintar o destino* is a modest film in Creole that begins in the port city of Mindelo on the island of São Vicente. The film gives considerable yet discreet attention to the island topography, with its broad, red-clay terrain and distant mountains. The first shot focuses squarely on the island's rust-red earth onto which a boy painstakingly shovels chalk from a bucket to form court lines for a soccer practice. The town's economic stagnation is succinctly conveyed in a follow-up shot of a rusted freighter stranded in the island's bay and in many references to grog as Cape Verde's chief export. Despite the many years since the revolution, communication with the outside world comes almost entirely from a bar radio tuned to a Lisbon station and from the occasional newspapers that arrive from Portugal. These bits of information are the sources for

Mané's few regular customers, who eagerly await the game coverage on the radio and the league scores printed in the papers. Despite being a home away from home for customers, whose main activities are playing cards and talking about sports, the small bar does little business. As the cup finals near, a raffle for a bicycle is being planned. In the meantime, Mané's dream of traveling to Lisbon for the cup becomes a reality. He uses his and his wife's life savings to buy a plane ticket and makes arrangements to stay with his son, who emigrated to Lisbon, like thousands of young men before him, and now is married and has a child.

In many ways *Fintar o destino* is about an ironic form of *saudade*. Mané experiences a lifetime longing for a place he has never visited but has imagined, a utopia far removed from his disappointing and seemingly loveless relationship with his wife, Lucy (Betina Lopes), whose unexpected pregnancy prevented him from leaving Mindelo. The second part of the film takes place in Lisbon, where Mané steps onto the totally different terrain of the long-awaited utopia. Not just the soil but everything is different from Mindelo: shiny, new, modern structures are everywhere visible—signs of the economic prosperity promised by Portugal's entry into the European Union. Like a stranger in a familiar yet foreign land whose language he speaks, he marvels at the city sights. But in a small, dark apartment, he sits uncomfortably alongside his son, daughter-in-law, and grandchild as they silently watch mind-numbing *telenovelas*. Because of their years of separation and possibly the son's feelings of guilt for his father's life sentence on the island, their verbal exchanges are few.

Just as troubling as the fragile family ties is Mané's growing realization that the Pasárgada-like city of his dreams has a dark side. When he attempts to negotiate a contract for Kalu at the Benfica stadium, he is treated with patience yet condescension by team administrators, who have no memory of his once being invited to play for the team. When he tries to buy a ticket for the cup finals, Mané discovers that the stadium is sold out. Next he encounters a crooked scalper, who takes his money and fails to deliver the ticket. Then he misses the boat back to the city and ends up watching the match on television. Perhaps his greatest surprise is discovering that his childhood friend, Américo, after his short, unsuccessful soccer career, lives in a shantytown and dreams about the faraway home that he lost.

For Mané the sweet moments in Lisbon are few, although he and his son ultimately reconcile over a drop of grog that he brings as a present and reminder of Mindelo. Compared to his voyage out, his return to the island is almost joyous, beginning with a ride home with friends from the airport. Back at the bar, he places the Portuguese Cup ticket alongside the dusty trophies and other honors that he won when he played soccer. His friends congratulate him for getting to see the final match in the stadium; to spare their disappointment and to save face, he keeps his counsel and never disabuses them. His most cantankerous customer, who always supports Benfica's opponent, wins the raffle but in a loving gesture decides to give the bicycle to a young boy. The film ends as a contented Mané borrows the bike for a ride along the bay. The final shot shows him slowly peddling his way toward the distant mountains, like a navigator en route to a newfound land.

~ SEVEN ~

War in Africa and the Global Economy
LEAVING HOME AND RETURNING

While war was raging in different parts of Lusophone Africa, Guadeloupian filmmaker Sarah Maldoror made a film about colonialism and the liberation struggle from the point of view of rural poor and working-class Angolans. The text she chose as the basis for the script, partly written by her husband, the MPLA leader Mário Pinto de Andrade, was Luandino Vieira's *A vida verdadeira de Domingos Xavier* (1971) (*The Real Life of Domingos Xavier* [1974]), a novella about Angola at the cusp of the armed struggle, in 1961. Ironically, war did not stop migration from Portugal in the 1960s and early 1970s, especially to Angola, where government-assisted *colonatos* (migrant settlements) for agricultural production, along with mining in ore (manganese and copper) and the development of an oil industry, were transforming the country's economy.[1]

Maldoror's film, *Sambizanga* (1972), named after a *musseque* (shantytown) outside Luanda's colonial center, was made in the Congolese capital of Brazzaville, an early MPLA base of operations across the border from Angola. Departing from the novella, whose protagonist, Domingos Xavier, is a construction worker and activist, Maldoror shifts the film's principal focus to Domingos's wife, Maria (Elisa Andrade), and her long journey to find Domingos (Domingos Oliveira). He has been taken from their rural village by the secret police and imprisoned in Sambizanga.[2] Her search is a metaphor for the journey of a marginalized population coming to awareness of an organized liberation movement. As Maria travels from one village to another for information on her husband's whereabouts, she employs different strategies suggested by female relatives and friends. At one police station she upbraids a former village acquaintance who now works for the police, charging him with complicity as an *assimilado*. The

7.1. *Maria in* Sambizanga

film moves back and forth between long takes of Maria's anguished search, largely on foot and with her baby son strapped to her back, and Domingos's interrogations and torture by the PIDE. Although there is a significant difference between the vast landscape that Maria crosses and the small, dark cell and prison yard that Domingo paces, perhaps Maria more than Domingos is the one most entrapped by a ubiquitous colonial power that eludes her questions.

Domingos's death in a prison cell becomes a rallying point when, at a community get-together of like-minded activists, the news is announced that he has been beaten and killed. The film ends with a sorrowful celebration and the planning of the February 4, 1961, attack on the Sambizanga prison, one of six targets marked for the official beginning of the colonial wars. As Maldoror makes clear, Maria's search and those of other women

who aid and encourage Maria in her unrelenting defiance of police bureau-
cracy and brutality will ultimately lead to freedom. The film also shows
the commitment of individuals not normally associated with war, especially a young boy named Zito (Dino Albelino) and his elderly, disabled
friend Petelo (Jean M'Vondo), who are the eyes and ears for information
for Maria and others on the whereabouts of political prisoners swept away
by the police.

Maldoror has been recognized over the years as a trailblazer, not only
because of the subject matter of her film but also because at the time of
filming, few African movies were being made and even fewer received
international distribution. Interestingly, while Maldoror was preparing
her award-winning film, three women in Lisbon were working together on
a book that would also defy a government-imposed silence about the dele-
terious effects of the colonial wars. Their critique of the wars was part of a
broader condemnation of patriarchy and authoritarianism, both of which
were fundamental to a decades-old dictatorship.

A considerable amount of material has been written about *Novas cartas portuguesas* (1972) (*The Three Marias* [1975]), which brought international attention to Maria Isabel Barreno, Maria Teresa Horta, and Maria
Velho da Costa. Known as "the three Marias," the authors were arrested
and put on trial by the dictatorship for having written an "obscene" book.[3]
Although it is well known that their work is based on *Lettres portugaises*
(1669) (*The Letters of a Portuguese Nun* [1893]),the published correspondence long attributed to Mariana Alcoforado, a nun abandoned by her
French lover, *Novas cartas portuguesas* harks back even further to a critique of the patriarchal order associated with the *cantigas de amigo*, many
of which, as we have seen, describe the unhappy condition of women who
worry and wait whenever the king commands their men to go to war.

What is especially striking about *Novas cartas portuguesas* is the way
the three writers decided to approach the minefield of a dictatorship that
at the time was sending thousands of young men to Africa to fight a mis-
guided, unpopular, and unwinnable war—often compared with the later
U.S. war in Vietnam. Although their book is largely about the status of
women under patriarchy and about letter writing as a means to give voice
to female oppression and desire, the authors decided to represent the war
in a letter by a bereft soldier in Africa, António Moutinho, to an unknown
woman in Lisbon whom he addresses as "Menina Maria" (Miss Maria).
António does not know her personally. His letter reveals that her name
and address were given to him by Júlio, their mutual friend who is serving
alongside António in Africa. António asks if Maria might consider being

his "madrinha da guerra" (wartime godmother) by entering into a correspondence that would offer him comfort and solace.

The entire tradition of Portuguese literature associated with brave men, noble deeds, and imperial warfare, as exemplified by such works as *A morte do lidador*, *Os lusíadas*, and historiographies by chroniclers, is challenged in this single two-page missive about a man's fear, loneliness, and alienation. Portugal's last-ditch effort to retain the African territories by means of a modern-day *fossado* becomes an enormous failure.[4] As we learn in the very first paragraph of António's letter, he is not the only soldier in despair. Even more desperate is Júlio, who has lost a leg and is recovering in a hospital. António confides to Maria that Júlio worries about returning home. A peasant farmer with no other talents, Júlio knows that he will no longer be able to push a plow. He cries day and night. António also describes the trauma of soldiers who vomit uncontrollably from the strains of war and who must be carried off the field of battle.

What the three Marias were describing challenged not only the literary canon but also the secrecy campaign mounted by the dictatorship to keep the public at home from knowing about the fears of troops and the number of bodily injuries and deaths. The continuing need for more troop buildup and the raging financial costs of the war were less easily disguised. Public opposition to the war gained ground, especially when General António Spínola, vice chief of staff of the armed forces, proclaimed in February 1974 that the war, now in its thirteenth year, was unwinnable.[5] With the April 25 revolution that same year, the troops gradually returned home.

The official proclamation of independence for the former African colonies resulted in another mass movement to Portugal by white settlers, many of whom were born in Africa, as well as black Africans who had fought on the side of Portugal or worked on behalf of the colonial government. As with most wars, a shroud of silence fell over what hundreds of thousands of soldiers had experienced in battle. Portugal celebrated a long-awaited democracy, but the arrival of the large civilian population from Africa known as *retornados* was regarded by many as an unwanted added burden to a nation struggling to recover from more than four decades of dictatorship and the protracted war. Not surprisingly, literature about these subjects was not immediately forthcoming; and it took several more years before the war and its effects appeared on screen. More than forty years after the revolution, these topics continue to preoccupy artists and intellectuals in Portugal and are repeatedly brought to the fore as a way of thinking about the nation's future and its relations with the former colonies.

7.2. *Maria Velho da Costa, Maria Isabel Barreno, and Maria Teresa Horta*

A FAREWELL TO ARMS × 3

Although a few films addressed the subject of the war during the dictatorship, Portuguese director João Botelho was the first filmmaker after the revolution to lay bare the war's tragic consequences in *Um adeus português* (1985) (*A Portuguese Farewell*), which was released ten years after the colonies became independent nations.[6] There are certain similarities between Botelho's film and Miguel Gomes's more recent feature *Tabu* (2012) (*Taboo*), which received considerable international attention. In different ways and degrees, both treat the subject of the Portuguese presence in Africa and its aftermath, and both use black-and-white footage to represent the colonial past. (Botelho shifts to color whenever his film moves forward in time to present-day Portugal.) Both films are beautifully photographed, and each has its experimental touches. Both also focus on the loss of a loved one in Africa and the impact of that loss, especially in women's lives, despite the passage of many years and even decades.

Um adeus português is an eerily quiet film that juxtaposes a couple of days in the lives of a small patrol of Portuguese soldiers in Africa in 1973 with a few days in the lives of an elderly couple, Piedade (Isabel de Castro) and Raul (Ruy Furtado), from the northern Minho region, in 1985. The couple travels to Lisbon to visit their youngest son, Alexandre (Fernando Heitor), and their widowed daughter-in-law, Laura (Maria Cabral), who was married to their eldest son and whom they have not seen for several years. Botelho uses rich black-and-white footage and dramatic close-ups to depict the African scenes that show the young armed soldiers, both black and white, slowly and cautiously searching jungle and plains for an enemy that never appears on screen. With very little dialogue and long tracking shots, the film captures the monotony and futility of their minuscule patrol's mission in the vast wilderness and their fear of attack, which is somewhat relieved during breaks with occasional small talk and cigarettes.

One night a sleep-deprived sergeant walks into a clearing, strikes a match to light a cigarette, and is immediately shot in the head. In the 1985 section of the film we learn that the soldier is Fernando (João Perry), Piedade and Raul's eldest son and the husband of Laura. When her in-laws come to stay with her, Laura chooses to hide the possibly painful news that she has found someone else to love. Alexandre, who left his newspaper job to write fiction for a soft-porn publisher, also spares his parents knowledge of his new job and girlfriend, Rosa (Cristina Hauer). It has been several years since he has visited his parents, whose comfortable farmhouse is a

7.3. *The long goodbye*

7.4. *A fatal shot in the dark in* Um adeus português

somber place filled with memories and photographs of the son who died in the war.

The older couple's visit to Lisbon rekindles the memory of the suffering they all experienced more than a decade earlier. Throughout, Botelho frames interior scenes to draw attention to windows that show a world alive outside, contrasting with the mournful stasis of the family members indoors. At one point the mother despairs openly that their son died in Africa for nothing. Her generally silent husband replies that it was far better for him to die a solider than in bed, although his looks betray an unspoken grief. The visit with Laura and Alexandre is tense but also has a cathartic effect. Ailing for some time, Piedade encourages Laura to marry again, thus providing both women with a measure of solace. Alexandre takes his father to a nightclub, where the father dances for the first time in years. His partner in the dance is a woman whom his son has invited to join them. Seeing his father happy and knowing that his mother is ill, Alexandre promises to visit them soon, as if the specter of Fernando's death has somehow lifted. He also confides to Rosa that his brother was killed in the war and not in an accident, as reported by the dictatorship.

Once back at the couple's farmhouse, the father visits his son's grave for the first time, as if finally able to face the source of his deep-seated grief. There, on Fernando's tombstone and engraved in stone, is the truth, rarely spoken, that he died in combat in Africa. The African war and its consequences have been an uncomfortable subject for the nation as a whole. In its quiet, gentle way, Botelho's groundbreaking film, suggesting that the time has come for Portugal to face the truth, urged frank discussion to help a society heal.

As I have indicated, the colonial war also meant the displacement of Africans who fought for and against the Portuguese, as well as civilians who were forced to flee their homes. Over a decade after the country's independence, the filmmaker Flora Gomes of Guinea-Bissau made *Mortu nega* (1988) (*Death Denied*), which, like Maldoror's *Sambizanga*, is a testimony and tribute to women who left home and took risks to find loved ones. In *Mortu nega*, which was filmed in Creole, Diminga (Bia Gomes) is back in Guinea after a stay in Guinea Conakry (former French Guinea), across the border, where she was treated for injuries when her village was attacked by Portuguese troops. We learn later in the film that her children were killed in that raid.

Instead of returning home, Diminga travels alongside liberation troops searching for a patrol that includes her husband, Sako (Tunu Eugénio Almada), whom she has not seen for some time. Their march through fields and along dirt paths is a treacherous one involving fatal encounters with landmines and enemy war planes. Undaunted, Diminga, with an older woman named Lebeth (M'Make Nhasse) and a few youths who are bearers of supplies, finally meets up with Sako's group. The couple's tender rendezvous is cut short by a helicopter attack that kills the leader of Diminga's patrol. The combined patrols then launch a rocket attack against enemy troops who, left to guard a nearby town, quickly surrender. Ironically, the captured troops left behind by the Portuguese are black soldiers who fought against their own compatriots. The year is 1973, we learn from a troop radio announcing the assassination of revolutionary leader Amílcar Cabral. One of the film's most moving scenes takes place not long afterward, when dozens of youngsters shout and laugh as they play war in the ruins of an old Portuguese fort. Having parted from Sako, who remains with his company while nursing an old foot wound, Diminga approaches the fort and shouts that the war is over. Amazed, the boys and girls drop to the ground in unison and cry out, "Viva!" This part of the film ends as Diminga returns to her village, where surprised friends and new residents greet her warmly after her long absence.

The second and shorter part of the film focuses on the villagers' lives once independence is declared. Diminga sets out with the help of others to clear and plant her patch of land. Exhausted from a decade of fighting, Sako returns home, but his wounded foot is worse. Government trucks bring supplies to the village. Some of the women demand more than their share and then sell the surplus locally at black-market prices in a scene that contrasts sharply with the neighborly goodwill of women who bonded with the returning Diminga. A drought makes planting difficult, and wells run dry. Sako becomes dangerously ill and only wants to be treated in Bissau by a doctor and former comrade-in-arms who is currently away. Sako is marked by the ravages of war that go beyond his wound, and he now trusts only in those whose friendships date back to the struggle. He begs Diminga to track down two former army buddies to help him find lodging in the city and wait for the doctor's return. To Diminga's disgust, one former comrade now denies knowing any Sako, as if the war had never happened, but the other helps the couple with a place where they await the doctor's return.

Three scenes that appear at different moments in the film have particular resonance. As Diminga readies to leave Sako and his patrol prior to the war's end, she passes a makeshift outdoor classroom, where young adults are being instructed in Portuguese about the evils of colonialism. In her village at war's end, we see a second outdoor classroom, where vil-

7.5. *Diminga in wartime Guinea-Bissau*

lagers are being taught Portuguese. The teacher asks what the word *luta* (struggle) means. The word has long referred to the colonial war, but a woman's reply to the question shows the degree to which things have changed. She talks not about the war but about the daily fight to keep her family fed. The scene is immediately followed by a shot of a group of youngsters who, in the African tradition, listen to one of their number tell a parable about two animals. One of the children gently interrupts the tale to correct the storyteller's errors. What the film seems to suggest with these scenes is that while change is inevitable, and literacy and the Portuguese language are important parts of that change, there is also a need to reaffirm the African identity, preserving the spirit of comradeship and community as well the instructive oral cultural tradition. The significance of tradition is made especially clear in the film's extended final sequence of a ritual with music and dance. Shortly after this ceremony, a long-awaited rainstorm breaks over the village. Hope is communicated not only by the rain but also by the children, who excitedly race into the downpour to celebrate its arrival.

More than twenty years after Botelho's *Um adeus português* and over a decade following Flora Gomes's *Mortu nega*, Miguel Gomes's *Tabu* returns to the colonial past in the form of a love story recounted by an elderly Gian Luca (Henrique Espírito Santo) about his long-ago African love affair with Aurora (Laura Soveral), whom he never saw again. Two other important characters in the film are Pilar (Teresa Madruga), a lonely, middle-aged, pious woman who is a social activist and Good Samaritan neighbor of the elderly Aurora, and Santa (Isabel Muñoz Cardoso), Aurora's strong-willed Cape Verdean maid. Santa and Pilar occasionally confer over Aurora's in-

7.6. *The intrepid explorer in* Tabu

creasingly troubling and erratic behavior, which includes heavy drinking, gambling at the nearby Estoril casino, and accusing Santa of putting
a curse on her. Finally, Aurora's condition becomes so extreme that Pilar
and Santa rush her to the hospital. There, a dying Aurora asks Pilar to track
down Gian Luca, whom Pilar ultimately finds in a retirement home. But
Aurora dies before he can reach the hospital.

Unlike *Um adeus português*'s explicit critique of the colonial presence
in Africa, *Tabu* adopts a more indirect, ironic attitude, revealing a certain
postcolonial nostalgia and romanticism on the part of whites who settled
colonial Africa. In the film's oblique prologue, a brief, grainy-textured
black-and-white sequence centering on an "intrepid Portuguese explorer"
in Africa, we see a white man in a pith helmet, accompanied by native
bearers, wandering the wilderness as he suffers from the loss of his beloved
wife. He finally decides to end his misery and, after waving to his bearers,
jumps into a river, where a submerged crocodile awaits him. His suicide
elicits a celebration by the Africans, who dance and sing. Later, the explorer's tragic love becomes a legend and produces tales of repeated sight-
ings of a woman with a crocodile. The prologue ends as the camera suddenly shifts to the present day. A captivated Pilar, alone in a movie theater,
raptly watches the black-and-white melodrama.

Exoticism, melodrama, and crocodiles are also central ingredients in
Gian Luca's love story, which is told on-screen with black-and-white footage not unlike the film that Pilar watches in the theater. This flashback

to the early 1960s in Africa, titled "Paradise," is centered on Italian adventurer Gian Lucas's offscreen recounting of his affair as a young man
(Carloto Cotta) in Africa with the beautiful Aurora (Ana Moreira). The
daughter of Portuguese settlers who grew up comfortably near a fictional
Mount Taboo, Aurora is a capable outdoorswoman and keen shot. Her
first meeting with Gian Luca takes place at the plantation home of her new
husband (Ivo Müller), who is often away on business and has just given her
a baby crocodile as a present. Shortly after their initial meeting, Gian Luca
and Aurora begin a torrid romance, and the ensuing scenes of wild passion and betrayal seem to parody classic Hollywood romantic melodramas
about *amour fou* in the tropics. All this may simply be how Pilar imagines
the story that Gian Luca tells her. As suggested by the prologue, the lonely
Pilar is a devotee of women's melodramas, which provide her with the excitement and passion she lacks. For this reason, she rejects the advances
of a kindly but portly suitor (Cândido Ferreira), a mediocre painter who
unromantically snoozes by her side at the movies.

Miguel Gomes's portrait of the Portuguese plantation class in Africa is
both humorous and unsettling. In one scene, Aurora and her friends dance
the twist as a vulgar paterfamilias sits toying with a loaded pistol and sip-
ping a poolside whiskey served by a formally attired black manservant.
A nearby musical group led by Gian Luca's close friend Mário (Manuel
Mesquita) covers 1960s pop hits, including the Ronettes' "Be My Baby."

7.7. Gian Luca and Aurora

At one point the band members strike a silly pose in a large African tree for a photograph to promote their music. These and other white, leisure-class activities, such as Aurora and Gian Luca's romantic romp, take place within the larger context of a country whose impoverished black majority rarely appears except as domestic servants or field hands.

Despite Mário's advice to the contrary, the young and handsome Gian Luca continues to see Aurora even after he returns from a tour with the band and finds her pregnant. Their later, desperate attempt to run away together is foiled by Mário, who tracks them down and fights with Gian Luca. The heavily pregnant Aurora witnesses the struggle and shoots Mário dead; the trauma induces her labor, and she gives birth to a daughter with the help of native midwives in a nearby village. A bereaved Gian Luca sends word to the husband, who arrives and takes Aurora and the child home. Although Gian Luca is prepared to take the blame for Mário's death, radio propaganda attributes the killing to the increasing political tensions and espionage that eventually lead to the outbreak of war.

Perhaps the most compelling shot in the movie takes place as Aurora's husband drives from the village with her and their child, carrying Mário's corpse in the rear of their truck. From the back of the vehicle, the camera focuses on the smiling, laughing faces of a large group of village children who race after the truck as the radio announcement of the death and a lively African music are heard offscreen. The children's gaiety harks back to the movie prologue, in which blacks celebrate the white explorer's sacrificial demise. The children's swelling numbers as they run after the truck also anticipate the growing popular liberation movement and its drive to chase the Portuguese out of Africa. Shortly thereafter, Gian Luca leaves the country, never to return, while Aurora remains until independence, when, like thousands of Portuguese settlers, she relocates to Portugal. A couple of letters are exchanged between the former lovers and are read offscreen, but the two never meet again.

Tabu is less playful in the postcolonial sequences, titled "Paradise Lost."[7] Despite her reduced lifestyle after she leaves Africa, Aurora still maintains a black domestic servant. But unlike the silent and subservient African workers in "Paradise," Santa is pursuing an education that includes writing classes; in a highly ironic scene, we see her leisurely reading about the colonial encounter in *Robinson Crusoe* as she relaxes on a sofa smoking a cigarette. Pilar's life, on the other hand, has little gratification; her attempts to fill in for Aurora's absent daughter, who lives in Canada, are sometimes welcomed and other times rebuffed. Although she is an ardent social activist, she seems sadly alone at a candlelight peace demonstration. Her repeated attempt to host a young Polish woman on an ecumenical visit to Lisbon also comes to naught. Despite Pilar's efforts, Aurora dies in the hospital without seeing Gian Luca by her side one last time. This conclusion reflects the opening prologue, in which an intrepid explorer's death is turned into a myth of the African colonial past and a source of nostalgia or *saudade* for a supposed paradise that has no more to do with the African reality than the romantic pastiche we have seen on a movie screen.

BACK TO THE HOMELAND

Agora somos retornados.

(Now we are returnees.)

RUI IN *O RETORNO*, DULCE MARIA CARDOSO, 2011

Shortly after the revolution, nearly a half-million people left Africa and settled in Portugal, constituting close to 5 percent of the country's population at the time. Sixty percent of the *retornados* arrived from Angola and more than 30 percent from Mozambique (R. Pires, *Portugal*, 50).[8] The returnees included plantation and small-farm owners born in Africa as well as more recent émigrés who went there in the 1960s. Many of them were well educated and led comfortable, successful lives, especially in Angola, where a fast-expanding economy translated into well-paying jobs for professionals. Although not every white Portuguese citizen who left Africa did so after independence, the great majority did, and with some haste, leaving much of what they owned behind. A few managed to ship crates of belongings to Portugal, but most left with nothing but an airplane ticket and a suitcase.

The fortunate returnees had family in Portugal to help with housing and the transition to a new environment. Others had no one and relied upon the IARN (Instituto de Apoio ao Retorno dos Nacionais [Institute for the Repatriation of Nationals]) for food and rooms set apart for them in hotels while they searched for work to begin life anew. The angst of leaving home for the far-off homeland was accompanied by feelings of resentment toward a government that had betrayed them by granting independence to the colonies. The returnees' reception in Portugal was also a complicated matter since many locals felt that those who went to Africa

7.8. Decolonization *(1975), by Alfredo Cunha. Returnee possessions dockside in Lisbon with Monument to the Discoveries in the background. Courtesy of Alfredo Cunha.*

had benefited greatly from colonial rule and had led far better lives than those who stayed in Portugal. There was also resentment because the country now had to support thousands who were associated with the former dictatorship and the war that had drained the nation's coffers and sent young men to their deaths.

Partly because of these tensions, the late 1970s and early 1980s witnessed the emergence of a new postrevolutionary literary generation who wrote engagingly about the once taboo subject of the war. Two of the most important early works to appear were António Lobo Antunes's *Os cus de Judas* (1979) (*South of Nowhere* [1983]; *The Land at the End of the World* [2011]), about a former soldier who is irrevocably damaged by his two-year tour as an army doctor in Angola, and Lídia Jorge's *A costa dos murmúrios* (1988) (*The Murmuring Coast* [1995]), which likewise looks back to the war for its colonial critique. Jorge's novel is narrated from the point of view of a woman who traveled to Mozambique to wed her soldier-fiancé. The novel describes the futility and violence of the war, including atrocities committed by Portuguese troops that are covered up by the dictatorship. Jorge's narrator deconstructs the official (male) version of the war, which appears in the prologue of the novel, replacing it with a personal account of the war's devastation and effects on the private lives of soldiers and their wives.[9]

While the dictatorship and war were unpopular prior to 1974 and ripe for examination after the revolution, the subject of the *retornados* remained an uneasy one, especially given the history of resentments on both sides. Lobo Antunes was again in the forefront with his 1988 novel *As naus* (*The Return of the Caravels* [2003]), a complex, satirical work that conflates the heyday of empire with its ignominious end. The story focuses on the return of the earliest Portuguese colonists, among them Vasco da Gama, Diogo Cão, and Camões, along with women and children who arrive in caravels from the provinces and enter a modern-day Portugal that has no memory of or use for them. Settling into the backstreets of Lisbon, they live disillusioned and marginalized lives as gamblers, pimps, beggars, prostitutes, and wastrels. Lobo Antunes's indictment of the vicissitudes of colonialism ends ironically as a small group of tubercular patients looks for signs of Dom Sebastião, who was long prophesied to return from defeat in Africa and save the nation. But just as there is no going back to Africa, there is no looking forward to a hero who can save the nation.

As naus's disquieting portrait of an inglorious return is a subtle homage to Camões's Old Man of Restelo in *Os lusíadas*, who predicted the folly to be visited on a nation driven by conquest and greed. But despite Lobo Antunes's considerable knowledge, skill, and boldness in tackling a delicate topic in *As naus*, a more realistic treatment of the *retornados* had to wait nearly a decade before he published *O esplendor de Portugal* (1997) (*The Splendor of Portugal* [2011]), a novel about a mother who remains in Angola after independence and her three adult children, who were sent to Lisbon once civil war broke out. Their relationships are irremediably torn apart by the effects of the colonial past.

An even more straightforward narrative and possibly the most compelling treatment of the subject to date took more than another ten years to appear. Dulce Maria Cardoso's *O retorno* (2011) (*The Return*) is narrated in first person by a fifteen-year-old named Rui, who arrives in Portugal along with Dona Glória, his psychologically troubled mother; his slightly older sister, Milucha; and the few belongings they brought from Angola. Without family or friends to support them, they are temporarily housed by the IARN in a five-star hotel in Estoril, a lush seaside resort outside Lisbon. Rui's father, a business owner and racist who threatens to burn down his house in retaliation for their forced, empty-handed exit, is not with them. A case of mistaken identity has resulted in his arrest outside their house just as the family is about to depart for the airport. A guilt-ridden Rui watches as his father is taken away with his hands tied behind his back, but he never tells his mother or sister about that unsettling detail. The family writes desperate letters to Rui's Uncle Zé, a former soldier who supports independence and remains in Angola, to ask him to inquire about the father's whereabouts and welfare. Their letters go unanswered.

Rui's narrative captures the estrangement of arriving in a country that was long the focus of school lessons, classroom maps, and songfests. His imagination of a distant, bucolic homeland collides with the reality of a somewhat dingy, chaotic postcolonial Portugal that embraces him as its own yet deposits him like an inconvenient guest in a remote hotel, where he and others, suspended in time, anguish about what to do and what their future holds:

> Foi esquisito pisar na metrópole, era como se estivéssemos a entrar no mapa que estava pendurado na sala de aula. Havia sítios onde o mapa estava rasgado e via-se um tecido escuro ou sujo por trás, um tecido rijo que mantinha o mapa inteiro e teso. Não sabíamos o que havíamos de fazer e era como se estivéssemos a entrar no mapa rasgado, ou então nas fotografias das revistas, nas histórias que a mãe estava sempre a contar, nos hinos que cantávamos aos sábados de manhã no pátio do colégio. (76–77)

> (It was strange to step into the metropole, as if we were entering the map that was hanging on the classroom wall. There were places where the map was torn and you could see the dark or dirty cloth underside, a stiff cloth that kept the map together and taut. We didn't know what we were supposed to do, and it was as if we were entering the torn map, or the magazine photographs, or stories Mother was always telling us [about Portugal], or the hymns that we sang on Saturday mornings on the school's patio.)

Cardoso briefly shifts from Rui's point of view to a short speech by the hotel manager speaking privately with his family. She praises the facility, informs the family that she is responsible for their housing, and tells them that they are fortunate not to have been placed in a campsite or miserable boardinghouse like so many who have returned from the former colonies. She also sets forth a series of house rules and assumes they will be followed because, as she declares at one point, surely in Angola "não viviam numa selva" (69) (they didn't live in a jungle). Dona Glória's anxious questions that occasionally interrupt this speech are never directly quoted—a stylistic decision that shows the returnee has no real voice—and are merely implied by the manager's impatient, dismissive responses.

The strangeness of the situation is intensified in almost Kafkaesque fashion by the unfamiliar acronym IARN that the hotel management repeatedly uses in responses to questions by the newly arrived. The mystery surrounding this omnipresent agency is somehow linked to the fact that they are now all *retornados*, a puzzling term that has no meaning for them:

> Em quase todas as respostas, uma palavra que nunca tínhamos ouvido, o **IARN**, o **IARN**, o **IARN**. O **IARN** paga as viagens para a terra, o **IARN** põe-nos em hotéis, o **IARN** paga os transporte para os hotéis, o **IARN** dá-nos comida, o **IARN** dá-nos dinheiro, o **IARN** ajuda-nos, o **IARN** aconselha-nos, o **IARN** pode informar-nos. Nunca tínhamos ouvido tantas vezes uma palavra, o **IARN** parecia mais importante e mais generoso do que deus. Explicaram-nos, **IARN** quer dizer Instituto de Apoio ao Retorno dos Nacionais. Agora somos retornados. Não sabemos bem o que é ser retornado mas nós somos isso. Nós e todos os que estão a chegar de lá. (77)

> (In almost all their responses was a word we had never heard before, the **IARN**, the **IARN**, the **IARN**. The **IARN** pays for the trips here, the **IARN** places us in hotels, the **IARN** pays for transportation to the hotels, the **IARN** provides us with food, the **IARN** gives us money, the **IARN** helps us, the **IARN** advises us, the **IARN** can inform us. We had never heard a word so many times; the **IARN** seemed more important and more generous than God. They explained to us, **IARN** means Institute to Assist the Return of Nationals. Now we are returnees. We don't know for sure what a returnee is, but that's what we are, we and everyone else who comes from back there.)

Unlike older returnees, who argue about political events, Rui has little understanding of what has happened to him. An innocent who feels neither shame for having been part of the colonial enterprise nor resentment about being forced to leave, he believes the recent official announcement of Angolan independence means that his father, like the empire itself, is dead; although he wishes his father were with them, there is no more reason to hope for his return. His words "Não consigo viver à espera que o pai chegue. Ninguém consegue viver sempre à espera de uma coisa assim" (154) (I can't go on waiting for father to come. No one can live always waiting for something like that) are wise beyond their years and contrast sharply with Lobo Antunes's description in *As naus* of an ailing and expectant community that awaits Sebastião's return. At the same time, Rui suffers the stigma of being a returnee. Angered by his teacher's condescension and feeling that he lags behind peers in class, he drops out of school. His sister Milucha continues to study and avoids using words and expressions associated with Angola. She is deeply ashamed of her status and prefers to go hungry rather than show the IARN card that guarantees her a free lunch at the school canteen.

Rui spends his free time daydreaming in a hideaway in the hotel and talking to the kindly doorman, who gives him a secondhand bicycle, comic books, and cigarettes. After meeting the doorman's young, attractive wife, he begins an affair at her instigation that lasts for months, well into her pregnancy. In the meantime, his nervous and forgetful mother suffers a breakdown, while his sister continues her efforts to adapt, which now include dating a local. Rui's world seems on a crash course of constant truancy, smoking, and sex when, after a year in the hotel, his father, thought to be long dead in Africa, unexpectedly appears.

Like the long-awaited arrival of Sebastião from the Africa crusade, the father's return, to which the novel's title also refers, saves his family—in particular Rui, who is relieved of his sense of guilt over his father's arrest as well as his duty to be the man of the family. Slowly the family's life begins to change for the better as they plan for their departure from the hotel and their resettlement in a small, one-bedroom house. The father succeeds in getting an IARN loan for a cement factory that he proposes as a cooperative with a few other returnees. His earlier deep-seated resentments have given way to a firm conviction that his family can rebuild their lives in Portugal. At no time does the family talk about what happened to him in Angola, although scars on his body speak for what is not said. They learn from Zé, who has returned because of civil war, that the father was released once the case of mistaken identity was resolved.

We might read the family's uneasy silence about the father's imprisonment as Cardoso's way of representing the reluctance of a nation on the mend to address the conflicting feelings of former colonists and newly liberated Portuguese citizens during the period of decolonization. Although autobiographical accounts of African life by former colonists occasionally appeared, *As naus* defined the return as emblematic of the *non* that inspired Manoel de Oliveira's 1990 film *Non, ou a vã glória de mandar*, about defeats caused by the "vainglory of a nation to command" and their consequences.[10] In *O retorno*, Cardoso elides both sentimentality and moral judgment, offering a more nuanced view of loss from the perspective of a teenager who has little understanding of the history that led to his family's repatriation. His story is as much or more about loss of innocence in a strange new world where nothing is certain and everything is in flux.

LEAVING HOME: DIASPORIC ADVENTURES
IN A GLOBALIZED WORLD

Quatrocentos anos de presença portuguesa em Macao e ninguém fala português.

(Four hundred years of Portuguese presence in Macau and no one speaks Portuguese.)

JOÃO PEDRO RODRIGUES AND JOÃO RUI GUERRA DA MATA,
A ÚLTIMA VEZ QUE VI MACAU, 2012

We normally think of the diaspora in terms of mass movements of people who, for various reasons, leave one part of the world for another. In 1986, José Saramago published *Jangada de pedra* (*The Stone Raft* [1994]), a fantasy novel about an enigmatic cataclysm that severs the entire Iberian Peninsula from its European anchorage and launches the landmass into the open seas in search of a new harbor. Also set in motion by the seismic split are the novel's characters, who come from different parts of the peninsula and encounter one another as they travel like passengers on a sailing ship. Written on the eve of Portugal's entry into the European Union, the novel served as Saramago's warning shot over the nation's bow about the problems of forging an economic alliance with powerful countries to the north that could easily compromise Portugal's political and cultural identity. Like the Old Man from Restelo, Saramago worried about what might befall Portugal and Spain when yielding to the dubious promise of riches, if not glory.

Lídia Jorge had already painted a less-than-attractive picture of globalization's impact on Portuguese cultural identity in her second novel, *O cais das merendas* (1984) (*Picnic Quay*), about rural villagers in the southern Algarve whose language and customs are transformed by proximity to British tourists and owners of luxury hotels. The novel shows that as time passes, locals employed in the coastal resorts as hotel staff have increasingly less in common with their families back home in the rural areas than with the foreigners whose language they now speak. Saramago's novel is about the possibility of the European Union's far greater power to transform the locals; although the peninsula is still on the move at the end of his book, it shifts to a southerly course, toward Latin America (Brazil) and West Africa (Angola), which promised a more suitable and rewarding geopolitical, economic, and cultural alliance.

Not long after joining the European Union in 1986, Portugal experienced a steadily increasing migration from Brazil. What had begun in the 1970s with a small, largely upper-middle-class population seeking political asylum from a military dictatorship (1964–1985) and a haven from soaring inflation continued in the late 1980s with the arrival of professionals drawn by attractive job opportunities created by EU funds to modernize the nation. The Brazilian population more than tripled in Portugal during this time, from an estimated 3,500 in 1980 to around 12,000 in 1990. Under an austerity program launched by Brazilian President Fernando Collor de Mello in 1990, working-class Brazilians also looked to Portugal for jobs and economic security. Political persecution, civil war, and jobs also brought thousands of Africans to Lisbon from the former colonies, the PALOP states (Países Africanos de Língua Oficial Portuguesa), the Portuguese-Speaking African Countries group initiated in 1992. In 1996, Portugal, Brazil, and the PALOP states formed the CPLP (Comunidade dos Países de Língua Portuguesa [Community of Portuguese Language Countries]) to strengthen diplomatic and cultural relations, with special emphasis on language and culture—an alliance suggested in Saramago's novel about a free-floating peninsula. The year 1996 was also when Brazilian directors Walter Salles and Daniela Thomas released *Terra estrangeira* (*Foreign Land*), about the crossings and confluence of different Portuguese-speaking groups in Lisbon.

Perhaps because he lived outside Brazil for much of his early life, Salles seems especially drawn to the theme of *dépaysement*, a term that denotes "leaving home" and connotes cognitive estrangement. As in Cardoso's *O retorno*, estrangement is a central theme in *Terra estrangeira*, in which the two central protagonists leave home in search of something that may or may not exist. Co-produced with Portugal, the film dramatizes the idea of *saudade* and deals with the encounter between Latin America, Europe, and Lusophone Africa. A film noir shot in black and white, it features gangsters, a young man down on his luck and on the lam, a femme fatale, and a hidden cache of diamonds. These familiar ingredients, however, are a pretext for the depiction of a sometimes bewildering space in which Portuguese speakers from different countries are thrown together and old assumptions about the new world and the old world are reversed or revised.

The protagonist of the film is Paco (Fernando Alves Pinto), a lackluster student and aspiring actor who lives with his seamstress mother (Laura Cardoso) in a drab São Paulo apartment facing the dystopian inner-city throughway called the Minhocão (the big earthworm). Paco's mother dreams of returning to her native Basque town of San Sebastián. Paco is insensitive to this lifelong wish for which his mother has scrupulously saved until he discovers her in front of the television set, dead from a heart attack after learning that Collor has frozen all savings accounts. (The reference to Collor's handling of the economy functions at least indirectly as a self-reflexive comment on the circumstances under which Salles's feature-film career began.) Going through her belongings, he comes across cherished picture postcards and photographs of her native land and decides, out of guilt and sorrow, to make the journey she had planned. To pay for the trip he agrees to carry a package containing an old violin to Lisbon for the shady character Igor (Luís Melo), an antiques dealer and diamond smuggler. In a storeroom piled with run-of-the-mill antiques and what he calls "relics of colonization," Igor waxes enthusiastic about Brazil's rich colonial heritage and laments the decline of a national memory. The country has become an "empire of mediocrity" obsessed with Americanized shopping malls and filled with "Sydney Sheldon readers." Turning to Paco, he declares, "It's the end of the world." He nevertheless wants to move illegal goods across borders, in imitation of global trade.

A parallel story line about *dépaysement* involves a young, middle-class Brazilian woman named Alex (Fernanda Torres) who has left Brazil because of its declining economy and the promise of a better life in the European Union. Settling in Lisbon, she shares an apartment with her Brazilian boyfriend, Miguel (Alexandre Borges), and waitresses in a modest restaurant under the watchful eye of a brutish Portuguese boss. Alex feels alienated in Lisbon, declaring at one point, "The more time passes, the more I feel like a foreigner." Her equally alienated boyfriend, a drug addict and frustrated musician, is employed by Igor to pick up packages smuggled from Brazil. He occasionally plays trumpet in a bar, although his improvisations go unappreciated by the young black and white clientele, who become enthusiastic only when he takes his break and piped-in African music begins. Miguel derides the bar, where Brazilians, Angolans, and Guineans congregate, as a "colonial cabaret," and snidely comments on their tastes: "Next time I'll mix bossa nova with rap."

212 ~ *The Portuguese-Speaking Diaspora*

During the opening of the film, Salles cuts back and forth between São Paulo and Lisbon to create parallels between Paco and Alex, who will become a romantic couple. Paco applies for a passport, while on the other side of the Atlantic, Alex sells her passport to raise funds. This part of the film once again serves as a self-reflexive commentary on the economic conditions of Brazilian cinema and the need for foreign exchange. Alex is shocked when her Spanish-speaking buyer remarks that Brazilian passports aren't worth anything and offers three hundred dollars instead of the three thousand she expected. When she argues that the passport has been recently renewed, the Spaniard shrugs and counters, "It's Brazilian."

The film's parallel narratives merge once Paco arrives at the Hotel dos Viajantes (Travelers Hotel) in Lisbon and, after waiting days to hand over the package containing the violin, leaves in search of his contact, Miguel. In the meantime, Miguel boosts a cache of Igor's diamonds and is killed by Igor's henchmen before he can escape. While searching for Miguel, Paco meets Loli (Zeka Laplaine), a black Angolan who lives at the Travelers Hotel with other Angolans, and their awkward encounter on a side street is an ironic reminder that race relations are not easy in the now more racially diverse Lisbon. When Paco nervously steps back from a smiling Loli, he registers surprise: "What, you're afraid of me? Hey, this isn't São Paulo or Rio de Janeiro."

Ultimately Paco finds a grieving and distrusting Alex, who dispatches Miguel's Portuguese friend Pedro (João Largato) to the Travelers Hotel to pick up the smuggled package. In the meantime, she misleads and distracts Paco by offering to take him to a place outside Lisbon where he can meet Miguel's contacts. Their trip to the solitary, windswept Cape Espichel turns into an overnight tryst, with some of the most powerful imagery in the movie. The wide camera angles show the smallness of Paco and Alex against the sprawling coastline, plunging cliffs, and churning sea. Seated near the promontory's edge, Alex echoes a line we have heard the gangster Igor speak earlier: she tells Paco that they are "at the end of the world," as the Portuguese once believed about their own country. She praises the ancient mariners who dreamed of a paradise across the ocean and went in search of it, but she adds with a scoff, "Poor Portuguese . . . they ended up discovering Brazil."

After a night of lovemaking on the cape, Alex is cool to Paco. When he returns to his hotel, he discovers the violin is gone and is disconcerted by a note from Igor telling him to deliver what he no longer has to a Mr. Kraft (Tchéky Karyo). Hearing music from Loli's room above his own, he looks to the Angolan for consolation. He and Loli step out onto a balcony,

7.9. *Loli and Paco's postcolonial encounter in Lisbon*

where Paco complains that Alex "me comeu" (ate me). Unfamiliar with the Brazilian slang for sex, Loli asks, "How did she eat you?" Paco simply replies, "She ate me." Loli laughs: "Oh, I get it. . . . Leave it to you Brazilians. Hah! And yet we're supposed to be the cannibals." When Paco says that the strangest things have happened to him since he arrived in Lisbon, Loli asks, "But what were you expecting in Lisbon, Brazilian?" Paco replies, "I don't know . . . at the very least to discover something. Wasn't it from here that they discovered the whole world?" Laughing and pointing at the bridge that spans the Tagus River, Loli remarks, "Portugal? They take three hours to get across the fucking bridge. You're kidding!"

Much of the Lisbon action takes place in and around the Alfama, the oldest part of the city, along the Tagus. The film takes full advantage of the district's noir atmosphere, showing Paco running through its maze of dark, narrow alleyways pursued by the French-speaking Kraft, his Portuguese henchman Carlos (João Grosso), who earlier murdered Miguel, and Igor, who has suddenly arrived from Brazil to make the final deal for the diamonds that have been hidden in the violin case. When Paco rediscovers Alex, she tells him that she has given the violin away. Pedro, who is in love with Alex, lends the couple his car and advises them to head for the Spanish border; when Alex blurts out that she has sold her passport, Pedro suggests that they go through Boa Vista, where the border is less heavily guarded. On the run and driving back roads at night, Alex and Paco turn to small talk that gradually becomes intimate. When they stop for a rest,

7.10. *Paco and Alex on the beach*

they make love in the car and fall asleep. The next morning, Alex finds Paco standing nearby on a deserted beach where an old freighter rests, stranded on its side like an enormous beached whale. Inspired by her newfound love and the magnificence of the ruined maritime sculpture, Alex turns to Paco and says, "Let's head for San Sebastián."

Somewhat like the Portuguese mariners of old, Alex and Paco envision a paradise beyond the edge of Portugal, but they travel in an easterly direction. Arriving in Boa Vista, they decide to stop at a roadside restaurant until nightfall, when the nearby border is left unguarded. After torturing Pedro for the information, Carlos and Igor catch up to the couple. Alex manages to wound Igor and Paco kills Carlos, but not before Carlos shoots him in the stomach. Dragging Paco's bleeding body into the car, Alex cradles his head in her lap, takes off for the border, and tries to comfort him with the tearful refrain "I'm taking you home, I'm taking you home. . . ." As the car demolishes the flimsy wooden barrier that marks the divide between nations, the film suddenly provides its one and only aerial shot (an echo of Nicholas Ray's Hollywood noir, *They Live by Night* [1949]), revealing the indistinguishable terrain on either side of the border and the car speeding north toward a home somewhere beyond the wilderness.

We never know if Paco survives his wound, and most viewers probably infer that, like the typical couples in love-on-the-run noirs, Paco and Alex are ultimately doomed. The shot of the car crossing the border, however,

has a somewhat liberating effect, as if the film were gesturing toward a utopian freedom that cannot be imagined except in a natural landscape. Salles
then cuts from the car racing beyond the border to a bustling underground
station in Lisbon, where an old blind man plays the smuggled violin and
passing commuters occasionally toss him coins. When the violin case is
accidentally upended, Igor's hidden cache of black-market diamonds
spills onto the ground, an echo of the ironic conclusions of such US films
as John Huston's *Treasure of the Sierra Madre* (1948) and Stanley Kubrick's
The Killing (1956). The valuable and coveted merchandise that crossed an
ocean and precipitated chaos and death goes unnoticed by the passersby,
whose feet scatter the gems. City dwellers in transit, their attention is on
getting back home.

Like Salles and Thomas, Angolan novelist José Eduardo Agualusa en-
visions the possibility of new communities and relationships that break
down conventional boundaries and assumptions—a world in which
humans, and not simply money and commodities, cross borders and
make discoveries. Agualusa is also a migratory sort who makes his home
at different times in Luanda, Rio, and Lisbon. Similar to *Terra estrangeira*
and other Salles road films, Agualusa's works often treat imaginary alli-
ances with neighboring or related cultures and emphasize the need to leave
home to fully understand the places where we usually live. A good example
is his postmodern pastiche *Nação Crioula*. A more recent one is his novella
Um estranho em Goa (2000) (A stranger in Goa), a postcolonial chronicle
about the crossings and moorings of Portuguese-speaking people in Goa,
the cultural capital of the territory once known as Portuguese India.

The history of *Um estranho em Goa* has some bearing on its content.
Agualusa entered a competition for writers sponsored by the Fundação
Oriente (Orient Foundation) in Lisbon for funds to travel to a place in Asia
of their choosing and then write books about their experiences. Agualusa's
proposal to travel to Goa was selected, and the resulting novella, which
appears in the Fundação Oriente's Oriental Series, is a fictional recounting of this sojourn by the narrator, José, who plans to write a book about
his travel experience. The book's plot turns on José's long-standing fascination with an Angolan named Plácido Domingo, a former captain in the
Portuguese army, who switched sides during the colonial war to become
a celebrated MPLA guerrilla. Years after the war, José found Domingo in
the Amazon, where he had been hiding since the revolution. During their
interview, Domingo reveals that he had infiltrated the MPLA as an under-

cover agent for the PIDE. Now years later, José learns that Domingo has settled in Goa and decides to write a book about what has happened to him.

There are interesting plot similarities between Salles and Thomas's film *Terra estrangeira* and Agualusa's novel *Um estranho em Goa*. Like the innocent Paco, José unknowingly becomes involved in a global black-market scheme that, instead of diamonds, involves relics stolen from Saint Francis Xavier's supposedly uncorrupted body, which lies in the Basílica do Bom Jesus in Goa. According to Domingo, the church long ago had certain body parts removed as relics for saintly display in Rome and Macau; later dealings between the church and well-heeled locals have reduced the saint to a few remains. Shady characters whom José meets through a friend, Jimmy Ferreira, offer him the saint's "beating heart" for a bargain three thousand dollars. Meanwhile, a Portuguese femme fatale conducts archival research for the aged Domingo, who is writing a book about the devil. His personal story becomes enigmatic when he informs José that he was betrayed by individuals in the liberation movement who falsified his name on PIDE documents and denounced him as a spy. A murder takes place involving the religious contraband. José flees Goa after learning that Jimmy has been killed. José's future, like that of the wounded, fleeing Paco in the Salles and Thomas film, seems less than bright when a stranger on the plane hands him a mysterious package that he fears is a Pandora's box.

The backdrop for the book's sometimes dark, sometimes comic and ironic twists and turns is a place whose Portuguese heritage, somewhat like Saint Francis Xavier's body, is held sacred by many but is slowly disappearing. This is especially true of the descendants of the old Catholic aristocracy, whose names, according to José, "são tão portugueses que nem em Portugal existem mais" (20) (are so Portuguese than they don't even exist in Portugal any longer). José notes that, like the historic landmark Grande Hotel do Oriente where he stays, once sumptuous colonial buildings are largely in ruins. Among the few exceptions are the many Baroque churches that continue to serve the sizable Catholic population.

Among the fascinating characters whom he meets during his visit is Sal, Salazar Barata de Sousa, a taxi driver who considers his namesake "um grande português" (24) (a great Portuguese). Although his knowledge of Portuguese is limited to "bom dia," he is a fervent Catholic, as suggested by his car's dashboard, featuring a miniature altar replete with a blinking statue of the Virgin Mary, a crucifix, and a replica Saint Francis urn. What surprises José more than the Catholic icons is the tiny flag that hangs from the front mirror bearing the name of an obscure Oporto soccer team.

The taxi also sports a Portuguese flag on the rear window and the name "Princesa de Goa" (Princess of Goa), which Sal has written in gold-painted script on both of the car's doors.

Sal is an admirer of Xanana Gusmão, the East Timor politician who resisted Indonesian occupation following the island's decolonization by the Portuguese. The novella gives considerable attention to Goans like Sal, who believe that they should have fought to remain independent and resisted their so-called 1961 liberation by the Indian Union. José notes signs of still others' resistance in the form of houses whose interiors resemble museums dedicated to preserving the Portuguese past. Even older Hindi residents whom he meets confess to a certain *saudade* for the Portuguese language and a bygone era when streets were quiet and safe. That same *saudade* is felt by Vasco, an Angolan who emigrated twenty years earlier to escape the civil war back home. Despite these various lamentations, José seems bombarded by reminders of what was once Portugal's omnipresence: names of people, churches, streets, and shops such as Vasco's fusion-style restaurant, A Ferradura (The Horseshoe), which serves both traditional Goan and Portuguese cuisine, including *churrasco*, *caldo verde*, and chicken soup. Leaving the restaurant one day, José happens upon a chorus of twenty men in the middle of the street who are singing a hymn in Portuguese. Like an anthropologist who has come across a major find, he races back to the hotel for a tape recorder, only to discover when he returns that the men have vanished.

Um estranho em Goa has a ludic, sometimes rollicking quality typical of Agualusa and nicely captures the slightly chaotic world of chance encounters between different Portuguese speakers in a changing and increasingly globalized Goa. The style also brings to the fore the anachronistic nature of a modern-day chronicler's contact with a local community steeped in the past and still practicing the language and faith of the colonizer, whose retreat from their now tourist-ridden shores they continue to debate and even mourn.

For the young professional class in Portugal forced to leave their Euro-struggling homeland for employment, Macau has become a small twenty-first-century mecca. Ranked in 2014 as the world's leading economic performer out of three hundred major international cities, Macau combines a reputation as a UNESCO World Heritage Site with that of a fast-growing international gambling capital.[11] The city's luxury hotel-casinos, with world-class cuisine, high-end boutiques, spas, and museum-level artwork, attract annually thirty million tourists from nearby mainland China, Hong

Kong, and around the globe.[12] Gambling has created jobs in the service sector as well as higher-level technical and professional openings that appeal to Portuguese speakers in a city where Portuguese is the co-official language with Cantonese. Although signage throughout the city is in both languages, Portuguese is spoken only by the small Macanese community and occasionally by resident Jesuits.

Interestingly, Macau's legal code was, until recently, only in Portuguese, which means that lawyers and civil servants needed to know the language. This is where the Macanese have had a long-standing advantage over Chinese locals. Nowadays, China's economic and diplomatic interests in Lusophone countries, especially oil-rich Angola, are behind the relatively recent rise in Portuguese language training programs, which are attracting greater numbers of students in Macau. As a result, the sharp decline in Portuguese instruction shortly after the 1999 handover has reversed, and a language taught at just six universities in Macau and throughout China in 2005 is now offered in twenty-six institutions, including large programs at the Universidade de Macau and the Centro Pedagógico e Científico de Língua Portuguesa.[13]

For those Portuguese who lived in Macau prior to the handover, returning after many years can be disorienting. This is the crux of João Pedro Rodrigues and João Rui Guerra da Mata's feature film, *A última vez que vi Macau* (2011) (*The Last Time I Saw Macao*), a noirlike adventure whose protagonist, also named Guerra da Mata, gets mixed up with a woman in distress, shady characters, and murder in a city that never seems to sleep. The film pays discreet homage to Josef von Sternberg's noir classic *Macao* (1952), which stars Jane Russell as a sassy nightclub singer and Robert Mitchum as a drifter and war veteran, both of whom are caught up in the mayhem of the city's corrupt gambling world. The Portuguese film of six decades later begins in a Macau nightclub with Candy, a sexy transgender singer in a tight Chinese silk dress, lip-synching Leo Robin's sprightly tune "You Kill Me," which was sung by Russell in *Macao*. Unlike Russell, whose easygoing, playful performance brings out the tune's sly humor, Candy is apprehensive, mouthing lyrics that have a far darker significance for her. Underworld figures have killed a friend; fearing for her safety, she contacts Guerra da Mata, a close friend back in Lisbon, who returns to his childhood home after thirty years to help her.

As in *The Maltese Falcon*, the plot of *A última vez* centers on an object—in this case, a covered birdcage—that passes from one hand to another and provokes subterfuge and murder. The cage is a McGuffin used to forward the plot, and there is no reference to what makes the cage

7.11. *Friendly Chinese tigers in* A última vez que vi Macau

desirable. In one scene, the cage's cover is partially opened, and a bright glow radiates from its interior—no doubt a reference to Robert Aldrich's 1959 noir *Kiss Me Deadly*, which ends with the radioactive brilliance released from a coveted Pandora's box. Like the contents of the cage, the identity of the rival villainous factions is mysterious; the film deftly elides most faces, including the protagonist's, and advances the action by focusing on the movements of arms and legs. Ultimately, Guerra da Mata's quest to save Candy fails, and she is murdered. He gets a gun, seeks out her killers, and ends up with the cage, the contents of which are never divulged.

The film's murky approach to characters and plot is in keeping with the otherworldliness that Guerra da Mata experiences as he winds his way through a Macau barely recognizable from his childhood, a place where he constantly gets lost and no one understands Portuguese. His frustration is palpable: "Quartocentos anos de Portugal em Macau e ninguém fala portugues." (Four hundred years in Macau and no one speaks Portuguese.) At the same time, China is everywhere present and overwhelms the city's celebration of Christmas, a remnant of the Portuguese presence that is still a public holiday. The film focuses briefly on a little Chinese girl dressed in a red Santa Claus costume while all around the city are gigantic balloon displays of tigers, a major cultural symbol in China. Two real tigers appear in a cage behind Candy and heighten the sense of lurking danger as she sings, but the balloon tigers are cuddly cartoon figures and convey the friendliness being extended by China to its neighbor and recent territorial acquisition.[14]

A *última vez* is as much a document of the Portuguese past in Macau as it is a film about a fictional crime. Guerra da Mata's walks through the city include stops at landmarks such as the Camões Garden and Grotto, a large park with a bust of the poet and stone tablets with verses from *Os lusíadas*, which purportedly was written in Macau. Now daily activities there entail locals performing morning exercises and walking their otherwise caged birds. (Not surprisingly, the film's mysterious birdcage makes an appearance in the garden.) Childhood memories of Macau, in the form of discolored Polaroid photos of a young Guerra da Mata and his family, appear onscreen alongside the film's own stills of statues, forts, and other monuments, some with patriotic wording in Portuguese, now dwarfed by monolithic casinos. His visit to the once popular and now empty Military Club has a ghostly feel as he gazes at its gallery of old photographs, with their images of smiling Portuguese officers socializing in dress uniform. Even his childhood home in the nineteenth-century building called the Moorish Barracks is off limits. A UNESCO Heritage Site, it is occupied by the maritime administration and no longer open to the public. In many ways, Guerra da Mata is another ghost from the past. Unable to communicate, he has no personal interactions during his solitary wanderings through streets with Portuguese names like Travessa da Saudade (Nostalgia Lane), and he seems invisible to those around him. The only beings that sense his presence are stray dogs and an occasional cat, which appear repeatedly onscreen as they make their own unnoticed way through the city.

Despite its largely bleak tone and pervasive nostalgia, A *última vez* might be understood in a broader sense as a film about the resilience of the past; it is a contemporary movie that quotes classic Hollywood films and is part of a fascination with noir today that seems unlikely to fade away any time soon. The film is also about a people who circumnavigated the globe and left their mark in remote places like Macau and Goa regardless of whether their presence and designs were welcomed there. Although nostalgia is not always a good thing nor accurate in what is recalled, it is very much associated, for better or worse, with the Portuguese empire and everything it signified for the small country in the sixteenth century.

Epilogue

THE PORTUGUESE-SPEAKING
DIASPORA AND "LUSOFONIA"

Although the era of empire is long over, different forms of diaspora continue within the Portuguese-speaking world, including the economic migration of young professionals from Portugal and Brazil to Macau and Angola and an increasing tourism that brings wealthy Angolans to shop in Lisbon's designer stores along the Avenida da Liberdade. Literature about diaspora continues to be published and often sells quite well. A case in point is Miguel Sousa Tavares's novel *Equador* (2003) (*Equator* [2010]), in its thirty-fifth edition in 2013, about the enslavement of Angolans brought to work the São Tomé cocoa fields at the turn of the twentieth century. A more recent novel about diaspora is João Pedro Marques's *Uma fazenda em África* (2012) (A farm in Africa), about Portuguese who leave the Brazilian Northeast to establish a colony in Moçâmedes, in southern Angola. Both novels are based on historical events. *Equator* is about the British threat to boycott São Tomé cocoa if the Portuguese Crown fails to halt slave practices and to satisfy an inspection "para inglês ver" (for the English to see) reminiscent of earlier British searches of Portuguese ships suspected of illegal slave trafficking. The fictional 1848 rebellion in Pernambuco that initiates the migration of Portuguese to West Africa in *Uma fazenda em África* is based on the Praieira revolt of that year, which was partly directed at the Portuguese who controlled trade in the Brazilian Northeast. The Portuguese government supported the colonization of Moçâmedes by providing sea passage and financial aid to those who emigrated from Brazil.

The nineteenth century is also the starting point for Raquel Ochoa's *A casa-comboio* (2010) (The house-train), about four generations of an Indo-Portuguese family whose migratory trajectory includes the Portuguese cities of Daman, Diu, and Silvassa in India and finally Lisbon in

1961 after Portugal's defeat in Goa by the Indian Union. Ochoa's characters represent different attitudes of a people who for centuries have not only spoken Portuguese and practiced Portuguese customs but also regarded Portugal as the homeland. When asked by his young son Rudolfo if Portugal is very far away, the paterfamilias, Honorato Carcomo, who dreams of traveling to the Alentejo, replies, "Ó que disparate! Portugal é aqui!" (24). (What nonsense! Portugal is here!) Honorato's grandson Baltazar, who serves in the Indian army, has a different idea of Portugal after he is taken prisoner in Goa. He is frustrated by Portugal's delay in liberating the captured soldiers; not long after his less-than-welcoming arrival in Lisbon, he is sent to fight in Angola and then Guiné, where he is wounded and assigned to a job in the morgue. Baltazar's daughter Clara, born in Lisbon after the 1974 revolution, is curious about India, a land about which her parents rarely speak. While touring India in 2001, she meets Juscelino, a distant cousin whose family remained in Goa. Not unlike Honorato at the turn of the twentieth century, Juscelino identifies with Portugal and longs to migrate, but he lacks a visa. Cognizant of the paradoxical nature of his feelings about Portugal, he asks Clara, "Acha normal eu sentir saudades de uma coisa que não conheço?" (316). (Do you think it's normal for me to feel nostalgic about something I don't know?) Clara's response has a certain Fifth Empire resonance emanating from an imperial nostalgia: "Não é muito normal, não. Mas acontece. Há quem lhe chame saudades do futuro" (361). (No, it's not very normal. But it happens. There are those who call it a nostalgia about the future.)

The Brazilian Luiz Ruffato's tongue-in-cheek *Estive em Lisboa e lembrei de você* (2009) (I was in Lisbon and remembered you), a "depoimento, minimamente revistado" (13) (minimally revised testimonial) of Sérgio de Souza Sampio, centers on a working-class protagonist from Minas Gerais who, like many Brazilians before him, leaves his home for a presumably better life in Lisbon. With little education and few skills, Sérgio has expectations of becoming rich and returning to Brazil that collide with the realities of daily life in his new homeland; after more than six years spent working in a modest restaurant, he finds himself no further ahead and ultimately out of work.

Estive em Lisboa's humor derives from Sérgio's well-meaning misreadings of his new environment. For example, when he notices that no one is behind the reception desk at the boardinghouse where he takes a room, he rings the service bell not once but several times in agitation. When the irritated manager appears and asks what he wants, Sérgio explains that he was simply worried that with no one behind the counter the place might be robbed. Angered, the manager brusquely replies, "Isso aqui não é o Brasil" (43) (This here isn't Brazil). The novella also describes Sérgio's struggles with European Portuguese and his relief when he meets Segafredo, a fellow Brazilian who helps him to adapt: "Puxa vida, que bom encontrar alguém que fala a mesma língua da gente" (47). (Gosh, it's good to find someone who speaks our language.) The story calls attention to Sérgio's gradual adoption of a European vocabulary with terms such as *chapéu-de-chuva* (umbrella), *telemóvel* (cell phone), and *parvo* (stupid), all of which appear in bold print in the narrative. Unfortunately, his growing knowledge and fluency do not help him advance. He is dismissed from his waiter job because he is monolingual and not white. He is to be replaced by a better-educated and white Eastern European migrant who knows French and English and would be preferable for the restaurant's growing international clientele.

The Portuguese language, which is central to Ruffato's novella, is a recurring topic of discussion today in Portuguese-speaking nations competing in the global marketplace. The CPLP, founded in 1996 after the creation of PALOP in 1992, is a coalition of eight nations formerly constituting the Portuguese empire, with the recent addition of Equatorial Guinea, with the objective of ensuring that all citizens, especially in rural areas in Africa, are fluent in Portuguese, the language used in all diplomatic and economic negotiations between the member nations.[1] The greater dispersion and adoption of the language could be described as a form of diaspora prescribed by the CPLP for its populations and for countries like the United States, Canada, and Australia with historically large immigrant communities. The ultimate aim of the CPLP is a linguistically unified community of considerable size and reach that will have a greater presence and role in the global economy.

The term *lusofonia* (Lusophony), which grew out of the CPLP and circulates widely today, especially in Lisbon, refers ostensibly to the multicultural and multiracial richness that resulted from Portugal's long history and postdemocratic union with the former colonies represented by the CPLP, whose primary attribute and common denominator is the Portuguese language. According to Portuguese journalist and politician José Carlos de Vasconcelos, the first dictionary definition of *lusofonia* appeared in Brazilian Aurélio Buarque de Holanda's *Novo dicionário da língua portuguesa* (1988). It is defined as the adoption of the language by those for whom it is not the vernacular, and the example is given of countries colonized by the Portuguese. Vasconcelos comments that this early definition is curious because it excludes both Portuguese and Brazilians. He also cites the 2001 definition given by Brazilian Antônio Houaiss in his dictionary that specifies the group of countries in which Portuguese is the official or dominant language, including areas where a form of the language is spoken, among them Macau, Goa, Daman, and Timor. Vasconcelos adds that the term has come to mean different things: "[S]ão muitos os sentidos ou não sentidos que lhe são dados, os díspares juízos valorativos e as previsões quanto ao futuro" ("Lusofonia," 101). (There are many meanings and non-meanings given to it, disparate value judgments and forecasts about the future.)

During a visit to Lisbon in May and June 2015, I asked university and other professionals how they might define the word *lusofonia*. There was no consensus about the meaning of the term despite the fact that the city was celebrating a festival dedicated to Lusofonia not long afterward, the Dia da Lusofonia (Lusophony Day), also known as Dia Internacional da Língua Portuguesa (International Day of the Portuguese Language), which is officially recognized on May 5. An Angolan I interviewed expressed his disapproval of the term because of its emphasis on *luso*, or Lusitanian. His reaction is not unique and represents concerns about the potential neocolonial implications of a project whose moniker places Portugal front and center. His comment also disagrees with Vasconcelos's opinion that the term has gradually become more acceptable over time and no longer places Portugal in first place among the nations (101). Portuguese political scientist Maria Sousa Galito concurs with Vasconcelos in the sense that the generation born after the 1974 revolution is more focused on the present and less preoccupied with or knowledgeable about the colonial past ("Conceito de Lusofonia," 15–16).

The five-day Festival da Lusofonia de Lisboa in May 2015 featured a wide range of events in art, dance, literature, music, film, and gastronomy sponsored by various cultural entities, including *casas* (houses) representing communities that migrated from the former colonies (Casa do Brasil, Fundação Casa de Macau, Casa de Goa, and so forth), ethnic group associations (like the Associação Caboverdeana and the Associação Guineenese da Solidariedade), organizations such as the UCCLA (União de Cidades Capitais de Língua Portuguesa),[2] the international youth group Conexão Lusófona (Lusophone Connection), and local government in the form of the Câmara Municipal (Municipal Chamber).

What should we make of the present-day celebration of Lusofonia, given its possible connections with the centuries of colonialism that produced the widespread diffusion or diaspora of not only people but also the Portuguese language? On the one hand, Lusofonia seems to posit a sort of melting pot of Portuguese-speaking peoples and cultures; on the other hand, the term's Lusitanian reference prioritizes Portugal in this mix. Portuguese anthropologist Miguel de Vale Almeida has written extensively on Lusofonia, describing it as a rhetoric rising out of Portugal's attempt to maintain its position of authority in the postdemocratic era while also generating a sense of community and goodwill with the former colonies:

> Contrary to what could have been expected, the Portuguese State did not reconfigure itself as a small European territory, as an Austria or Denmark, so to speak. Rather, it constructed for itself and the population an image of a bridge or platform of connection between Europe, on the one hand, and Brazil and Africa on the other. It offered both sides a specific type of culture and historical capital, that of the colonial experience, decontextualized in time and space (that is, with no differentiation between the early colonization of Brazil or the harsh and brutal wars in Africa), and that of a common language. Language became the main symbol, resource and fetish in this reconstruction of identity and the Portuguese state invested in the creation of a Commonwealth, the CPLP, and branded the term Lusophony to define a transnational community of Portuguese speakers. In school books, the expansionist and chauvinistic discourse was replaced by a humanist, universalist version, but one that has always left untouched the role of Portugal as a center, a point of diffusion. ("Portugal's Colonial Complex," 8)

Maria Sousa Galito argues that any concern about Portugal's postimperial aspirations is baseless given Brazil's greater international presence as one of the BRICS (Brazil, Russia, India, China, and South Africa) and Angola's oil-rich economy. In fact, she notes, Portugal is the nation that risks being colonized ("Conceito de Lusofonia," 14).

While Lusofonia and the festivals named in its honor tout the linguistic ties that bind racially and culturally diverse nations, the problems born of a centuries-long colonial past remain in evidence. Despite the celebration of a commonly spoken language, there are interesting political differences within the CPLP, one of which has to do with the 1990 orthographic agreement to reduce the two separate Portuguese orthographies (one European-African and another Brazilian) to one, in accordance with the organization's transatlantic unifying objectives.[3] Although Portugal ratified the agreement, there is unhappiness and resistance in Portugal—as well as in African nations—about an orthography that privileges Brazil, Portugal's former colony, and threatens the Portuguese national identity.[4]

Efforts are under way in the CPLP to turn Portuguese into a language of the global marketplace and an official language of the United Nations. International conferences and celebrations of Lusofonia project a spirit of fellowship within the CPLP, with an emphasis on multiculturalism; nevertheless, the legacy of colonialism persists in not-so-subtle racial tensions, broad economic disparities, and, one might say, even in the way a plan for a common orthography is perceived.[5] As William Faulkner famously said, "The past is never dead. It's not even past." One might also say that diasporic culture never ends, and its determinants persist. This is true for both older and more recent works of art, which, like Raquel Ochoa's novel *A casa-comboio* or Goya Lopes's prints or Pedro Costa's films, deploy the past in different ways and for different ends to elicit new modes of thinking. Whether representing movement back in time or travel in the present, they reveal the continued dispersion, comingling, and sometimes conflict of peoples and cultures in the far-reaching Portuguese-speaking world.

Notes

INTRODUCTION

1. For details on the values and peaks of remittances received, consult Rui Pena Pires, editor, "Migrations and Remittances," *Portugal*, 98–99.

2. The Forum Angola-Portugal was recently announced as a new program sponsored by the Geographic Society in Lisbon. Its purpose is to serve as mediator and adviser to international companies that seek Portugal's help in establishing relations with businesses in Angola.

CHAPTER ONE

1. Unless noted otherwise, all translations that appear in this book are my own.

2. Nineteenth-century novelist, poet, and historian Alexandre Herculano edited a two-volume collection titled *Lendas e narrativas* (1851) (Legends and narratives) that includes "A morte do lidador," "A dama pé-de-cabra" (The cloven-hoofed lady), and other stories from the medieval *IV Livro de linhagens* (Fourth book of lineages).

3. Madeira was the first land to be discovered and claimed as part of the Portuguese empire, in 1419.

4. The beginning of Portuguese romanticism is generally associated with Almeida Garrett's long poem titled *Camões* (1825).

5. Camões purportedly wrote part or all of *Os lusíadas* in Macau. A park with a grotto there is named in his honor and contains a bust of the poet and stone tablets on which several of his poems appear.

6. When presented with good news or some form of tribute, kings regularly responded by giving the presenter money, land, or a title or fulfilling a request. Josiah Blackmore makes a case for the importance of Álvaro Velho's *Relação da viagem de Vasco da Gama (1497–1499)* to Camões's poem; Blackmore, *Moorings*, 56–63.

7. Pires was named Portugal's first ambassador to China shortly after the Portu-

guese arrived there in 1513. For a discussion of Paes and Nunes, see Joan-Pau Rubiés, *Travel and Ethnology in the Renaissance.*

8. There was also the fear of how a woman and family would survive without the legal head of the household. Harking back to the expansionist period, the expression "viúvas dos vivos" (widows of the living) continued to be used well into the twentieth century to describe women whose husbands emigrated to Brazil, the United States, and other places for economic reasons and often never returned. The literature on this topic is considerable. See Caroline Bethell, *Men Who Migrate, Women Who Wait,* among other studies. Elvira Azevedo Mea, in "Mulheres nas teias da expansão," discusses what happened to those women during the empire who remarried after years of waiting and whose first husbands, believed to have died abroad, suddenly reappeared. This is also the plot of Almeida Garrett's play *Frei Luís de Sousa,* written in 1843; Garrett, *Obras,* vol. 2.

9. Bacchus feared that his escapades and conquests in India would be diminished by the arrival of the Portuguese fleet there.

10. Camões's portrayal of the Portuguese disinterest in other cultures differs radically from pronouncements made by then Brazilian president Fernando Henrique Cardoso and former Portuguese president Mário Soares. They concur that fundamental to the Portuguese identity is an innate curiosity about and interest in the Other. See their conversation on this topic in Cardoso and Soares, *O mundo em português,* 276–277.

11. Madalena is a good example of a "viúva do vivo" who is punished for remarrying. Although she waited many years for Dom João's return, her "sin" is all the greater because she fell in love with Dom Manuel prior to João's departure for the fateful encounter at Alcácer-Quibir.

12. The duke of Ferrara commissioned Alberto Cantino to arrange for the map. Cantino paid a Lisbon cartographer who had access to Portugal's highly guarded maritime charts. Wealthy Italians like the duke were eager to know as much as possible about Portugal's overseas activities. The map can be found in the Biblioteca Estense de Modena.

13. Anthony Disney writes about this community near the Niger Delta in "Portuguese Expansion, 1400–1800," 296. A. J. R. Russell-Wood's seminal *World on the Move* refers to the Benin plaques and other artistic and literary works produced as a result of Portuguese expansionism in Africa, Asia, and Brazil; see especially his chapter titled "Movement in Word and Image," 209–221.

14. For more on early African-Portuguese artwork, consult Nicholas N. Bridges, "Loango Coast Ivories."

15. Later plundering by the British in Nigeria meant that numerous Benin bronzes that were prized and not traded would be cached in private collections and museums outside Africa, especially in England and the United States. More recently there has been a reverse migration to Nigeria of Brazilians whose ancestors were enslaved by the Portuguese and shipped to Brazil; see Milton Guran, *Agudás: Os brasileiros do Benin.* There is considerable scholarship on the Benin bronzes. A recent source of information is Neil MacGregor, *History of the World in 100 Objects,* 498–502. An excellent, concise

commentary on the ivories is Luís de Moura Sobral's "Expansion and the Arts," 397–404. Other sources include William R. Flagg, *Afro-Portuguese Ivories*; Maria Helena Mendes Pinto, ed., *Marfim d'além-mar no Museu de Arte Antiga*; and Kathy Curnow, *Afro-Portuguese Ivories*.

16. Canto X refers to both commerce and Christianity under the Portuguese in Japan: "E Japão, onde nasce a prata fina,/ Que ilustrada será com a lei divina" (line 131). (And Japan with its trove of fine silver,/ How illustrious it will be once under divine law.) For the moment, "the Orient" was of primary interest despite the founding of Brazil. Although Pero Vaz de Caminha's fascinating letter about New World peoples provides a unique ethnographic study of inhabitants of the "Land called Vera Cruz," Brazil's significance was ancillary to the spice trade. Pedro Álvares Cabral commanded a thirteen-ship armada, more than four times the size of Vasco da Gama's fleet and with larger vessels, or *naus*, to bring Indian goods back to Lisbon.

17. In his book *Imaginary Geographies*, Luis Madureira notes the centrality of the *roteiro* subgenre to the image of the growing Portuguese empire (34).

18. The Jesuit Manuel da Nóbrega wrote to the king in 1552 to ask that he send Portuguese women to the colony to marry and to help keep settlers from straying from the Church and "going native." To respond to this request, the Crown sent a number of orphans to Brazil who were known as "órfãs d'El Rei" (orphans of the king). Orphaned females whose fathers had died in service to the Crown were also sent to India to help populate the colony there. In the latter case, dowries of land and titles were often part of the package. Ana Miranda's historical novel *Desmundo* (1996) is about the adventures of a convent-raised orphan who is sent with others to marry colonists in Brazil.

19. The *década* is a classical form and refers to a volume divided into ten books. The Roman Livy (Titus Livius) used this approach in writing his multivolume history of Rome often referred to as the *Décadas*. Only a few of the original 142 volumes survived; they were translated into Spanish by Pedro López de Ayala in the late fifteenth century.

20. Mina was the name given to the region in West Africa associated with the mining of gold and other precious metals.

21. Bragança, *Lições de literatura portuguesa*, 539–540.

22. An equally unattractive view of the Portuguese in late sixteenth-century India is Francisco Rodrigues Silveira's *Memórias de um soldado da Índia* (Memoirs of a soldier from India), posthumously published in 1877.

The historian Panduronga S. S. Pissurlencar wrote about the Portuguese presence in early Indian literature. The images in poems and chronicles written in Sanskrit, Tamil, Persian, Arabic, and other languages of the continent are largely disparaging. The author also calls attention to more favorable aspects of the Portuguese in India, including their introduction of the first printing press in Goa in 1556. Other contributions include plants, especially a type of mango called *portuguesas*, and construction methods used in building Catholic churches, which were the first examples of European architecture in India; Pissurlencar, "Os portugueses nas literaturas indianas."

23. Machado, *O mito do Oriente*, 39. The words are originally attributed to the

Roman general Scipio the African, who grew disillusioned with the empire and died far from home.

24. In a prefatory note, Mendes Pinto states that he wrote *Peregrinação* so his family would have a record of his youthful adventures abroad. He finished the manuscript, but it was not published during his lifetime and only appeared in 1614, some thirty years after his death.

25. Joan Pau Rubiés, "Oriental Voices of Mendes Pinto," 29.

26. In his *Portugueses das sete partidas*, novelist and critic Aquilino Ribeiro states that the António de Farias character allows Mendes Pinto to divulge the kinds of despicable acts committed by Portuguese abroad. The seafaring Faria is the obvious antithesis of the mariner-hero Vasco da Gama, and Faria's privateer type is roundly criticized in Couto's *Décadas da Ásia*.

27. Different approaches were taken to colonizing new lands. As historians Vimala Devi and Manuel de Seabra have observed, the Portuguese in India immediately destroyed all works written in the vernacular, razed temples, and banned Hindu festivities. The Portuguese language was imposed on the local population in the schools, although the people continued to speak Konkani. Because the vernacular was never taught, locals remained largely illiterate. Mass Christian indoctrination sessions were held on Sundays; to ensure conversion, non-Christians were excluded from holding public office, while converts were extended employment and other privileges; *A literatura indo-portuguesa*, 1:46–47, 55, 74–75.

28. See Villiers, "The Portuguese and the Trading World of Asia," 3–4.

29. In his book *Mary and Misogyny*, Charles R. Boxer observes, "The Portuguese Crown, unlike the Castilian, tended to discourage women from going to the Asian and African 'conquests' [colonies] . . . The average male emigrant to the East could not have afforded to take his wife and/or daughters to India, without a monetary grant (*ajuda de custo*) from the Crown. The impecunious Portuguese monarchs neither would nor could grant these on a lavish scale . . . [N]o wife of a Portuguese viceroy or governor-general of India accompanied her husband to Goa between 1549 and 1750" (64–65).

30. For more information on Catholic art and architecture in India, see Jorge Flores, "They Have Discovered Us," 184–197. One of the most famous contemporary examples of Indo-Portuguese religious art is the painting by Goan artist Ângelo da Fonseca. In his *Virgem e o menino* (1961) (Virgin and Child), Mary is wearing an Indian sari.

31. See Luis Moura Sobral, "Expansion and the Arts," 404–416, for more information on furniture, textiles, and porcelains.

32. In his essay "Early Ming Images of the Portuguese," K. C. Fok notes that some of the first such images were far from favorable. Sixteenth-century Chinese documents refer to the Portuguese as "cruel and crafty," cannibalistic "lovers of children's flesh," and practitioners of "outrageous acts" that included enslaving the Chinese (145–147).

33. The word *nagasaki* means "long cape." The Japanese called one vessel "the black ship," after the black-clothed Jesuits who controlled Nagasaki; Teixeira, "Japo-

neses em Macau," 201. For more information on Nagasaki art of the time, see Alexandra Curvelo, "Nagasaki."

34. Consult *Portugal Japão*.

35. According to one source, the Saint Lawrence cannon was given to the *vice-rei* of Canton and later taken by the British following the occupation of the city in 1841. It is now in the Tower of London; C. A. Montalto de Jesus, *Macau histórico*, 83.

36. Paul Guedes, "Weapons of Yesteryear."

37. The lotus is the sacred flower of Buddhists and Daoists and is a symbol of purity. A popular motif in Chinese art, it regularly appears on porcelains. An early and exceptionally beautiful example is a twelfth-century bowl from the Song Dynasty in the Dr. Anastácio Gonçalves Museum in Lisbon. A photograph of the bowl appears in Pinto de Matos and Desroches, eds., *Chinese Export Porcelain*.

38. The first Jesuit church was erected in Kyoto in 1568.

39. See Jay Levenson, ed., *Encompassing the Globe, Reference*, 116, for a brief discussion of the Jesuit image in art located in Lisbon's famous São Roque church and museum. For an in-depth study of Jesuits who left Portugal to establish missions in China, see Liam Matthew Brockey, *Journey to the East*.

40. Under Dom João III, Portugal established the first *coleginho* (college) for Jesuits, and in 1546 it became the first administrative province for Jesuits worldwide; António Lopes, "História da Província Portuguesa da Companhia de Jesus," 37. These and other initiatives were part of João III's plan to train and send missionaries to all parts of the empire. Lopes has found that 351 missionary expeditions left Lisbon between 1541, when Xavier went to India, and 1756. In addition to India, the Far East, and Brazil, Jesuits were in Angola by 1560 and in Cabo Verde by 1604 (38).

41. José Manuel Garcia credits António José de Figueiredo's 1862 article in *Arquivo pitoresco* for initiating the nineteenth-century vogue; Garcia, *O Japão visto pelos portugueses*, 12.

42. Fróis's study includes a letter of complaint from the Japanese leader Hideyoshi to the Jesuit Gaspar Coelho on the Portuguese enslavement of Japanese. It states,

> [E]u tenho sabido que os portugueses e os siões e combojas que vêm a estas partes fazer suas fazendas, compram grande número de gente e a levam cativa para seus reinos, desnaturando os japoneses de sua pátria, de seus parentes, filhos e amigos, e isto é coisa insofrível. Pelo que o Padre faça que todos os japoneses que até agora se venderam, para a Índia e para outras partes remotas, sejam outra vez restituídos a Japão, e quando isto não for possível por estarem longe em reinos remotos, ao menos os que agora os portugueses têm comprado os ponham em sua liberdade, e eu darei a prata que lhe custaram. (In Fróis, *História de Japam*, vol. 4 [1583–1587], 402)

> (I have learned that Portuguese, Siamese, and Cambodians who come to our shores to trade are buying a great number of people, taking them captive to

their kingdoms, tearing the Japanese away from their homeland, families, children, and friends, and this is insufferable. Would the Padre ensure that all those Japanese who have up until now been sold in India and other distant realms be returned again to Japan? And if this is not possible, because they are far away in distant kingdoms, then at least have the Portuguese set free those whom they have bought recently, and I will provide you with the money that this costs you.)

See Zhidong Hao, *Macau*, 60–61, 86–87, for commentary on the Chinese slaves sent by the Portuguese to Macau and India.

43. For more information on these debates, see Helmut Feldmann, "As disputas de São Francisco Xavier com bonzos da doutrina *Zen*," 70–78.

44. Valignano's appointment was controversial because he was Italian-born. But the Portuguese government required that Jesuits born outside Portugal live for a time in the country and learn the language before taking up service in the empire. Established in the 1550s, the Colégio de Santo Antão became one of the premier learning centers in Europe and was renowned for its "aula da esfera" in mathematics and the sciences. For more information on this school, see Henrique Leitão, *A ciência na "aula da esfera."*

45. The Spanish-Japanese version is titled *Vocabulário de Japon declarado primero en Portugues por los Padres de la Compañia de Jesus de aquel reino, y ahora en Castellano en el Colegio de Santo Thomas de Manila* (1630). A copy can be found in the Charles R. Boxer Collection in the Lilly Library at Indiana University–Bloomington.

46. These works are cited in Luís de Rebelo, "Language and Literature in the Portuguese Empire," 374.

47. The letter in its entirety is cited in João de Deus Ramos, "A província do Japão da Companhia de Jesus após o século cristão," 97–103.

48. The Cardim document is archived in the Boxer Collection (mss II) in the Lilly Library. Charles Boxer wrote on the binding's back inside cover that there are Japanese versions of this episode as well.

49. Paulino and Oliveira e Costa, eds., *O Japão visto pelos portugueses*, 117.

50. See Andrew C. Ross, *A Vision Betrayed*, for more information on Xavier and the Jesuits in Asia. José Eduardo Franco, in his essay "Jesuítas e Inquisição, complicidades e confrontações," analyzes opposing views of the Society of Jesus's relationship with the Holy Office.

51. Boxer mss I, Lilly Library, Bloomington, IN.

52. In 1955 the bibliophile Alfonso Cassuto published a bibliography of "sermões da auto-da-fé" (sermons read at the auto-da-fé) from his extensive collection of Judaica; *Bibliografia dos sermões de autos-da-fé*.

53. Vieira, "Proposta," *Obras escolhidas*, 4:1–26. For a concise discussion of Vieira's many writings on the topic of shoring up the economy, see Novinsky, "Padre António Vieira."

54. Among the many scholars who discuss these particular writings are José van

den Besselaar (*António Vieira: o homem, a obra, as ideias* and *O sebastianismo: história sumária*) and Thomas Cohen (*The Fire of Tongues*).

55. See Luis Moura Sobral, "Expansion and the Arts," for commentary and bibliography on religious architecture of the empire (420–455, 458–459).

56. Simão de Vasconcelos's *Crônica da Companhia de Jesus* (1663) has an extraordinary example of frontispiece engraving.

57. See Sanjay Subrahmanyam, *Portuguese Empire in Asia*, 212–215, for a discussion of the East India Company and its takeover of the Indian Ocean and other trade routes. Founded in 1641, the semigovernmental Dutch West India Company, which also had shareholders, controlled the sugar trade with Brazil during the Dutch occupation of the Northeast.

58. Loss of life at sea is a theme in Portuguese literature dating back to the earliest poems, many of which were compiled by Garcia de Resende in the *Cancioneiro geral* (1516). A good example is João Ruiz de Castelo Banco's verse "E quantos este mar tem/ sumidos, que não parecem, e quão cedo cá esquecem,/ sem lembrarem a ninguém" (And how many have disappeared in the sea/ seems unimaginable, and how quickly they are forgotten here,/ never to be remembered by anyone).

59. In 1946, during the Salazar dictatorship, the film *Camões* was made by José Leitão de Barros. Like *O descobrimento do Brasil* (1937), directed by Humberto Mauro during the Vargas dictatorship in Brazil, *Camões* celebrates important figures associated with empire. One of the most dramatic scenes in the Barros film is the shipwreck, with Camões struggling to hold the manuscript above the waves. His love interest, who appears in a tender scene with the poet prior to the disaster, simply disappears, and there is no further reference to her.

60. In this case, the survivors were the ship's watchman Álvaro Fernandes and three female African slaves. For in-depth studies of the *História trágico-marítima*, see Angélica Madeira, *Livro dos naufrágios*, and Josiah Blackmore, *Manifest Perdition*.

61. Gil Vicente's plays are unusual in this regard. They focus mainly on the commoner and minor nobility, figures he could satirize while writing under court patronage.

CHAPTER TWO

1. East African slaves from Mozambique were transported to Goa shortly after the Portuguese settlement was established there in 1510. For a discussion of the term "Mina," consult Robin Law, "Ethnicities of Enslaved Africans in the Diaspora." For more information on African slave trafficking in Portuguese Asia, see Rudy Blaus, "The Portuguese Slave Trade from Mozambique to Portuguese-India and Macau and Comments on Timor."

2. Edmund Abaka, *House of Slaves and "Door of No Return."*

3. Another example appears on an early sixteenth-century map by Pedro Reinel

titled "Africa Amina," where the castle is bedecked with several Portuguese flags. This image appeared on a 1960 Angolan stamp to commemorate the five-hundredth anniversary of the Infante Dom Henique's death.

4. In her essay "O negro e a negritude na arte portuguesa do século XVI," Maria José Goulão lists other examples of the *cabeça de negro* that appear in buildings of the Manueline period.

5. In his "Carta do achamento do Brasil" (1500), Pero Vaz de Caminha writes about the Indians' good noses in comparison to those of the Africans.

6. Religious conversion of Africans was a basic rationale as well as subterfuge for the capture of slaves, who were considered "barbarous," meaning lacking in knowledge of Christianity and therefore potential recruits to the faith, as opposed to North African "infidels," considered the Christians' enemies. The Vatican sanctioned these distinctions and approved African enslavement as a means to save innocent and otherwise lost souls; the monarchy also mandated the conversion of all slaves, although not every owner complied with the law. For more discussion of this topic, see Tinhorão, *Os negros*, 55–58.

7. In her essay about the black regiment, Hebe Mattos states that Dias had the titles and other awards transferred to his sons-in-law to avoid an investigation that would deny such honors if his parents had been manual laborers or were of mixed race; "'Black Troops' and Hierarchies of Color in the Portuguese Atlantic World," 9.

8. Two twentieth-century Brazilian portraits of Henrique Dias appear in Heitor Martins's article "Um primitivo documento inédito da consciência negra em língua portuguesa." In the portrait by Vicente do Rego Monteiro, Dias is white; in the other, by the painter Manuel Bandeira, he is black. The article examines an unpublished poem (*silva*) about Henrique Dias by the eighteenth-century black writer Alexandre Antônio Lima, who was born in Portugal. According to Martins, the poem is likely the first literary treatment of a heroic figure born in Brazil and the first time a black author wrote about a representative of his own race.

9. Da Gama was suspected of being a Jansenist and arrested and condemned to exile in Angola. His long poem written for the daughter of the marquis of Pombal spared him that tribulation.

10. In 2014, Angolan novelist José Eduardo Agualusa published *A Rainha Ginga*, about the "black wars" between Angola and Portugal that involved Ginga (also known as Ngola).

11. In 2012 children from Harlem Park Elementary and Middle School in Baltimore, Maryland, were asked to paint a picture based on the sixteenth-century Alfama fountain scene, a painting of which was exhibited at the Walters Art Museum. The students' painting appears, along with the original, in Robin Cembalest, "From Kongo to Othello."

12. For more information on Rocha's work, see Casimiro, "Uma nova etapa da pedagogia."

13. Charles Boxer translated and wrote about this pamphlet in 1964 in the journal *Race*.

14. The eighteenth-century Brazilian essayist Nísia Floresta Brasileira Augusta, considered the country's first feminist, took a similar approach to the topic, viewing slavery as an ill that affected the health and well-being of the slaveholding population. In an essay on the nineteenth-century black poet Luís Gama, Heitor Martins states that Gama's contemporaries, including José de Alencar in *O demônio familiar* (1858), Joaquim Manuel de Macedo in *As vítimas-algozes* (1869), and Bernardo Guimarães in *A escrava Isaura* (1875), were also less concerned about the slave than slavery's impact on Brazilian slaveholders (Martins, "Luís Gama," 90).

15. Da Gama wrote about the Guarani war in his epic poem *O Uraguai* (1769). As Heitor Martins mentioned in one of our conversations, da Gama should also be recognized as the first writer to compose major works about all three races.

16. Tinhorão, *Domingos Caldas Barbosa*, 29, 41.

17. See Martins's edited volume *Neoclassicismo*, especially page 183.

18. The word is sometimes spelled *lundu*. It was frequently referred to as *batuque*, a percussion-based song and dance from Cape Verde from which the African *lundum* partly derives. See "Lundu" in the *Dicionário Cravo Albin da música popular brasileira* for more information on the form.

19. Bocage and other neoclassical poets wrote occasional pornographic poems, but these tended to circulate separately from their other works and, similar to many medieval *cantigas* of a similar nature, were left out of the canon. Perhaps because he was a clergyman, Caldas Barbosa never wrote erotic verse.

20. There is no evidence that these medieval *cantigas*, which were written only in manuscript form, were known at the time, aside from oral variations sung by the *povo*.

21. The two Caldas Barbosa volumes are composed of booklets that were printed individually. References to the volumes are to the respective booklet and page number.

22. The Portuguese explorer Major Serpa Pinto wrote a variation on this Caldas Barbosa tribute in his African travel memoir, *Como eu atravessei a África* (1881); both volumes are translated as *How I Crossed Africa* (1881), the source of the translations I quote in this present work. In his description of the young female Ambuela dancers, he states, "Impressionou-me o tipo daquelas raparigas, que era perfeitamente europeu, algumas vi que, com a mudança de cor, fariam de inveja a muitas formosas europeias, a quem igualmente em beleza e excederiam em formas e elegancies naturais" (1:271) (I was much struck with the type of those girls, which was perfectly European, and I saw several whose forms, as they undulated in the dance, would have raised envy in the hearts of many European ladies, whom they equaled in beauty and surpassed in grace of motion) (1:326). The translation omits the point that that they would be the envy of European ladies if not for their color. I discuss Serpa Pinto further in chapter 4.

23. For more information on the rhyme schemes and rhythms that distinguish the *lundum* and *modinha*, consult José Ramos Tinhorão, *História social da música popular brasileira* and *Domingos Caldas Barbosa*.

24. For additional information on early cultural and religious transferences, see James Sweet, *Recreating Africa*.

25. Sadlier, *Brazil Imagined*, 132–149.

26. Gonçalves Dias's *Primeiros cantos*, with prologue and "Canção do exílio," are in his *Obras completas* and reproduced online at http://objdigital.bn.br/Acervo_Digi tal/livros_eletronicos/primeiroscantos.pdf.

27. In 1849, Nísia Floresta Brasileira Augusta wrote a long poem titled *A lágrima de um caeté* that is in keeping with the romantic treatment of the Brazilian Indian at the time. In her later *Opúsculo humanitário* (1853) she uses verses from that earlier work to denounce the institution of slavery. The verses are as follows: "Deus que nenhuma raça fez / Para sobre uma outra ter / Revoltante primazia, / Ilimitado prazer" (*Opúsculo*, 116) (God who made no race / to have a revolting advantage / unlimited pleasure / over another).

28. The same year that Gama's *Trovas* appeared, Maria Firmina dos Reis, using the pseudonym "Uma maranhense" (a woman from Maranhão) published *Úrsula* (1859), the first novel by a black writer on the condition of slaves and women in general and a pioneer abolitionist work. The novel has received considerable critical attention since its recovery in the form of a facsimile edition in 1975 and its reprint in 2004.

29. The poem can be found in Machado de Assis, *Obra completa*, at http://ma chado.mec.gov.br/images/stories/html/poesia/maps03.htm#SABINA.

30. The title was a reference to the eighteenth-century French newspaper, also known as the *Gazette d'Amsterdam*, that was published in Holland and had far more liberal leanings than the *Gazette de France* published in Paris. For the *Gazeta de Holanda*, see Machado de Assis, *Obra completa*, at http://machado.mec.gov.br/images/stories /html/poesia/maps04.htm.

31. "O caso da vara," Machado de Assis, *Obra completa*, at http://machado.mec .gov.br/images/stories/html/contos/macn006.htm#o_caso_da_vara_embaixo.

32. Joaquim Nabuco, *O abolicionismo*, 52.

33. Ibid., 59.

34. Jean-Baptiste Debret wrote of these racial attitudes in his *Viagem pitoresca e histórica ao Brasil* (1834–1839), which also contains a list of the different races and ethnicities in Brazil organized according to their supposed degrees of civilization. Gregório de Matos, in his famous poem "Descreve o que era naquele tempo a cidade da Bahia," about the colonial city of Bahia, dedicates a stanza to the mulatto:

Muitos mulatos desavergonhados
Trazidos sob os pés dos homens nobres,
Posta nas palmas toda a picardia. (*Poemas escolhidos*, 41)

(Many shameless mulattos
Rise on the backs of noble men,
By knowing every dirty trick in the book.)

35. For a brief discussion of the economy of Maranhão, see the introduction by Daphne Patai and Murray Graeme MacNicoll to the translation *Mulatto*.

36. For more on Azevedo's female characters, consult Elizabeth Marchant, "Naturalism, Race, and Nationalism."

37. In her book *Writing Identity*, Emanuelle K. F. Oliveira cites a 1995 *Folha de São Paulo* survey on racial attitudes that indicated African Brazilians' discriminatory practices toward members of their own race (36).

38. Araipe Júnior praised *O mulato* months after its release in Rio's *Gazeta de Notícias*; others who wrote favorably included Sílvio Romero, José do Patrocínio, and Raul Pompéia. According to Fernando Góes, the novel received only one local review in Maranhão's *A Civilização*; written by Euclides de Faria, the review counseled Azevedo to give up writing and take up manual labor (Góes, "Introdução," 25).

39. Because of their often esoteric and otherworldly concerns, symbolist poets were sometimes referred to as *nefelibatas*, or "cloud dwellers."

CHAPTER THREE

1. Once the Portuguese settled in Macau in the mid-sixteenth century, the port became the conduit for trade goods between China and Portugal and through the Portuguese to other parts of Europe. Goods were also traded between the Japanese and Portuguese though Macau until Japan closed its doors to the Portuguese presence in 1639.

2. An unrivaled example of the decorative function of sixteenth-century and later Chinese porcelains is the Porcelain Room in the Santos Palace, now the French Embassy in Lisbon. Decorated between 1664 and 1687, the room contains 263 dishes that are artfully displayed on the ceiling and walls.

3. In 1518, more than two and one half tons of Chinese silk alone were shipped to Portugal; Maria João Pacheco Ferreira, "Chinese Textiles for Portuguese Tastes," 48.

4. Chinoiserie textiles were produced much earlier in Portugal and likely by Asians trained in the art and who, in the early seventeenth century, constituted twenty-three percent of the slave population in Lisbon. For more on this topic, consult Jorge Fonseca, *Escravos e senhores na Lisboa quinhentista*. Ferreira quotes from a Florentine merchant's 1578 letter that comments on the character and artisanal talents of both Japanese and Chinese captives in Lisbon; "Chinese Textiles for Portuguese Tastes," 54–55.

5. Maria Helena do Carmo's *Bambu quebrado* is a novel based on Amaral's life story.

6. For a discussion of the origins and some of the literary aims of this generation, see my essay "Modernism and Modernity."

7. Adam Smith's *Theory of Moral Sentiments* (1790) is regarded as the source for this theme; Honoré de Balzac's *Le Père Goriot* (1835) includes a conversation in which the proposition of gaining wealth by killing off a Mandarin is posed; Eric Hayot, *Hypothetical Mandarin*. Eça had never been to China, though as a diplomat he had contact with the large Chinese coolie population in Havana, where he was consul in 1872. There

he worked to arrange Portuguese citizenship papers for Chinese workers who sailed from Macau. Ming K. Chan has found that around twenty-two thousand Chinese left Macau annually, and between a quarter and a half million were sent to Cuba between 1859 and 1873 ("Luso-Macao Dimensions of Sun Yat Sen's Modern Chinese Revolution," 93).

8. This situation is interesting to consider in relation to Fernão Mendes Pinto's critique in *Peregrinação* of Portuguese mistreatment of Muslims in China.

9. S. C. M. Paine, *Imperial Rivals*, especially 112–129.

10. The Orientalist works of French novelist Pierre Loti, the nom de plume of Julian Viaud, were popular reading in Portugal. The brothers Goncourt and Michel Revon were others who wrote about the Far East. The Greek-born Lafcadio Hearn's works about Japan were even more widely read at the turn of the century.

11. For two commentaries on Eça's essay "Chineses e japoneses," see Orlando Grossegesse, "O fantasma do chinês deschinesado," and José Carvalho Vanzelli, "Uma leitura da China."

12. Following the building of the Transcontinental Railroad, the United States put a halt to Chinese migration with the Chinese Exclusion Act of 1882.

13. Moraes's correspondence was immense and also includes posthumously published collections of his letters to various friends in Portugal.

14. See, for example, Moraes's "Vestígios da passagem dos portugueses no Japão" in *O culto do chá*, 61–78, and *Fernão Mendes Pinto no Japão*.

15. For more information on Moraes's work on legends, see Anabela Chaves, "Japanese Legends and Wenceslau de Moraes."

16. This is also true of Machado de Assis in his story "O segredo do bonzo" (1882) (The bonzo's secret), in *Obra completa*; the story is purportedly an unpublished chapter from Fernão Mendes's Pinto's *Peregrinação*. In his portrayal of the colonial East-West encounter, Machado focuses on the art of deception through false and empty rhetoric and human gullibility and greed.

17. Moraes's friend Feliciano Francisco Rosário served as intermediary for letters between Moraes and his sons, who were sent to school in Hong Kong; Leopoldo Danilo Barreiros, *A "paixão chinesa" de Wenceslau de Moraes*.

18. For more on this subject, see K. David Jackson, "Recordações das musas."

19. The children of Portuguese and Chinese or Macanese often identified more closely with Portugal than with China. Around 20 percent of the Macanese migrated to Portugal in 1999, when the city was handed over to China. Few had ever visited Portugal.

20. For an early important study of the Portuguese-speaking diaspora, see David Lopes, *A expansão da língua portuguesa no Oriente*.

21. The films are *A ilha dos amores* (1982) and *A ilha de Moraes* (1983).

22. The information on Pessanha's son and companions is based on Daniel Pires's preface to *Camilo Pessanha* and introduction to Pessanha's *Correspondência*.

23. Baudelaire's reference to this instrument in his verse is often cited as the source for the book's title.

24. The only poem in *Clepsidra* that refers to China explicitly is "Viola chinesa." As Pessanha's own observation attests, the title's indirect reference to his "exile," the only "exotic" reference in the work, becomes entwined in the poem's theme of profound sadness. A few critical studies discuss the possible relation of *Clepsidra* to Buddhist and Taoist thought. Published in 1914, his Portuguese translations of eight Chinese elegies are another example of the relation between exile and melancholy.

25. Writing more than a decade after Eça, Pessanha had the advantage of witnessing the defeat of the Qing Dynasty in southern China and the establishment of the Republic of China in 1911. As he himself declares, he had this advantage over his friend Dr. Palha, who wrote his book prior to the revolution.

CHAPTER FOUR

1. For more information on nineteenth-century military interventions, see Malyn Newitt, *Portugal in Africa*.

2. Serpa Pinto is especially warm in his acknowledgement of Stanley as inspiration and mentor in his memoir *Como eu atravessei a África*.

3. In the epigraph and throughout, citations of Serpa Pinto's *Como eu atravessei África* are from the 1998 Europa-América reprint. English quotes are from the 1881 Lippincott translation by Alfred Elwes.

4. See María Emília Madeira Santos, "Das travessias científicas," for a discussion of the society's exploration aims and expedition support. Along with other documents, the society's web page, "Exploração científica em África na época de Serpa Pinto," presents a map that illustrates nineteenth-century Portuguese expeditions in Africa, at http://www.socgeografialisboa.pt/wp/wp-content/uploads/2010/01/Apresenta%C3%A7%C3%A3oCinf%C3%A3es1.pdf.

5. Boaventura de Sousa Santos has described the historic and uneven relationship between England and Portugal in terms of Shakespeare's Prospero and Caliban. He argues that despite its global empire, Portugal was economically and politically a subaltern in its treaties and other dealings with England; "Between Prospero e Caliban" (2002). This argument, which builds on Perry Anderson's thesis in "Portugal and the End of Ultra-Colonialism" (1962), is debated by Éric Morier-Genoud and Michel Cahen in *Imperial Migrations* (2012). Morier-Genoud and Cahen refer to W. G. Clarence-Smith's observations in his book *The Third Portuguese Empire* (1985) that Portugal had regular disputes with its ally and was never Britain's subordinate; *Imperial Migrations*, 5.

6. Serpa Pinto was adamant about the difference between the Portuguese military and those troops in Africa that represented the Portuguese government:

O nosso exército da metrópole é bom, porque o Português é bom soldado;
o nosso soldado das colónias é mau porque o Preto é mau soldado; e os brancos que ali servem de mistura com pretos são piores ainda do que estes . . . . Hoje,

mesmo em Lisboa, três batalhões estão sempre prontos a marchar para as colónias e já lá têm ido; o que prova sabermos nós que o ter exército no ultramar, tal como ele é, não passa de velha costumeira. (*Como eu atravessei a África*, 1:62)

(Our home army is good, because the Portuguese are good soldiers; our colonial army is bad, because the blacks, of which it is composed, are bad soldiers, and the few whites that are mixed up with them are even worse than the negroes. . . . Even at the present time in Lisbon there are three battalions always ready to start for the colonies, and who have in fact already been there; a proof, in my opinion, that keeping up an army abroad, on its present footing, answers to no other purpose than that of perpetuating a bygone usage.) (*How I Crossed Africa*, 1:37–38)

His view of local military differs significantly from earlier writings about Africans in service to the Portuguese Crown as well as from contemporary histories by Newitt and others.

7. Serpa Pinto describes at one point an African called Alves: "José António Alves é um preto (*pur sang*) de Pungo Andongo, que, como muitos dali e de Ambaca, sabe ler e escrever. No Bié chamam-lhe branco, porque, ali todo o preto que usa calças e sapatos de liga e guarda-sol é tratado assim" (1:173). (José António Alves is a negro *pur sang*, born in Pungo Andongo, who, like many others trading from that place and from Ambaca, knows how to read and write. In the Bié they call him white, because they bestow that name upon every man of color who wears trousers and sandaled shoes and carries an umbrella [1:202].) In a footnote to this passage in his memoir, he quotes a statement made to him by Ivens: "Em eu vendo entrar meu campo preto de sapatos de liga e guarda-sol, já sei que é branco e estou logo a tremer" (1:172). (I saw . . . a jet black negro come into my camp with sandals on, and a parasol in his hand, so I knew he was a white man, and trembled accordingly [1:202].)

8. The English translation leaves out Serpa Pinto's phrase about their skin color and changes other wording: "they do not look like Portuguese in their coloring, they are natives, without education." In his letters back home, Camilo Pessanha was especially critical of members of the Luso-African population, some of whom landed in Macau: "Eu também detesto a nossa África Ocidental, *a pérola das nossas colónias*, pelo que dela me posso figurar: negociantórios boçais, militarejos ladrões, magistradórios acomodatícios, todos mais ou menos negreiros, todos mais ou menos mulatos, todos mais ou menos degredados. Alguns tenentesórios que com escala por lá têm ido bater a Macau, vê-se-lhes na dentuça a obsessão do imposto de palhota" (*Correspondência*, 19). (I also detest our Western Africa, *the pearl of our colonies*, for what I can glean of it: coarse, disreputable businessmen, military-thieving types, easily accommodating little magisterial appointees, all more or less Negroid, all more or less mulattos, all more or less criminals in exile. Some little lieutenant types from there who have been stopping over in Macau, and recognizable because you see in their bucktoothed grin their obsession with property tax.)

9. For more discussion of the Staden text, see chapter 1 in my book *Brazil Imagined*.

10. It is perhaps not surprising that African and other tribal communities frequently resisted being photographed, in the belief that the camera would steal their souls. Serpa Pinto comments on the difficulties of transporting the heavy camera equipment into the interior, and despite the inclusion of the Monteiro photographic plates, he acknowledges the native population's resistance to being captured on film: "Supondo, porém, que se podiam mais ou menos facilmente empregar os meios fotográficos, qual era o indígena do interior que deixava apontar uma máquina e estava um momento firme da objectiva da câmera escura?" (1:270). (And even supposing that the difficulty were got over, and that photography could be effectively employed, where is the native of the interior who would allow an apparatus to be set up, and stand before it as a subject for the camera obscura? [1:324])

11. An explorer contemporary with Serpa Pinto, Capelo, and Ivens was Henrique de Carvalho, who traveled from 1884 to 1888 between Angola and the Congo. His archive can be found at the Sociedade de Geografia de Lisboa.

12. Fradique was born out of discussions in the 1860s among Eça, Ramalho Ortigão, Antero de Quental, and Jaime Batalha Reis, who became known as the Portuguese Generation of 1870. In 1867, a short biography of Fradique and a few of his poems appeared in the Portuguese newspaper *Revolução de Setembro*, and in 1870, he appeared briefly as a character in Eça and Ortigão's collaborative novel *O mistério da estrada de Sintra*. Nearly two decades later, in 1888, a few more letters by Fradique appeared in newspapers in Lisbon and Rio; these were followed four years later by the publication of an additional five in Lisbon. In 1900, shortly following Eça's death, a biographical note about, and sixteen letters, by Fradique were published as *A correspondência de Fradique Mendes*.

13. The word *alegre* means "happy" as well as "drunk," "showy," and "not serious." In addition to the incapable architect-senator, another of those "slaphappy elements" to whom Fradique snidely refers is a bureaucrat whose bricklaying skills have been recommended to Fradique.

14. According to the long biographical note on Fradique that serves to introduce the novel and whose narrator has all the earmarks of Eça, Fradique died in 1888.

15. Carlos Mayer, whom Fradique addresses as Carolus Mayerensis, was a well-known Lisbon aesthete and a possible model for both Fradique and Jacinto, the protagonists of two of Eça's last works.

16. With few exceptions, Fradique's letters are written from Paris. For sixteen years, Eça wrote letters from London that appeared in the Portuguese *Gazeta de Notícias*. They were collected in his posthumously published *Cartas da Inglaterra* (1905).

17. Agualusa, "Interview."

18. This accepting, adaptive power of the Portuguese, which in colonial times involved sexual relations with African, Asian, and Brazilian indigenous females, became the central argument of Gilberto Freyre's Lusotropicalism, discussed further in chapter 6.

19. Agualusa focuses on the Atlantic triangle of relations among Portugal, Brazil, and Africa that is central to contemporary discussions about lusophone issues such as language and orthography, culture, and commerce. Eça was more focused on Portugal from the perspective of a reluctant native son who lived abroad, traveled incessantly to distant lands, and only occasionally returned to Portugal.

20. Citations in Portuguese are from the Dom Quixote 2004 *Nação Crioula* 4th edition and in English from Daniel Hahn's translation, *Creole*, published by Arcadia in 2007.

21. Ana's exiled husband is a slave owner and trafficker whose name, Vitorino Vaz de Caminha, is an obvious playful reference to Pero Vaz de Caminha, who wrote the letter of 1500 on the founding of Brazil.

22. With regard to women, Fradique's epistolary relationship with Clara in Eça's work has certain affinities with a later "romance" in letters between Fernando Pessoa "himself" and Ofélia. In Fradique's case, his passion for women resides in the cult of the "eterno feminino" (eternal feminine) or "Mulher" (Woman) rather than in actual physical contact.

23. Translations of the *Emigrantes* quotes are mine except the few mentioned later from Dorothy Ball's 1962 translation, *Emigrants*.

24. This is the same nativist attitude represented in scores of literary works about the homeland, most famously Gonçalves Dias's "Canção do exílio."

25. Hollinshead, "Tourism and the Restless Peoples." Also see Tim Coles and Dallen J. Timothy, "'My Field Is the World,'" 7. The ship's community in Ferreira de Castro's *Emigrantes* is composed primarily of Italians, Portuguese, and Spaniards, reflecting the principal ethnic groups that migrated to Brazil at the turn of the twentieth century. Between 1908 and 1936, more than a quarter of a million Portuguese had passed through the port of Santos in the state of São Paulo. The majority, like Manuel, arrived without their families; Herbert S. Klein, "European and Asian Migration to Brazil." Among the emigrants whom Manuel encounters in São Paulo are the Japanese, who came to work on the plantations and in the city. When he first sees Japanese in the streets, he remarks: "Que homens tão esquisitos!" (*Emigrantes*, in *Obra completa* 1:388–389). (What strange-looking men!) I list Dorothy Ball's translation in this book's bibliography. But it contains questionable modifications, one of which involves Manuel's initial reaction to the Japanese, which she translates as, "What ugly devils they are!" (*Emigrants*, 125). Ball even embellishes on Manuel's few words and has him state, "If I ever met a face like that at a lonely crossroad at night, I should take to my heels" (125). Manuel's reaction in the original is one of surprise at a people who look strange to his provincial eyes. Ball's version makes Manuel appear crude and explicitly racist when, in fact, he is in awe of most everything around him. For purposes of greater accuracy, I have provided my own translations of the novel.

26. Ferreira de Castro says nothing about the history of Indians enslaved by landowners in the Amazon; in this sense, his novel resembles early colonial works about the Brazilian "savage." The novel *A selva* is far more sensitive about the mixed-race *caboclo*

population whose river and agrarian lifestyle he portrays in idyllic terms compared to that of the rubber tapper.

27. Although *A selva* does not give the details, Japanese companies paid travel and settlement expenses for migrants in exchange for land grants. For a brief history on this subject, see Hiroaki Maruyama, "Japanese Migrants in the Amazon."

28. Tizuka Yamasaki's film *Gaijin: Os caminhos da liberdade* (1980) (*Gaijin: Roads to Freedom*) is a powerful portrayal of the first Japanese to work on the Brazilian coffee plantations; I discuss the film in *Brazil Imagined*, 262–263. In 2002 Leonel Vieira adapted *A selva* to the screen. The adaptation has a certain heightened sense of melodrama not unlike the *telenovela*. Vieira even invents a torrid love affair between Alberto and the wife of senhor Guerreiro, replete with nude scenes, to substitute for Alberto's occasional sexual fantasies in the novel.

29. For a good overview and bibliography for the subject, consult Xenia Vunovic Wilkinson, "Tapping the Amazon for Victory." In the years prior to and after World War II, the struggles of the Northeastern migrant would become one of the prominent themes in Brazilian literature. Those works were influential in the rise of neorealist literature in Portugal, which was equally focused on the hardships of internal migration carried out mainly by a peasant population.

30. Among those who wrote about the Portuguese in Brazil were Joaquim Paço D'Arcos, Aquilino Ribeiro, José Rodrigues Miguéis, and Miguel Torga; for a brief discussion of their works on the topic, see Eulália Maria Labmeyer Lobo, *Imigração portuguesa no Brasil*, 188–192. Also see Mário Quartin Graça, "A imagem do Brasil na literatura portuguesa." For a broader view of the ways that Brazil and Portugal saw one another, consult Nelson H. Vieira, *Brasil e Portugal*.

CHAPTER FIVE

1. These individuals included members of the French-trained Movimento Matemático group and writer-academics such as Adolfo Casais Monteiro, Jorge de Sena, and Victor Ramos. Another, less studied but important writer in exile was Maria Archer, whose fiction was censored by the Salazar regime. For more on political exiles in Brazil, see Douglas Mansur Silva, "Portuguese Writers and Scientists Exiled in Brazil."

2. See Cláudia Castelo, *Passagens para África*.

3. Various laws were introduced to promote assimilation in the colonies; one was the Ato Colonial (1930), which placed further restrictions on who received funding and administrative positions in the *ultramar*. Also, students with little or no financial means to continue their educations were often sponsored by local organizations, including the Protestant church and neighborhood groups.

4. Historian Pires Laranjeira writes that a CEI de Moçambique and a CEI de Angola had already been established in Coimbra in 1941 and 1942, respectively ("Introdução," xvii). Over the years, the CEI in Lisbon had more than two thousand mem-

bers; later houses established in Coimbra in 1944 and Oporto in 1958 had one thousand members and two hundred members, respectively (xviii). The largest community was from Angola. Membership data is provided by the União das Cidades Capitais da Língua Portuguesa (UCCLA) in the information section titled "Documentação histórica" from its conference program "Homenagem aos Associados da Casa dos Estudantes do Império" in May 2015.

5. For his valuable support, Caetano was named honorary president of the CEI by its student membership (Castelo, "Casa dos Estudantes do Império," 28).

6. Because of the smaller number of students from India, Macau, and Cape Verde at the time, their houses were located within the CEI de Angola.

7. Faria, *A Casa dos Estudantes*, 31; Castelo, "Casa dos Estudantes," 24. Following World War II, Portugal was frequently attacked at meetings of world leaders for maintaining its colonies. One of venues was the famous Bandung Conference held in Indochina in 1955. The "civilizing mission" continued to be a trope in Portugal's responses in defense of its overseas agenda. Two examples of the official stance on the benefits of Portuguese colonization were published in a 1955 issue of the *Boletim da Sociedade de Geografia de Lisboa*: Joaquim Moreira da Silva Cunha, "O caso português e a crise da colonização," and Adriano Moreira, "A Conferência de Bandung e a missão de Portugal."

8. Although the early Salazar regime did not agree with Brazilian sociologist Gilberto Freyre's landmark study, *Casa grande e senzala* (1933) (*The Masters and the Slaves* [1946]), in which Freyre claimed the Portuguese were naturally inclined toward miscegenation, in the post–World War II years it embraced Freyre's Lusotropicalist thesis to argue against decolonization. For Salazar, the *ultramar* was an integral part of Portugal precisely because of the country's long history in building and promoting a multiracial and pluricontinental nation-state, as I discuss in chapter 6.

9. The January 1949 circular published by the house lists the names of the recently elected administration: "Presidente—Telmo Crato Monteiro (Cabo Verde), Vice-Presidente—José A. de S. Carvalho (Moçambique), Tesoureiro [Treasurer]—João Soares (Macau), Secretário-Geral—Jorge Pinto Furtado (Angola), Vogal [Voting member]—Rui Nazaré (Índia)" (*Mensagem*, CEI, 17).

10. Pires Laranjeira states that Brazilian Fernando Mourão was an active participant in the late 1950s. He also lists the names of several Portuguese who supported the CEI, among them Alfredo Margarido, Eduardo Medeiros, Luís Franciso Rebelo, Jorge de Sena, José Augusto França, and Urbano Tavares Rodrigues ("Introdução," xvii, n10).

11. *Mensagem* was published by the CEI's cultural division; other units were dedicated to administration, information, sports, and medical and other assistance. Between 1947 and 1953, the CEI in Coimbra published a bulletin called *Meridiano*. A digitized copy of its 1953 issue can be found at Fundação Mário Soares, http://www.fm soares.pt/aeb_online/visualizador.php?nome_da_pasta=04354.006.001&bd=Docu mentos. In 1950, another Coimbra publication, *Momento: Antologia de literatura e arte*, appeared.

12. Interview of Tomás Medeiros by the author, October 16, 2014, Quinta Grande,

Amadora. A longtime resident of Parede, outside Lisbon, Maria Augusta de Figueiredo recalled regularly eating lunch at the canteen with her husband. The food was inexpensive, she said, and the CEI was well located, close to the Instituto Técnico Superior, which her husband attended; interviews by the author, October 18 and November 20, 2014.

13. The volumes of transcribed issues of *Mensagem* and the untitled bulletin are missing several numbers. Critic Manuel Ferreira spent years scouring rare-book venues, used-book stores, and archives in search of the ephemeral issues; CEI, *Mensagem*. For additional information on the history of the collection, see Orlanda Amarílis's preface in volume 1 of the series, v–viii.

14. In honor of the 2014–2015 celebrations of the CEI in Lisbon and Coimbra, UUCLA reissued all the CEI publications, including *Mensagem*.

15. The title does not appear on the cover of transcribed issues of *Boletim* from this period.

16. A chronology in the 1994 special issue dedicated to *Mensagem* refers to the 1957 to 1959 bulletins as the beginning of the second series of *Mensagem*. But the bulletins in the actual volume have no such reference to *Mensagem*.

17. Tomás Medeiros has discussed the importance of the library to the students' education and their clandestine acquisition of books that were banned by the regime. He specifically mentioned the Livraria Buchholz, where students used code language to purchase books sold under the counter. He expressed enthusiasm especially about their acquisition of novels by Jorge Amado, Graciliano Ramos, and other politically engaged writers; interview by the author, October 16, 2014, Lisbon.

18. Works cited from *Mensagem* and *Boletim* are referenced according to the month and year of the issue they appeared. Page numbers refer to their locations in the transcribed volumes.

19. Organized by the Angolan section, the commemorative circular issue marked the three-hundredth anniversary of Portugal's defeat of the Dutch, who occupied Luanda from 1641 to 1648. An afterword refers to the issue as a "testemunho espiritual" (spiritual testimony) of Angola, which is celebrated as "a mais portuguesa das colónias portuguesas" (88) (the most Portuguese of the Portuguese colonies).

20. Lara commends the Portuguese Catholic and Protestant missionaries who serve the indigenous populations in the interior, who, she states, are more religious than the Portuguese settlers (5). What is not said is that proselytizing was often accompanied by submission and enslavement, as was the case in colonial Brazil.

21. Interestingly, an essay about the feminist movement in India ("O movimento feminista na Índia contemporânea"), by Ricardo Fernandes, appears immediately after Lara's article in *Mensagem*. In our conversation, Tomás Medeiros made a number of points about Lara's comments on women. Most important, he said, was that only one of the many Angolans in the CEI married a Portuguese woman because Angolans were unacceptable in Portugal as spousal candidates even if they were white. He was most likely referring to Agostinho Neto, who returned to his studies in 1958 after his imprisonment by the regime in 1951. He married Maria Eugénia da Silva, who was born in

Trás-os-Montes. Medeiros stated that mixed-race and black students were considered far below Lusophone African whites in the racial hierarchy; interview by the author, October 16, 2014.

22. In 1952, Lara and her husband, Orlando Albuquerque, collected Dias's thirteen stories for the volume titled *Godido e outros contos*, which was published by the CEI.

23. The title "Rumo" is based on an important line from Dias's story: "Godido precisava outros rumos" (Godido needed other bearings).

24. The poem originally appeared in the Mozambican weekly titled *O Brado Africano*, which introduced the works of many important poets from the country.

25. In 1980, Vítor Evaristo wrote an essay for the Lisbon journal *África* about his early friendship with João Dias in Mozambique and their student days in Coimbra and Lisbon. Evaristo writes poignantly of Dias's isolation as a black student in Coimbra, where even white Mozambicans ignored him, and the difficulties of finding housing in Lisbon after he fled Coimbra. The portrait is both moving and sad and provides a glimpse of the difficulties and alienation experienced by black Africans in Portugal; Evaristo, "João Dias." That racial tension was depicted in 1951 by Vera Micaia/Noémia de Sousa in her poem "Godido," based on João Dias's story.

26. The subsequent issue of *Mensagem* uses Cabral's letter to his friend Arlindo António as an introduction to António's article "Hoje e amanhã." Written during World War II, the essay discusses the need to build a better future for children. Cabral's letter suggests his own growing awareness of the crises and struggles in Portuguese-controlled Africa. He is discreet in his letter, stating that he would expand upon his thoughts in a later, private missive to his friend.

27. José Eduardo Agualusa's *Nação Crioula* offers a variation on this historical lover-father reality. Fortunately, the former slave Ana Olímpia is educated, and she and her daughter survive Fradique Mendes's return to Europe.

28. In the mid-1950s, Andrade, with Tomás Viriato da Cruz (1928–1973), founded the MPLA. Cruz, whose name appears in the circular, was a driving force in the Angolan publication titled *Mensagem (Luanda)* that appeared in 1951 and 1952.

29. After his arrival in Lisbon in 1948, Andrade also participated in the "Vamos descobrir Angola" (Let's discover Angola) movement begun in the mid-1940s by Viriato da Cruz and Agostinho Neto. Physician, historian, and former CEI member Edmundo Rocha writes in his essay "A Casa dos Estudantes" and his book, *Angola*, about the various associations and clubs with which many in the CEI had affiliations or contact. These included the MUD-Juvenil (the Portuguese Communist Party youth organization); the Centro de Estudos Africanos (Center for African Studies), an early and important organization created by the more politically radical black students in the CEI; and the Movimento Anti-Colonialista. In an interview on October 15, 2014, at his home in Massamá, Lisbon, Rocha also discussed the importance of the Clube Marítimo Africano (African Maritime Club), whose ship workers and stevedore members sailed between Lisbon and Luanda and brought back with them politically sensitive materials for CEI student club members, among them Angolans Lúcio Lara

(1929–), Agostinho Neto, and Amílcar Cabral. The workers were a prime example of a Portuguese-speaking diaspora whose travels out and back kept students who resisted the colonial cause informed. For more detailed information on these organizations, see Edmundo Rocha, *Angola: Contribuição ao estudo da génese do nacionalismo moderno angolano*.

30. Neves's lecture was presented in Luanda to members of the Clube Rádio Telégrafo-Postal de Angola on October 7, 1950.

31. Prior to the administrative takeover of the CEI, Mário Pinto de Andrade organized a collection of essays by CEI students titled "Les étudiants noirs parlent" (Black students speak) that appeared in 1953 as a special issue of the French journal *Présence Africaine*. Although the essays were unsigned because of their strong critiques of Portuguese colonialism, sources indicate that the authors included Agostinho Neto, Amílcar Cabral, Francisco José Tenreiro, Alda do Espírito Santo, and Mário Pinto de Andrade. For more on this publication, consult the Andrade section "Juventude: Investigação e textos," Fundação Mário Soares, http://www.fundacao-mario-soares.pt/. After moving to Paris in 1953, Andrade published with Tenreiro the anthology *Poesia negra de expressão portuguesa*; those poems plus others were published in a second anthology in France in 1958.

Edited by Salim Miguel, *Revista Sul* in Florianópolis published several writers associated with the CEI, including Angolans António Jacinto and José Graça (Luandino Vieira) and Cape Verdean Viriato da Cruz. Miguel sent many books to young Angolan, Mozambican, and São Tomé writers who were eager to receive literature from Brazil. In *Cartas d'África e alguma poesia* (2005), Miguel published some of their correspondence from the 1950s and 1960s. Especially interesting is a letter from Viriato da Cruz that gives specific information on how Miguel should package Brazilian works, including the novels of Jorge Amado and other Northeastern writers that were banned by the dictatorship, to avoid their being confiscated by customs inspectors.

32. Bandeira's poem had been appropriated earlier in the 1930s by Osvaldo Alcântara (the pen name of Cape Verdean author Baltasar Lopes) for his poem "Itinerário de Pasárgada" about Cape Verdean migration and the search for a better life. Alcântara's work became identified with what was called *evasionismo*. Later Cape Verdean poets took a different approach and wrote "anti-Pasárgada" poems about staying and improving life in the archipelago and fighting for its independence. A good example is Ovídio Martins's *Não vou para Pasárgada* (I won't go to Pasárgada) from the 1960s. Writers like Rui Knopfli from other provinces wrote their own variations on the Pasárgada theme. Consult Simone Caputo Gomes, "A poesia de Cabo Verde," and Tania Martuscelli, "Para uma discussão do lugar utópico."

33. In 1952, Cabral published an essay titled "Apontamentos da poesia caboverdiana" in which he lauds Fonseca alongside CEI member António Neto as the two leading figures in the vanguard of a new Cape Verdean poetry. He ends the essay by citing verses from Fonseca's work; Amílcar Cabral's essay is posted by Jorge Morbey in "In memoriam—Aguinaldo Fonseca," *Ponto Final* (blog), January 27, 2014, http://pontofinalmacau.wordpress.com/2014/01/27/in-memoriam-aguinaldo-fonseca/.

34. Luandino Vieira's work first appeared in the February 1958 issue with the poem "Canção para Luanda," which he signed with his birth name, José Graça.

35. In his essay "Uma ilha africana na Duque d'Ávila," Alfredo Margarido wrote, "Houve um momento, difícil de datar, que se coloca entre 1961 e 1962, em que a CEI decide por em funcionamento as suas prórpias regras: a ilha rebelara-se" (There was a moment, difficult to date, somewhere between 1961 and 1962, when the CEI decided to put into motion its own rules: the island had rebelled); in *Mensagem: Número especial*, Borges et al., 43. This shift had to have occurred after July 1961. According to Ana Maria Mão-de-Ferro Martinho, a second and much briefer government intervention in the CEI administration took place from January to July that year (51). She also notes that, beginning in January 1963, the Portuguese government imposed a professor onto the organization who had the right to veto initiatives ("Reflexões," 52). Martinho's essay includes a helpful listing of the *Mensagem* volumes, with dates and selected contents.

36. For a long commentary on these events, see Edmundo Rocha, "A Casa dos Estudantes do Império nos anos de fogo."

37. Rocha specifically references the help of a Bishop Black in Frankfurt; interview by the author, October 15, 2014.

38. Diana Andringa made a documentary film, *Operação Angola: Fugir para lutar* (2015), based on interviews with former CEI students about their escape from Portugal.

39. The CEI was under surveillance by the secret police, PIDE (Polícia Internacional e de Defesa do Estado). A document from its files shows that PIDE received detailed information on the students' escape to France after the fact; the document is published in *Mensagem: Número especial*, ed. Borges et al., 199. Edmundo Rocha says that in this and other instances CEI members successfully eluded PIDE surveillance by holding small-group meetings in cars that they drove around the city. Rocha also mentions the importance of an Angolan group in Brazil that included CEI member Fernando Mourão and that supported the MPLA efforts there; interview by the author, October 15, 2014. See also the personal testimonies at "A caminho da luta," *Buala*, http://www.buala.org/pt/mukanda/a-caminho-da-luta.

40. Four years later, in 1965, Vieira's short story collection titled *Luuanda* was awarded the Portuguese Writers Society prize named for Camilo Castelo Branco. The action resulted in the Salazar regime's suppression of the association. Although the book's publication was prohibited, a PIDE agent commissioned pirate copies to sell that were printed in Portugal but with attribution to a nonexistent publishing house in Belo Horizonte. Indiana University's Herman B. Wells Library has a copy of this rare edition. Heitor Martins, who was in Lisbon in 1965 shortly after the prize had been announced and the society was banned, recalled that Portuguese radio kept recycling the news about the "traitors" in the Writers Society who had bestowed the prestigious award on a "terrorist." He stated that the radio broadcasts avoided any reference to Luandino Vieira's name or the book's title, *Luuanda*; interview by the author, Bloomington, February 21, 2015. By that time, Vieira was officially regarded as a terrorist be-

cause of his support of the MPLA and had been incarcerated as a political prisoner at Tarrafal.

41. In 1992, Pepetela published *A geração da utopia*, a four-part novel, and based its first section, "A Casa (1961)," on his experiences in the CEI; he ends the section with the 1961 flight of the one hundred students from Portugal.

42. A *linóleo* is a waterproofed vinyl tile generally used for flooring. Vieira used *linóleos* for making prints that appear in his works.

43. During the writing of this chapter, numerous celebrations and commemorations were taking place to acknowledge the CEI and its former members. On October 28, 2014, a daylong roundtable took place in Coimbra that included Pepetela. On November 14, 2014, a long article titled "Longe da vista, perto do coração" (Far from sight, near the heart), by Susana Moreira Marques, appeared in the Angolan *Jornal de Negócios* in recognition of the CEI, its members, and their activities. A program of lectures took place on the CEI and the student movement on February 25, 2015, in Lisbon, and another, larger conference occurred in May 2015 in which former CEI members like Edmundo Rocha and Tomás Medeiros appeared alongside historians and others who have written about the CEI. For a listing of recent publications and programs on the CEI, consult "Homenagem aos Associados da Casa dos Estudantes do Império," União das Cidades Capitais de Língua Portuguesa (UCCLA), http://www.uccla.pt /sites/default/files/divulgacao_nos_ocs_16novembro2014.pdf.

CHAPTER SIX

1. For a detailed study of *O descobrimento do Brasil*, see Eduardo Morettin, *Humberto Mauro, Cinema, História*.

2. *Camões* was not Barros's first biopic; in fact, he made several earlier patriotic-style movies about famous figures, such as the eighteenth-century poet Manuel Maria Barbosa du Bocage (*Bocage* [1936]) and the doomed Inês de Castro (*Inês de Castro* [1944]), the love interest of Prince Pedro's whose execution by his father, the king, is poignantly rendered in Camões's *Os lusíadas*.

3. In the early postwar period, there was considerable discussion at the United Nations about the need to effect legislation that would liberate countries under colonial rule.

4. Despite its firm refusal to free the colonies, Portugal was accepted into the United Nations in 1955, its membership most likely granted because of the dictatorship's strong anticommunist position during the Cold War period. The reference to "a way of being Portuguese in the world" comes from Cláudia Castelo's *"O modo de estar português no mundo."* The bibliography on Lusotopicalismo is significant. Works that appeared in the 1960s by faculty members and graduate students at the Universidade de São Paulo were largely critical of Freyre's writing about race relations in Brazil; among these are Thales de Azevedo, *Cultura e situação racial no Brasil* (1966); Florestan

Fernandes, *A integração do negro na sociedade de classes* (1965); Fernando Henrique Cardoso, *Capitalismo e escravidão no Brasil meridonal* (1962); and Octavio Ianni, *As metamorfoses do escravo* (1962). Charles R. Boxer challenged Freyre in this period with his landmark study *Race Relations in the Portuguese Colonial Empire* (1963). Freyre's work has remained a focus of criticism and debate over the decades.

5. There is considerable information on Portugal's position on decolonization at this time and Freyre's importance to Salazar's mission to retain the *ultramar*. The most detailed is Cláudia Castelo's *"O modo português."* See also Portuguese foreign minister Franco Nogueira's *Portugal e as Nações Unidas* (1962) for his commentary on Portugal's defense of its colonial project to the United Nations.

6. Castelo cites the letter sent by Sarmento Rodrigues to Salazar about Freyre and Timor. She hypothesizes that Timor was a problem for the dictatorship because of repressive measures used to regain control of the island after the war; "*O modo português*," 89n105.

7. The diary was the springboard for Freyre's follow-up book, *Um brasileiro em terras portuguesas* (1955), which featured lectures Freyre presented during his tour.

8. Cláudia Castelo has commented that Freyre was already well known and admired by the Cape Verdean intelligentsia, and his early works were credited by them with introducing not only Brazilian poetry but also the Northeastern novel (*O modo português*, 80–81).

9. Examples of Orientalism include the Macau archway and pagoda structure in the former Overseas Garden. On the grounds of the Pestana Palace Hotel, originally a palace built by the marquis de Valle Flor in the early twentieth century, is a large pagoda building. Among the palace's public rooms is one dedicated exclusively to Orientalist furnishings and art. The palace is now a national monument.

10. Sardessi's story appears in the second volume of *A literatura indo-portuguesa*, edited by Vimala Devi and Manuel de Sousa, 355–359. The first-person account involves the growing friendship between the narrator, an Indo-Portuguese political prisoner, and his African prison guard. To the narrator's surprise, the guard marries an Indo-Portuguese woman, and he credits her for civilizing the African, whose brutishness in the story gives way to compassion.

11. In 1950, Nehru made a speech in which he stated that Portugal should allow Goa to join the newly independent India. Freyre agrees in his diary and writes that Goa should have greater contact with the rest of India, and vice versa. Eleven years later, in 1961, the Portuguese military was routed from the territory by Indian combat forces. After thirty-six hours of air, land, and sea battles, 450 years of Portuguese imperialism came to a close.

12. Admiral Carlos Pena Boto was head of the Anti-Communist Crusade in the 1940s and 1950s.

13. Freyre's description of Vilhena is at odds somewhat with a possibly family-related thesis on Vilhena that states he owned the largest private art collection in Portugal in the first part of the twentieth century; Carvalho, "As esculturas de Ernesto Jardim de Vilhena."

14. In Andrade's article "Qu-ést-ce que le lusotropicalisme?" *Presènce Africaine* 4 (October–November 1955): 24–35, he wrote under the name Buanga Fele. On January 11, 1962, Andrade continued his critique of Freyre and Lusotropicalism in an address titled "Literature and Nationalism in Angola" at Columbia University.

15. Baltasar Lopes, "Uma experiência românica nos trópicos," (1947). In his article "Gilberto Freyre contestado," João Medina comments on the irony of Freyre's position, pointing out that being Creole exemplified the very fusion of cultures and races that the Brazilian constantly promoted. He also notes that Freyre's Northeastern compatriot Rachel de Queiroz wrote to complain that Freyre's acceptance of the invitation gave support to Salazar's dictatorship; her critique, titled "Por terras além mar," appeared in an April 1952 issue of the Brazilian magazine *Cruzeiro*. Freyre replied to Queiroz's charge in a later issue of the same magazine, stating that he had met regularly with figures in the opposition during his travels. Cláudia Castelo cites the article titled "Carta a Gilberto Freyre" (*Correio da Manhã*, March 4, 1952), by Portuguese exile Tomás Ribeiro Colaço, who wrote that Freyre was being used by the dictatorship to support their agenda ("*O modo português*," 92). She also describes Freyre's pro-dictatorship activities following *Aventura e rotina*'s publication, such as writing a regular column for the Lisbon newspaper *Diário Popular* (91).

16. Historian Marcos Cardão notes that the dictatorship fostered the image of a paterfamilias nation-state by promoting star soccer players and hybrid-style music such as "fado tropical" from the colonies. He also discusses at length the Miss Portugal beauty contests that included contestants from the overseas territories; "'A juventude pode ser alegre.'"

17. This epigraph's source, Sousa's "Goa," is subtitled "Paródia à poesia 'Portugal' de E. P. e Alvim que parodiou a poesia de 'Brasil' de Antônio Gonçalves Dias, brasileiro." The Portuguese-Indian poet is imitating Gonçalves Dias's "Canção do exílio" verse of longing for a homeland.

18. Quoted in "Álbum de memórias: Índia Portuguesa, 1954.1962" from the exhibition Padrão dos Descobrimentos held in Lisbon from September 30 to December 30, 2012, in recognition of the fiftieth anniversary of the end of the Portuguese military presence in Portuguese India.

19. According to Vimala Devi and Manuel de Seabra, in the sixteenth-century, emissaries were sent from India to Portugal to learn the language and Christian doctrine. Books written in the vernacular were viewed by the Portuguese as pagan texts and banned. Unlike the development of a Creole language in Cape Verde, Portuguese was imposed on Goans but was never learned by the majority, who remained illiterate. The authors estimate that ten percent of the local language, Konkani, consists of Portuguese-derived words, while Portuguese vowel pronunciation was affected by contact with Konkani; *A literatura indo-portuguesa*, 1:39, 46, 55, 57.

20. Orlando da Costa's older contemporary Ángelo da Fonseca was one of the most important Goan painters of the period. He blended Hindu and Catholic iconography in paintings such as *A Virgem e o Menino*. According to some critics, this and other hybrid paintings by Fonseca displeased the Salazar dictatorship. For example,

in *A Virgem e o Menino*, Mary is wearing a sari, necklace, and earrings. Salazar may have been displeased with such representations, but Fonseca's work, along with other hybrid-style religious artworks by artists from China and Japan, were on display in a sacred-art exhibit at the Jerónimos monastery in 1951. An illustration of *A Virgem e o Menino* also appears in the volume on Goa, Daman, and Diu in the series *Antologia da terra portuguesa*, which was published by Livraria Bertrand in the 1960s. The series featured volumes on all the provinces in Portugal as well as the individual colonies as another means to reinforce the cohesiveness of the nation-state. Importantly, the volume on India, the first in the Ultramar series, appeared in 1960, just months before a takeover by the Indian Union.

21. Salazar is quoted in José Manuel Barroso, "Só soldados ou mortos." See also Moço, "Prisoneiros na Índia," 175n797.

22. A month earlier, Portuguese troops had fired on a passenger boat that was thought to be part of a military invasion. Two people were killed. International opinion turned against the Portuguese; in conjunction with the various conflicts waged between Portugal and the Indian Union by this time, the incident paved the way for the December invasion.

23. In *A literatura indo-portuguesa*, ed. Devi and Sousa, 2:397. The name Súria refers to the sun or sun divinity.

24. In some ways the focus on Mariana's desire and sexual experiences is a variation on the Portuguese (male) tradition of racial mixing with native inhabitants in the colonized topics.

25. Amália's character is a reminder that locals employed at Tarrafal often supported the prisoners. Perhaps the best-known case is that of Ana de Tchuntchum, a laundress at the prison who smuggled out Luandino Vieira's manuscripts and kept them until his release; José Vicente Lopes, *Tarrafal-Chão Bom*, 1:148–150. In 2013 Ana Margarida de Carvalho published the novel *Que importa a fúria do mar*, about the first political prisoners shipped from Portugal to Tarrafal in the 1930s.

26. In a 1962 speech published in Cape Verde, Overseas Minister Adriano Moreira praised Cape Verdeans as "o exemplo mais perfeita da cultura luso-tropical . . . e desde sempre um excelente veículo difusor da cultura nacional e devemos-lhe serviços inestimáveis no aportuguesamento da Guiné, Angola e S. Tomé" (the most perfect example of Lusotropical culture . . . and since forever an excellent vehicle for diffusing national culture and [for which] we owe them inestimable support for making Portuguese [the territories of] Guiné, Angola, and S. Tomé); "Partido português."

27. For an early commentary on *Colossal Youth*, see James Naremore, "Films of the Year, 2007." For a recent overview of Costa's films, consult Nuno Barradas Jorge, "Thinking of Portugal, Looking at Cape Verde."

CHAPTER SEVEN

1. See Photius Coutsoukis, "Angola."

2. Oliveira is an Angolan actor, and Andrade is Cape Verdean. The cast was a Lusophone collaboration that brought together professionals and nonprofessionals who were active in the liberation movement.

3. See my "Radical Form in *Novas cartas portuguesas*," in *The Question of How: Women Writers and New Portuguese Literature* as well as studies at Projecto Novas Cartas Portuguesas 40 Anos Depois, http://www.novascartasnovas.com/.

4. According to João Paulo Borges Coelho, there were around 100,000 Portuguese troops in Angola, Mozambique, and Guinea-Bissau at this time. Africans were also recruited to fight for the Portuguese homeland, and they numbered from 50,000 to 60,000 by the end of the war; "African Troops in the Portuguese Colonial Army."

5. Spínola's book *Portugal e o futuro* (1974) (*Portugal and the Future* [1974]) had a bombshell effect in Portugal and paved the way for the April 25 revolution.

6. Among the few prerevolutionary films that refer to the war is Paulo Rocha's family drama *Mudar de vida* (1966) (*Change of Life*), about a Portuguese soldier who returns to his fishing village community after the war to discover that his girlfriend has married his brother.

7. For a brief discussion of *Tabu*'s dialogue with the earlier F. W. Murnau film *Taboo* often mentioned in reviews of the film, see Carolin Overhoff Ferreira, "Imagining Migration."

8. A few years after the revolution, around 30,000 Portuguese of Indian descent who resided in Mozambique left that country and resettled in Portugal (Portugal, *Portugal Japão*, 53).

9. For more on these works by Lobo Antunes and Jorge, consult Helena Kaufman and Anna Klobucka, eds., *After the Revolution*.

10. Oliveira's film *Non, ou a vã glória de mandar*, also distributed as *No, or the Vain Glory of Command*, focuses on the futility of the colonial war within the context of a history of Portugal's defeats over the centuries.

11. See Paul Wiseman, "Macau Ranks No. 1."

12. Carlos Tavares Oliveira estimates that Macau's casinos make around thirty billion dollars per year. The Venetian in Macau is the largest casino in the world. There are more than thirty casinos to date crammed side by side into a relatively small area that includes Taipa to the south. That number continues to grow; "O papel de Macau."

13. Carlos André, "Centro de Macau vai formar professores." A 50 percent rise from 2010 to 2013 in Portuguese applications for temporary residency in Macau affected processing time; what used to take an average of three months for a permit in 2013 required at least a year. This longer waiting time continued despite an accelerated processing of Portuguese (and Chinese) passport holders seeking residency; Luciana Leitão, "A Desirable Home." For a discussion of Portuguese as legislative language in Macau, consult Zhidong Hao, *Macau: History and Society*, 169–172.

14. In 1999, in a gesture of friendship, the Chinese government gave Macau fifty-

six works of art that represent different regions and ethnic groups of China. Most of the works are huge; among them are rare sculptures in wood and precious stones, paintings, vases, and elaborately carved and painted furniture. The pieces can be found in the Handover Gifts Museum of Macau, which was built solely for the purposes of displaying them; http://www.icm.gov.mo/handovermuseum/index1.asp?Language=3.

EPILOGUE

1. Once under Portuguese rule, Equatorial Guinea's admission to CPLP membership angered many in Portugal's government. It was described as a case of checkbook diplomacy by which the country's rich oil reserves won over the CPLP's own statutes, which ban countries like Equatorial Guinea that are ruled by a dictator and have the death penalty.

2. Founded in 1985, UCCLA (União de Cidades Capitais de Língua Portuguesa) (Union of Portuguese-Speaking City Capitals, formerly called Luso-Afro-American-Asiatic Capital Cities) is a Lisbon-based organization that fosters cooperation among the cities for a range of projects such as cultural events, educational programs, and public health works.

3. The Portuguese Language Orthographic Agreement of 1990 is posted on Wikipedia at https://en.wikipedia.org/wiki/Portuguese_Language_Orthographic_Agreement_of_1990.

4. Michelly Carvalho and Rosa Cabecinha, "The Orthographic (Dis)Agreement and the Portuguese Identity Threat."

5. At a May 2015 conference in Lisbon with the curious title "O futuro da língua portuguesa discutido em bom português" (The future of the Portuguese language discussed in good Portuguese), former Portuguese president Jorge Sampaio talked about the goal of having Portuguese recognized as an official language of the United Nations. Note, however, his emphasis on Portugal as opposed to the commonwealth: "Para mim, continua a ser claríssimo que a língua é, para Portugal e para os portugueses, um grande desígnio nacional, que merece ser assumido plenamente pelo Estado e pela sociedade" (For me, it continues to be very clear that the language is, for Portugal and for the Portuguese, a great national project that deserves to be assumed fully by the State and by society); in "Não devíamos desistir de conseguir incluir o português entre as línguas oficiais das Nações Unidas," (Lisbon) *Diário de Notícias*, May 27, 2015, http://www.dn.pt/politica/interior.aspx?content_id=4591101.

Bibliography

Abaka, Edmund. *House of Slaves and "Door of No Return": Gold Coast/Ghana Slave Forts, Castles, and Dungeons and the Atlantic Slave Trade.* Trenton, NJ: Africa World Press, 2012.

Agualusa, José Eduardo. "An Interview with José Eduardo Agualusa." Interview by Paulo Polzonoff Jr. and Anderson Tepper. *Words without Borders*, September 2007. http://wordswithoutborders.org/article/an-interview-with-jos-eduardo-agualusa.

———. *Nação Crioula: A correspondência secreta de Fradique Mendes.* 4th edition. Lisbon: Publicações Dom Quixote, 2004. Translation by Daniel Hahn as *Creole* (Charleston, SC: Arcadia Books, 2007).

———. *A Rainha Ginga: E de como os africanos inventaram o mundo.* Lisbon: Quetzal, 2014.

———. *Um estranho em Goa.* Lisbon: Edições Cotovia, 2000.

Alcoforado, Mariana. *Lettres portugaises.* By Gabriel-Joseph Guilleragues. Paris: Claude Barbin, 1669. Translation from the French by Edgar Prestage as *Letters of a Portuguese Nun (Mariana Alcoforado)* (London: David Nutt, 1893).

Alencar, José de. *Iracema: Lenda do Ceará.* 1865. Reprint, Rio de Janeiro: José Olympio, 1965.

Almeida, Miguel Vale de. *An Earth-Colored Sea: "Race," Culture, and the Politics of Identity in the Post-Colonial Portuguese-Speaking World.* New York: Berghahn Books, 2004.

———. "Portugal's Colonial Complex: From Colonial Lusotropicalism to Postcolonial Lusophony." Queen's Postcolonial Research Forum. Queen's University, Belfast, April 2008. http://miguelvaledealmeida.net/wp-content/uploads/2008/05/portugals-colonial-complex.pdf.

Amarílis, Orlanda. Preface to *Mensagem: Boletim da Casa dos Estudantes do Império*, CEI, 1:v-viii. Lousã, Portugal: Edições ALAC, 1996.

Anchieta, José de. *De gestis Mendi de Saa.* Rio de Janeiro: Publicações do Arquivo Nacional, 1958.

Anderson, Perry. "Portugal and the End of Ultra-Colonialism." *New Left Review* 1, no.

15 (May–June 1962): 83–102; no. 16 (July–August 1962): 88–123; no. 17 (Winter 1962): 85–114.

Andrade, Mário Pinto de. "Qu-ést-ce que le lusotropicalisme?" *Presènce Africaine* 4 (October–November 1955): 24–35.

Andrade, Mário Pinto de, and Francisco J. Tenreiro, eds. *Poesia negra de expressão portuguesa*. Linda-a-Velha, Portugal: África-Literatura Arte e Cultura, 1982.

André, Carlos. "Centro de Macau vai formar professores de português na China." *Revista Macau*, January 21, 2015. http://www.revistamacau.com/2015/01/21/centro-de-macau-vai-formar-professores-de-portugues-na-china/.

Andringa, Diana. *Operação Angola: Fugir para lutar*. Film. Portugal/Mozambique, Persona Non Grata Pictures, 2015.

Arenas, Fernando. "Reverberações lusotropicais: Gilberto Freyre em África 1-Cabo Verde." *Buala*, May 16, 2010. http://www.buala.org/pt/a-ler/reverberacoes-luso tropicais-gilberto-freyre-em-africa-1-cabo-verde.

———. "Reverberações lusotropicais: Gilberto Freyre em África 2. *Buala*, June 28, 2010. http://www.buala.org/pt/a-ler/reverberacoes-lusotropicais-gilberto-freyre -em-africa-2.

Assis, Joaquim Machado de. *Crônicas. Obras completas de Machado de Assis*. Vol. 4 (1878–1888). Rio de Janeiro: W. M. Jackson, 1955.

———. *Obra completa*. Florianópolis, Brazil: Universidade Federal de Santa Catarina. http://www.machadodeassis.ufsc.br/apresentacao.html.

Augusta, Nísia Floresta Brasileira. *A lágrima de um caeté*. 1849. Reprint, 4th edition, edited by Constância Lima Duarte. Natal, Brazil: Fundação José Augusto, 1997.

———. *Opúsculo humanitário*. 1853. Reprint, São Paulo: Cortez Editora, 1989.

Azevedo, Aluísio. *O mulato*. 1881. Reprint, São Paulo: Livraria Martins, 1964.

Azevedo, Thales de. *Cultura e situação racial no Brasil*. Rio de Janeiro: Civilização Brasileira, 1966.

Barreiros, Leopoldo Danilo. *A "paixão chinesa" de Wenceslau de Moraes*. Lisbon: Agência Geral do Ultramar, 1955.

Barreno, Maria Isabel, Maria Teresa Hora, and Maria Velho da Costa. *Novas cartas portuguesas*. 1972. Reprint, Lisbon: Publicações Dom Quixote, 1998. Translation by Helen R. Lane as *The Three Marias: New Portuguese Letters* (New York: Doubleday, 1975).

Barreto, Luís Filipe, and Jorge Flores. *O espelho invertido: Imagens asiáticas dos europeus, 1500–1800 / The Inverted Mirror: Asian Images of the Europeans, 1500–1800*. Lisbon: Centro Científico e Cultural de Macau, 2007.

Barros, João de. *Década primeira–quarta da Ásia: de João de Barros, dos feitos que os portugueses fizeram no descobrimento [e] conquista dos mares [e] terras do Oriente*. Lisbon: Galharde, 1552–1615.

Barros, José Leitão de, dir. *Camões*. Film. Produções António Lopes Ribeiro, Lisbon, 1946.

Barroso, José Manuel. "Só soldados ou mortos." *Diário de Notícias*, January 2, 2001. http://www.supergoa.com.

Batalha, Luís. "Cape Verdeans in Portugal." *Transnational Archipelago: Perspectives on Cape Verdean Migration and Diaspora*, edited by Luís Batalha and Jorgen Carling, 61–72. Amsterdam: University of Amsterdam Press, 2008.

Beebee, Thomas O. "The Triangulated Transtextuality of José Eduardo Agualusa's *Nação crioula: A correspondência secreta de Fradique Mendes*." *Luso-Brazilian Review* 47, no. 1 (2010): 190–213.

Besselaar, José van den. *António Vieira: o homem, a obra, as ideias*. Lisbon: Instituto de Cultura e Língua Portuguesa, 1981.

———. *O sebastianismo: história sumária*. Lisbon: Instituto de Cultura e Língua Portuguesa, 1987.

Bethell, Caroline B. *Men Who Migrate, Women Who Wait: Population and History in a Portuguese Parish*. Princeton, NJ: Princeton University Press, 1986.

Blackmore, Josiah. *Manifest Perdition: Shipwreck Narrative and the Disruption of Empire*. Minneapolis: University Minnesota Press, 2002.

———. *Moorings: Portuguese Expansion and the Writing of Africa*. Minneapolis: University of Minnesota Press, 2009.

Blaus, Rudy, "The Portuguese Slave Trade from Mozambique to Portuguese-India and Macau and Comments on Timor, 1750–1850: New Evidence from the Archives." *Camões Center Quarterly* 6/7, nos. 1–2 (Summer–Fall 1997): 21–27.

Borges, João Paulo Coelho. "African Troops in the Portuguese Colonial Army, 1961–1974: Angola, Guinea-Bissau and Mozambique." *Portuguese Studies Review* 10, no. 1 (2002): 129–150.

Borges, P., A. Freudenthal, Tomás Medeiros, and H. Pedro et al., eds. *Mensagem: Número especial*. Lisbon: Associação da Casa dos Estudantes do Império, 1997.

Botelho, João, dir. *Um adeus português*. Film. Lisbon: Instituto Português do Cinema, 1985.

Boxer, C. R. *Mary and Misogyny: Women in Iberian Expansion Overseas; 1415–1815. Some Facts, Fancies, and Personalities*. London: Duckworth, 1975.

———. "Negro Slavery in Brazil: A Portuguese Pamphlet (1764)." *Race* 5, no. 3 (January 1964): 38–47.

———. *Race Relations in the Portuguese Colonial Empire*. Oxford: Clarendon Press, 1963.

Braga, Teófilo. *Filinto Elísio e os dissidentes da Arcádia: A Arcádia brasileira*. Oporto, Portugal: Livraria Chardron, 1901.

Bragança, António. *Lições de literatura portuguesa (Sécs. XII a XVII)*. 10th edition. Oporto, Portugal: Livraria Escolar Infante, 1980.

Brandão, Antônio Fernandes. *Diálogos das grandezas do Brasil*. 1883–1887. Reprint, Recife, Brazil: Imprensa Universitária, 1962.

Bridges, Nicholas N. "Loango Coast Ivories and the Legacies of Afro-Portuguese Arts." In *Blackwell Companion to Art History: Companion to Modern African Art*, edited by Gitti Salami and Monica Blackmun Visonà, 53–73. London: John Wiley and Sons, 2013.

Brockey, Liam Matthew. *Journey to the East: The Jesuit Mission to China: 1579–1724.* Cambridge, MA: Harvard University Press, 2009.

Cabral, Amílcar. "Apontamentos da poesia caboverdiana." *Revista Cabo Verde*, January 1952.

———. (As Abel Djassi). *The Facts about Portugal's African Colonies.* London: Union of Democratic Control, 1960.

Cabral, Manuel Villaverde. *Portugal na alvorada do século XIX: Forças sociais, poder político e crescimento económico de 1890 a 1914.* Lisbon: Regra do Jogo, 1979.

Caldas Barbosa, Domingos. *Viola de Lereno.* 2 vols. Lisbon: Tipografia Lacerdina, 1798, 1826.

Caldeira, Carlos José. *Apontamentos d'uma viagem de Lisboa à China e da China a Lisboa.* Lisbon: Tipografia G. M. Martins, 1852.

Camargo, Oswaldo de. *O negro escrito: Apontamentos sobre a presença do negro na literatura brasileira.* São Paulo: Imprensa Oficial do Estado, 1987.

Camões, Luís Vaz de. *Os lusíadas.* 1572. Edited by Emanuel Paulo Ramos. 3d edition. Oporto, Portugal: Porto Editora, 1974.

Capelo, Hermengildo, and Roberto Ivens. *De Angola à contra-costa: Descrição de uma viagem através do continente africano.* Lisbon: Imprensa Nacional, 1886.

———. *De Benguella às terras de Iaca.* 2 vols. Lisbon: Imprensa Nacional, 1881. Translation by Alfred Elwes as *From Benguella to the Territory of Yacca.* 2 vols. (New York: Negro Universities Press, 1882).

Cardão, Marcos. "'A juventude pode ser alegre sem ser irreverente': O concurso Yé-Yé de 1966–67 e o lusotropicalismo banal." In *Cidade e império: Dinámicas coloniais e reconfigurações pós-coloniais*, edited by Nuno Domingos and Elsa Peralta, 319–360. Lisbon: Edições 70, 2013.

Cardim, António Francisco. *Relaçaõ da gloriosa morte de quatro embaixadores portugueses, da cidade de Macao, com cinquenta e sete cristãos de sua companhia, degolados todos pela fé de Cristo em Nagasaki, cidade de Japão, a três de agosto de 1640: Com todas as circunstâncias de sua embaixada, tirada de informações verdadeiras e testemunhas de vista.* Lisbon: Oficina de Lourenço Anueres, 1643.

Cardoso, Dulce Maria. *O retorno.* Lisbon: Tinta-da-China, 2011.

Cardoso, Fernando Henrique. *Capitalismo e escravidão no Brasil meridonal: O negro na sociedade escravocrata do Rio Grande do Sul.* São Paulo: Difusão Européia do Livro, 1962.

Cardoso, Fernando Henrique, and Mário Soares. *O mundo em português: Um diálogo.* Lisbon: Gradiva, 1998.

Carmo, Maria Helena do. *Bambu quebrado.* Lisbon: Editora Chiado, 2014.

Carneiro, Edison. *Antologia do negro brasileiro.* Porto Alegre, Brazil: Editora Globo, 1950.

Carneiro, Roberto, and A. Teodoro de Matos, eds. *O século cristão do Japão: Actas do colóquio internacional comemorativo dos 450 anos de amizade Portugal-Japão (1543–1993).* Lisbon: Barbosa and Xavier, 1993.

Carvalho, Ana Margarida de. *Que importa a fúria do mar.* Lisbon: Teorema, 2013.

Carvalho, Maria João Crespo Pimental Vilhena de. "As esculturas de Ernesto Jardim de Vilhena: A constituição de uma coleção nacional," PhD diss. Universidade Nova, Lisbon, 2014. http://hdl.handle.net/10362/13889.

Carvalho, Michelly, and Rosa Cabecinha. "The Orthographic (Dis)Agreement and the Portuguese Identity Threat." *Portuguese Literary and Cultural Studies* (UMass-Dartmouth, Tagus Press) 25 (August 2013): *Lusofonia and Its Futures*, edited by João Cezar Rocha, 82–95.

Casa dos Estudantes do Império (CEI). *Boletim: Casa dos Estudantes do Império* (1957–1959). Reprint, Linda-a-Velha, Portugal: Edições ALAC, 1996.

———. *Mensagem: Boletim da Casa dos Estudantes do Império.* 2 vols. (1948–1952, 1959–1964). Lousã, Portugal: Edições ALAC, 1996.

Casimiro, Ana Palmeira Bittencourt S. "Uma nova etapa da pedagogia no Brasil colonial: O *Etíope resgatado.*" *Publicação Universidade Estadual de Ponta Grossa* 16, no. 1 (June 2008): 27–34. http://www.revistas2.uepg.br/index.php/sociais/article/viewFile/2832/2117.

Cassuto, Alfonso. *Bibliografia dos sermões de autos-da-fé: Descrição bibliográfica da coleção do autor.* Coimbra, Portugal: Tipografia Atlántida, 1955.

Castanheda, Fernão Lopes de. *História do descobrimento e conquista da Índia pelos portugueses.* 1551. Reprint, 4 vols. Coimbra, Portugal: Imprensa da Universidade, 1924–1933.

Castelo, Cláudia. "Casa dos Estudantes do Império (1944–1965): Uma síntese histórica." In *Mensagem: Cinquentenário da fundação da Casa dos Estuduantes do Império: 1944–1994,* 23–29. Lisbon: Associação dos Estudantes do Império, 1997.

———. *O modo português de estar no mundo: O lusotropicalismo e a ideologia colonial português, 1933–1961.* Oporto, Portugal: Edições Afrontamento, 1999.

———. *Passagens para África: O povoamento de Angola e Moçambique com naturais da metrópole (1920–1974).* Oporto, Portugal: Editora Afrontamento, 2007.

———. "Uma incursão no lusotropicalismo de Gilberto Freyre." Instituto de Investigação Científica e Tropical. *História Lusófona* (blog) 6, September 2011, 261–280.

Castro, João de. *Roteiro de Lisboa a Goa.* Lisbon: Academia Real das Ciências, 1882.

Castro, José Maria Ferreira de. *Emigrantes.* 1928. Translation by Dorothy Ball as *Emigrants* (New York: Macmillan, 1962).

———. *Obra completa.* 2 vols. Rio de Janeiro: Editora José Aguilar, 1959.

———. *A selva.* 1930. Translation by Charles Duff as *Jungle: A Tale of the Amazon Rubber-Tappers* (New York: Viking Press, 1935).

Catz, Rebecca. Introduction to *The Travels of Mendes Pinto,* xv–xlvi. Chicago: University of Chicago Press, 1989.

Cembalest, Robin. "From Kongo to Othello to Tango to Museum Shows." *Art News,* October 25, 2012. http://www.artnews.com/2012/10/25/image-of-africans-in-western-art/.

Chan, Ming K. "The Luso-Macao Dimensions of Sun Yat Sen's Modern Chinese Revolution." *Revista de Cultura* 41 (2013): 91–109.

Chateaubriand, François-René. *Le génie du christianisme*. 1802. 4 vols. Reprint, Paris: G. Ainé, 1859.

Chaves, Anabela. "Japanese Legends and Wenceslau de Moraes." *Bulletin of Portuguese/Japanese Studies* 9 (2004): 9–41.

Clarence-Smith, W. G. *The Third Portuguese Empire: 1825–1975*. Manchester, England: Manchester University Press, 1985.

Cohen, Thomas M. *The Fire of Tongues: António Vieira and the Missionary Church in Brazil and Portugal*. Stanford, CA: Stanford University Press, 1998.

Coles, Tim, and Dallen J. Timothy. "'My Field Is the World': Conceptualizing Diasporas, Travel, and Tourism." In *Tourism, Diasporas, and Space*, edited by Coles and Timothy, 1–29.

———, eds. *Tourism, Diasporas, and Space*. London: Routledge, 2004.

Cooper, Michael. "45 anos de memórias." In *Portugal Japão: 45 anos de memórias*, 5–9. Tokyo: Embaixada de Portugal no Japão, 1993.

Correia, Gaspar. *Lendas da Índia*. Oporto, Portugal: Lello e Irmão, 1975.

Costa, Orlando da. *O signo da ira*. Lisbon: Editora Arcádia, 1961.

Costa, Pedro, dir. *Casa de lava*. Film. Madragoa Filmes (Portugal), Gemini Films (France), Pandora Filmproduktion (Germany), 1994.

———, dir. *Juventude em marcha*. Film. Contracosta Produções, Lisbon, 2006.

Costa, Pedro, and Rui Chafes. *Fora/Out!* Serralves: Mecenas do Museu/Fundação de Serralves; Maia: Sersilito-Empresa Gráfica, 2007.

Couto, Diogo do. *Décadas da Ásia*. 3 vols. Lisbon: Oficina de Domingos Gonçalves, 1736.

———. *O soldado prático*, Lisbon: Livraria Sá da Costa, 1954. Originally published as *Observações sobre as principais causas da decadência na Ásia: Diálogo do soldado prático, que trata dos enganos e desenganos na Índia* (Lisbon: Oficina da Academia Real das Ciências, 1790).

Coutsoukis, Photius. "Angola: Background to Economic Development." February 1989. http://www.photius.com/countries/angola/economy/angola_economy_back ground_to_econom~97.html.

Cravo Albin, Ricardo. *Dicionário Cravo Albin da música popular brasileira*. Instituto Cultural Cravo Albin, n.d. http:// http://www.dicionariompb.com.br/.

Cruz e Silva, António Dinis da. *Poesias*. Lisbon. Tipografia Lacerdina, 1814.

Cruz e Sousa, João da. *Evocações*. 1898. Reprinted in *Obra completa*, Rio de Janeiro: Nova Aguilar, 1995. http://www.literaturabrasileira.ufsc.br/_documents/evocacoes -3-2.htm#dw040.

Cunha, Joaquim Moreira da Silva. "O caso português e a crise da colonização." *Boletim da Sociedade de Geografia de Lisboa* (April-June 1955): 147–158.

Curnow, Kathy. "The Afro-Portuguese Ivories: Classification and Stylistic Analysis of a Hybrid Art Form," PhD diss. 2 vols. Indiana University, Bloomington, 1983.

Curvelo, Alexandra. "Nagasaki: A European Artistic City in Early Modern Japan." *Bulletin of Portuguese/Japanese Studies* 2 (2001): 23–35.

Debret, Jean-Baptiste. *Viagem pitoresca e histórica ao Brasil (1834–1839)*. 3 vols. São Paulo: Livraria Martins, 1954.

Devi, Vimala, and Manuel de Seabra. *A literatura indo-portuguesa*, vol. 1 [history]. Lisbon: Junta da Investigação do Ultramar, 1971.

———, eds. *A literatura indo-portuguesa*, vol. 2: *Antología*. Lisbon: Junta da Investigação do Ultramar, 1971.

Dias, Antônio Gonçalves. *Obras completas*. São Paulo: Edições Cultrix, 1942.

Dias, João. *Godido e outros contos de João Dias*. Lisbon: África Nova (Casa dos Estudantes do Império), 1952.

Disney, Anthony. "Portuguese Expansion, 1400–1800: Encounters, Negotiation, and Interactions." *Portuguese Oceanic Expansion, 1400–1800*, edited by Francisco Bethencourt and Diogo Ramada Curto, 283–313. Cambridge: Cambridge University Press, 2007.

Durão, José de Santa Rita. *Caramuru*. Lisbon: Régia Oficina Tipográfica, 1781.

Evaristo, Vítor. "João Dias visto por quem o conheceu." *África* 10 (October-December 1980). Reprint, *(Maputo) Notícias*, January 28, 1982. http://www.mozambique history.net/lang_lit/literature/joao_dias/19820128_dias_visto_por_quem_o _conheceu.pdf.

Faria, António. *A Casa dos Estudantes do Império: Itinerário histórico*. Lisbon: Câmara Municipal e Biblioteca Museu República e Resistência, 1995.

———. *Linha estreita da liberdade*. Lisbon: Edições Colibri, 1997.

Feldmann, Helmut. "As disputas de São Francisco Xavier com bonzos da doutrina *Zen* relatadas por Luís Fróis, SJ e João Rodrigues, SJ." In *O século cristão do Japão*, edited by Carneiro and Matos, 70–78.

Fernandes, Florestan. *A integração do negro na sociedade de classes*. São Paulo, Dominus Editora, 1965.

Fernandes, Ricardo. "O movimento feminista na Índia contemporânea." *Mensagem*, July 1948.

Ferreira, Carolin Overhoff. "Imagining Migration: A Panoramic View of Lusophone Films and *Tabu* (2012) as Case Study." In *Migration in Lusophone Cinema*, edited by Cacilda Rêgo and Marcus Brasileiro, 17–39. New York: Palgrave Macmillan, 2014.

Ferreira, Maria João Pacheco. "Chinese Textiles for Portuguese Tastes." *Interwoven Globe: The Worldwide Textile Trade, 1500–1800*, edited by Amelia Pick, 46–55. New York: Metropolitan Museum of Art, 2013.

Figueiredo, Manoel de. *Hydrografia: Exame de pilotos*. Lisbon: Vicente Alvares, 1606.

Flagg, William R. *Afro-Portuguese Ivories*. London: Batchworth Press, 1959.

Flores, Jorge. "They Have Discovered Us: The Portuguese and the Trading World of the Indian Ocean." In *Encompassing the Globe*, edited by Jay Levenson, 181–194.

Fok, K. C. "Early Ming Images of the Portuguese." In *Portuguese Asia: Aspects in History and Economic History (Sixteenth and Seventeenth Centuries)*, edited by Robert Ptak, 143–155. Wiesbaden, Germany: Steiner, 1987.

Fonseca, Fernando Taveira. "The Social and Cultural Role of the University of Coimbra (1537–1820): Some Considerations." *E-Journal of Portuguese History* 5, no. 1 (Summer 2007). https://www.brown.edu/Departments/Portuguese_Brazilian_Studies /ejph/html/issue9/html/ffonseca_main.html.

Fonseca, Jorge. *Escravos e senhores na Lisboa quinhentista.* Lisbon, Edições Colibri, 2010.

Franchetti, Paulo. *Estudos da literatura brasileira e portuguesa.* São Paulo: Ateliê Editorial, 2007.

Franco, José Eduardo. "Jesuítas e Inquisição, complicidades e confrontações: Em Portugal, no Brasil e no Oriente (Sécs. XVI–XVII)." *Relações luso-brasileiros* issue, *Revista Convergência Lusíada* 19 (2002): 220–234.

Freyre, Gilberto. 1952. *Aventura e rotina: Sugestões de uma viagem à procura das constantes portuguesas de caráter e ação.* São Paulo: É Realizações, 2010.

———. *Um brasileiro em terras portuguesas.* Rio de Janeiro: José Olympio, 1953.

———. *Casa-grande e senzala: Formação da família brasileira e o regimen de economia patriarchal.* Rio de Janeiro: Maia & Schmidt, 1933. Translation by Samuel Putnam as *The Masters and the Slaves: A Study in the Development of Brazilian Civilization* (New York: Knopf, 1946).

———. *O mundo que o português criou: Aspectos das relações sociais e da cultura do Brasil com Portugal e as colônias portuquesas.* Rio de Janeiro: José Olympio, 1940.

———. *Sobrados e mucambos: Decadência do patriarcado rural no Brasil.* São Paulo: Companhia Editora Nacional, 1936. Translation by Harriet de Onís as *Mansions and the Shanties: The Making of Modern Brazil* (New York: Knopf, 1963).

Fróis, P. Luís. *Historia de Japam.* 5 vols. Edited by José Wicki. Lisbon: Biblioteca Nacional de Lisboa, 1976.

Galito, Maria Sousa. "Conceito de Lusofonia." (Centro de Investigação em Ciência Política e Relações Internacionais, Artigo de Investigação) *CI-CPRI, AI* 16 (2012). http://www.ci-cpri.com/wp-content/uploads/2012/10/Conceito-Lusofonia.pdf.

Galvão, António. *Tratado.* Lisbon: João da Barreira, 1563.

Gama, José Basílio da. *Quitubia.* Lisbon: Oficina de António Rodrigues Galhardo, 1791.

Gama, Luís. *Luís Gama e suas poesias satíricas.* Edited by J. Romão da Silva. Rio de Janeiro: Editora Cátedra, 1981.

Garcia, José Manuel. Introduction to *O Japão visto pelos portugueses*, edited by Francisco Faria Paulino and João Paulo Oliveira e Costa, 7–20. Lisbon: Comissão Nacional para as Comemorações dos Descobrimentos Portugueses, 1993.

Garrett Almeida, João Baptista da Silva Leitão. *Obras de Almeida Garrett.* 2 vols. Oporto, Portugal: Lello e Irmão, 1966.

Godinho, Vitorino Manuel. *Os descobrimentos e a economia mundial.* Vol 4. 2d edition. Lisbon: Editorial Presença, 1983.

Góes, Fernando. "Introdução." *O mulato*, by Aluísio Azevedo, 9–25. São Paulo: Livraria Martins, 1964.

Gomes, Flora, dir. *Mortu nega.* Film. KS Visions (France) and Marfilmes (Lisbon), 1988.

Gomes, Miguel, dir. *Tabu.* Film. Komplizen Film (Germany), O Som e a Fúria (Portugal), Shellac Sud (France), Gullane (Brazil), 2012.

Gomes, Simone Caputo. "A poesia de Cabo Verde: Um trajeto identitário." *Poesia Sempre* 23 (2006): 264–266.

Gomes de Brito, Bernardo, ed. *História trágico-marítima*. 1735–1736. 2 vols. Reprint, 2d edition, introduction and notes by Ana Miranda and Alexei Bueno. Rio de Janeiro: Lacerda Editores/Contraponto Editora, 1998. Translation by C. R. Boxer as *Tragic History of the Sea* (Minneapolis: University of Minnesota Press, 2001).

Gonçalves Dias, Antônio. *Primeiros cantos*. 1847. Reprint, Belo Horizonte: Autêntica, 1998. http://objdigital.bn.br/Acervo_Digital/livros_eletronicos/primeiroscantos .pdf.

Gonzaga, Tomás Antônio. *Cartas chilenas*. 1863. Belém, Pará: Universidade de Amazônia: Núcleo de Educação a Distância, n.d. http://www.dominiopublico.gov.br /download/texto/bv000300.pdf.

Goulão, Maria José. "O negro e a negritude na arte portuguesa do século XVI." In *A Arte na Península Ibérica ao tempo do Tratado de Tordesilhas*, edited by Pedro Dias, 451–484. Coimbra, Portugal: Comissão Nacional para as Comemorações dos Descobrimentos Portugueses, 1998. http://repositorio-aberto.up.pt/bitstream/10216 /56647/2/1482.pdf.

Graça, Mário Quartin. "A imagem do Brasil na literatura portuguesa." Lecture at Teatro Nacional Maria II, Lisbon, November 27, 2012. http://casamericalatina.pt/2012/11 /28/a-imagem-do-brasil-na-literatura-portuguesa/.

Granada, Luis de. *Guía de pecadores*. Madrid: Ediciones de "La Lectura," 1929.

Grossegesse, Orlando. "O fantasma do chinês deschinesado." Introduction to *Chineses e japoneses*, by José Maria Eça de Queirós, 7–26. Lisbon: Fundação Oriente, 1997.

Guedes, Paul. "Weapons of Yesteryear." *Macao Magazine*, October 2011, n.p. http:// www.macaomagazine.net/index.php?option=com_content&view=article&id=185 :weapons-of-yesteryear&catid=44:issue-9.

Guran, Milton. *Agudás: Os brasileiros do Benin*. Rio de Janeiro: Nova Fronteira, 1999.

Hao, Zhidong. *Macau: History and Society*. Hong Kong: Hong Kong University Press, 2011.

Hayot, Eric. *The Hypothetical Mandarin: Sympathy, Modernity, and Chinese Pain*. New York: Oxford University Press, 2009.

Herculano, Alexandre, ed. *Lendas e narrativas*. 1851. 2 vols. Reprint, Lisbon: Publicações Europa-América, 1989.

Hollinshead, Keith. "Tourism and the Restless Peoples: A Dialectical Inspection of Bhabha's 'Halfway Populations.'" *Tourism, Culture, and Communication* 1, no. 1 (1998): 49–77.

Ianni, Octavio. *As metamorfoses do escravo: Apogeu e crise da escravatura no Brasil meridional*. São Paulo: Difusão Européia do Livro, 1962.

Jackson, K. David. "Recordações das musas: *O-Yoné e Ko-Haru*: O delírio e a saudade." In *Por s'entender bem a letra: Homenagem a Stephen Reckert*, edited by Manuel Calderón, José Camões, and José Pedro Sousa, 395–404. Lisbon: Imprensa Nacional Casa da Moeda, 2011.

Jesus, C. A. Montalto de. *Macau histórico*. Macao: Livros do Oriente, 1990.

Jorge, Lídia. *O cais das merendas*. Lisbon: Publicações Europa-América, 1982.

———. *A costa dos murmúrios*. Lisboa: Publicações Dom Quixote, 1988.

Jorge, Nuno Barradas. "Thinking of Portugal, Looking at Cape Verde: Notes on Representation of Migrants in the Films of Pedro Costa." In *Migration in Lusophone Cinema*, edited by Cacilda Rêgo and Marcos Brasileiro, 41–57. New York: Palgrave Macmillan.

Kaufman, Helena, and Anna Klobucka, eds. *After the Revolution: Twenty Years of Portuguese Literature, 1974–1994*. Lewisburg, PA: Bucknell University Press, 1997.

Klein, Herbert S. "European and Asian Migration to Brazil." In *The Cambridge Survey of World Migration*, edited by Robin Cohen, 208–214. Cambridge: Cambridge University Press, 1995.

Lara, Alda. "Os colonizadores do século XX." *Mensagem*, July 1948.

Laranjeira, Pires. "Introdução: Uma casa de mensagens anti-imperiais." *Mensagem: Boletim da Casa dos Estudantes do Império*, CEI, 1:xi–xxxi. Lousã, Portugal: Edições ALAC, 1996.

Law, Robin. "Ethnicities of Enslaved Africans in the Diaspora: On the Meaning of 'Mina.'" *History in Africa* 32 (2005): 247–267.

Leitão, Henrique. *A ciência na "aula da esfera": No Colégio de Santo Antão 1590–1759*. Lisbon: Comissário Geral das Comemorações do V Centenário do Nascimento de São Francisco Xavier, 2007.

Leitão, Luciana. "A Desirable Home." *Macau Business*, April 2013, 110–111.

Levenson, Jay, ed. *Encompassing the Globe: Portugal and the World in the 16th and 17th Centuries*. 3 vols. (*Reference, Essays, Images*) Washington, DC: Arthur M. Sackler Gallery, Smithsonian Museum, 2007.

Lisboa, José da Silva. 1818. *Memória dos benefícios políticos do governo del Rei Nosso Senhor D. João VI*. Rio de Janeiro: Arquivo Nacional, 1940.

Littré, Emile. *Dictionnaire de la langue française*. 1863–1877. Reprint (*Le Littré*), Marsane, France: Redon, 1999.

Livro de Lisuarte de Abreu. 1563. Facsimile edition, Lisbon: Comissão Nacional para as Comemorações dos Descobrimentos Portugueses, 1992.

Lobo, Eulália Maria Labmeyer. *Imigração portuguesa no Brasil*. São Paulo: Editora Hucitec (Humanismo, Ciência e Tecnologia), 2001.

Lobo Antunes, António. *Os cus de Judas*. 5th edition. Lisbon: Editorial Vega, 1979. Translations by Elizabeth Lowe as *South of Nowhere* (New York: Random House, 1983) and Margaret Jull Costa as *The Land at the End of the World* (New York: W. W. Norton, 2011).

———. *O esplendor de Portugal*. Lisbon: Publicações Dom Quixote, 1997.

———. *As naus*. Lisbon: Publicações Dom Quixote, 1988.

Lopes, António. "História da Província Portuguesa da Companhia de Jesus." In *A Companhia de Jesus e a missionação no Oriente*, edited by Nuno da Silva Gonçalves, 35–52. Lisbon: Brotéria and Fundação Oriente, 2000.

Lopes, Baltasar. "Uma experiência românica nos trópicos." *Claridade* 4, no. 5 (January and September 1947): 15–22.

Lopes, David. *A expansão da língua portuguesa no Oriente nos séculos XVI, XVII e XVIII.* Barcelos, Portugal: Portucalense Editora, 1936.

Lopes, José Vicente. *Tarrafal-Chão Bom: Memórias e verdades.* 2 vols. Praia, Cape Verde: Instituto da Investigação e do Património Cultural, 2010.

MacGregor, Neil. *A History of the World in 100 Objects.* New York: Viking, 2011.

Machado, Álvaro Manuel. *O mito do Oriente na literatura portuguesa.* Lisbon: Instituto de Cultura e Língua Portuguesa, 1983.

Madéira, Angélica. *Livro dos naufrágios: Ensaio sobre a* História trágico-marítima. Brasilia: Editora Universidade de Brasília, 2005.

Madureira, Luis. *Imaginary Geographies in Portuguese and Lusophone African Narratives of Discovery and Empire.* Lewiston, NY: Edwin Mellen Press, 2006.

Magalhães, Domingos José Gonçalves de. *Suspiros poéticos e saudades.* 1836. Reprint, edited by Fábio Lucas, Brasília: Editora da Universidade de Brasília, 1999.

Magalhães Júnior, Raimundo. *Poesia e vida de Cruz e Sousa.* São Paulo: Editora das Américas, 1961.

Maldoror, Sarah, dir. *Sambizanga.* Film. French-MPLA (Movimento Popular de Liberação de Angola) co-production, Brazzaville, 1972.

Manuel I. *Gesta proxime per portugalenses in India. Ethiopia et alijs orientalibus terris.* Nuremburg, Germany: Johannem Weyssenburger, 1507.

Marchant, Elizabeth. "Naturalism, Race, and Nationalism in Aluísio Azevedo's *O mulato*." *Hispania* 83, no. 3 (2000): 445–453.

Margarido, Alfredo. "Uma ilha africana na Duque d'Ávila." In *Mensagem: Número especial*, edited by P. Borges, A. Freudenthal, Tomás Medeiros, and H. Pedro, 41–44. Lisbon: Associação Casa dos Estudantes do Império, 1997.

Marques, João Pedro. *Uma fazendo em África.* Oporto, Portugal: Porto Editora, 2012.

Martinho, Maria Mão-de-Ferro. "Reflexões em torno dos contributos literários na *Mensagem* da Casa dos Estudantes do Império." In *Mensagem: Número especial*, edited by P. Borges, A. Freudenthal, Tomás Medeiros, and H. Pedro, 51–61. Lisbon: Associação Casa dos Estudantes do Império, 1997.

Martins, Heitor. "Luís Gama e a consciência negra na literatura brasileira." *Afro-Ásia* 17 (1996): 87–97.

———. *Neoclassicismo: Uma visão temática.* Brasília: Academia Brasiliense de Letras, 1982.

———. "Um primitivo documento inédito da consciência negra em língua portuguesa." *Suplemento Literário do Minas Gerais* 15, no. 843 (November 27, 1982): 1–2.

Martuscelli, Tania. "Para uma discussão do lugar utópico: A Pasárgada bandeiriana habitada por caboverdeanos e portugueses." *Revista Abril*, 2, no. 2 (2009):114–121. http://www.revistaabril.uff.br/index.php/revistaabril/article/view/266/205.

Maruyama, Hiroaki. "Japanese Migrants in the Amazon: Their Dreams and Reality." Lecture, Japan-Brazil Symposium on Research Collaboration, Tokyo, March 15, 2013. http://www.fapesp.br/japanbrazilsymposium/pdf/1-1_Maruyama.pdf.

Matos, Gregório de. *Poemas escolhidos*. São Paulo: Editora Cultrix, 1976.

Mattos, Hebe. "'Black Troops' and Hierarchies of Color in the Portuguese Atlantic World: The Case of Henrique Dias and His Black Regiment." *Luso-Brazilian Review* 45, no. 1 (June 2008): 6–29.

Mauro, Humberto, dir. *O descobrimento do Brasil*. Film. Instituto do Cacau da Bahia, 1937.

Mea, Elvira Azevedo. "Mulheres nas teias da expansão." In *O rosto feminino da expansão portuguesa: Actas I*, 65–75. Cadernos Condição Feminina 43. Lisbon: Comissão para a Igualdade e para os Direitos das Mulheres, 1995.

Medina, João. "Gilberto Freyre contestado: O lusotropicalismo criticado nas colónias portuguesas como alibi colonial do salazarismo." *Revista USP* 45 (March–May 2000): 48–61.

Mendes Pinto, Fernão. *Peregrinação*. 1614. 2 vols. Edited by Neves Águas. Lisbon: Publicações Europa-América, 1983. Translation by Rebecca Catz as *The Travels of Mendes Pinto* (Chicago: University of Chicago Press, 1989).

Mendes Pinto, Maria Helena. *Biombos Namban*. 2d edition. Lisbon: Museu Nacional de Arte Antiga, 1988.

———, ed. *Marfim d'além-mar no Museu de Arte Antiga/Overseas Ivory in the Museu de Arte Antiga*. Lisbon: Crédito Predial Português, 1988.

Metcalf, Alida C. *Go-Betweens and the Colonization of Brazil, 1500–1600*. Austin: University of Texas Press, 2005.

Mexic Bigotte Chorão, Maria José, and Sylvie Deswarte-Rosa, eds. *Leitura nova de Dom Manuel I*. 2 vols. Lisbon: Arquivo Nacional do Torre do Tombo, 1997.

Miguel, Salim, ed. *Cartas d'África e alguma poesia*. Rio de Janeiro: Topbooks, 2005.

Miranda, Ana. *Desmundo*. São Paulo: Companhia das Letras, 1996.

Moço, Diogo Manuel Simões Roque. "Prisioneiros na Índia: 1961–1962." Master's thesis, Universidade de Lisboa, 2012.

Moraes, Wenceslau de. *Cartas do Extremo Oriente*. Edited by Daniel Pires. Lisbon: Fundação Oriente, 1993.

———. *O culto do chá*. 1905. Lisbon: Relógio D'Água Editores, 2008.

———. *Dai-Nippon: O grande Japão*. 1897. 2d edition. Lisbon: Seara Nova, 1923.

———. *Fernão Mendes Pinto no Japão*. Oporto, Portugal: Comércio do Porto, 1920.

———. *O-Yoné e Ko-Haru*. 1923. Oporto, Portugal: Renascença Portuguesa, 1923.

———. *Páginas africanas*. Oporto, Portugal: Editorial Cultura, 1952.

———. *Os serões no Japão*. 1926. Lisbon: Parceria A. M. Pereira, 1973.

Morais, Manuel, ed. *Música escolhida da Viola de Lereno (1799): Domingos Caldas Barbosa*. Lisbon: Edições Estar/CHA-UE, 2003.

Moreira, Adriano. "A conferência de Bandung e a missão de Portugal: Conferência realizada na Sociedade de Geografia para o encerramento da Semana do Ultramar." *Boletim da Sociedade de Geografia de Lisboa* (April–June 1955): 159–172.

———. "Partido português." *Boletim Cabo Verde*, September 5, 1962.

Morettin, Eduardo. *Humberto Mauro, Cinema, História*. São Paulo: Alameda Casa Editorial, 2013.

Morier-Genoud, Éric, and Michel Cahen, eds. *Imperial Migrations: Colonial Communities and Diaspora in the Portuguese World*. New York: Palgrave Macmillan, 2012.

Moura, Clóvis. *Dicionário da escravidão*. São Paulo: Editora da Universidade de São Paulo, 2004.

Nabuco, Joaquim. *O abolicionismo*. 1883. Reprint, São Paulo: Publifolha, 2000. http://www.dominiopublico.gov.br/download/texto/bv000127.pdf.

Naremore, James. "Films of the Year, 2007." *Film Quarterly* 61, no. 4 (summer 2007): 48–61.

Neves, Tomé Agostinho das. "A literatura negra." *Brado Africano*, December 23, 1950.

Newitt, Malyn. *Portugal in Africa: The Last Hundred Years*. London: C. Hurst, 1981.

Nogueira, Franco. *Portugal e as Nações Unidas*. Lisbon: Ática, 1962.

Nova e curiosa relação de um abuso emendado, ou evidências da razão, expostas a favor dos homens pretos em um diálogo entre um letrado e um mineiro. Lisbon: Oficina de Francisco Borges de Sousa, 1764.

Novinsky, Anita. "Padre António Vieira, the Inquisition, and the Jews." *Jewish History* 6, no. 1–2 (1992): 151–162.

Ochoa, Raquel. *A casa-comboio*. Lisbon: Gradiva, 2010.

Oliveira, Carlos Tavares. "O papel de Macau no intercâmbio sino-luso-brasileiro." *Portos e Navios*, November 4, 2012. Reprint, http://arquivo.jtm.com.mo/view.asp?dT=415002001.

Oliveira, Emanuelle K. F. *Writing Identity: The Politics of Contemporary Afro-Brazilian Literature*. West Lafayette, IN: Purdue University Press, 2007.

Oliveira, Fernando. *A arte da guerra do mar: Estratégia e guerra naval no tempo dos descobrimentos*. 1555. Reprint, Lisbon: Ministério da Marinha, 1969.

Oliveira, Manoel de, dir. *Non, ou A vã glória de mandar*. Portugal: Paulo Branco, 1990.

Oliveira, Simão de. *Arte de navegar*. Lisbon: Pedro Crasbeeck, 1606.

Orta, Garcia de. *Colóquios dos simples, e drogas e coisas medicinais da Índia*. Goa: Joannes de Endem, 1563.

Paine, S. C. M. *Imperial Rivals: China, Russia, and Their Disputed Frontier*. Armonk, NY: M. E. Sharpe, 1996.

Patai, Daphne, and Murray Graeme MacNicoll. Introduction to *Mulatto*, by Aluísio Azevedo, 7–26. Translation by Murray Graeme MacNicoll (Austin: University of Texas Press, 1990).

Paulino, Francisco Faria, and João Paulo Oliveira e Costa, eds. *O Japão visto pelos portugueses*. Lisbon: Comissão Nacional para as Comemorações dos Descobrimentos Portugueses, 1993.

Peard, Julyan G. *Race, Place, and Medicine: The Idea of the Tropics in Nineteenth-Century Brazilian Medicine*. Durham, NC: Duke University Press, 1999.

Pepetela, *A geração da utopia*. Lisbon: Publicações Dom Quixote, 1992.

Pereira, Nuno Marques. *Compêndio narrativo do peregrino da América*. 1728. 2 vols. Reprint, Rio de Janeiro: Academia Brasileira de Letras, 1939.

Pereira, Paulo Roberto, ed. *Os três únicos testemunhos do descobrimento do Brasil: Carta de Pero Vaz de Caminha, Carta de mestre João Faras, Relação do piloto anónimo*. 2d edition. Rio de Janeiro: Nova Aguilar, 1999.

Pessanha, Camilo. *China: Estudos e traduções*. Lisbon: Agência Geral das Colónias, 1944.

———. *Clepsidra: Poemas*. Lisbon: Edições Lusitânia, 1920.

———. *Correspondência, dedicatórias e outros textos*. Edited by Daniel Pires. Lisbon: Biblioteca Nacional de Portugal; Campinas, Brazil: Editora da Unicamp, 2012.

Pessoa, Fernando. *Mensagem*. Lisbon: Parceria António Maria Pereira, 1934.

Pinheiro, Pedro. *A última crónica da Índia*. Alenquer: Escritor, 1997.

Pinto de Matos, Maria Antónia, and Jean-Paulo Desroches, eds. *Chinese Export Porcelain: From the Museum of Anastácio Gonçalves*. London: Philip Wilson, 1996.

Pires, Daniel. Introduction to *Correspondência, dedicatórias e outros textos*, by Camilo Pessanha, edited by Daniel Pires, 9–34. Lisbon: Biblioteca Nacional de Portugal; Campinas: Editora da Unicamp, 2012.

———. Preface to *Camilo Pessanha: Prosador e tradutor*, by Camilo Pessanha, edited by Daniel Pires, 7–37. Macau: Instituto Português do Oriente and Instituto Cultural de Macau, 1992.

Pires, Rui Penna, ed. *Portugal: An Atlas of International Migration*. Lisbon: Tinta-da-China, 2011.

Pires, Tomé. *A Suma oriental de Tomé Pires. E O Livro de Francisco Rodrigues*. 1944. Edited by Armando Cortesão. Coimbra, Portugal: Editora da Universidade de Coimbra, 1978. Translation and edited by Armando Cortesão as *The Suma Oriental of Tomé Pires . . . and The Book of Francisco Rodrigues*. 2 vols. (London: Hakluyt Society, 1944).

Pissurlencar, Panduronga S. S. "Os portugueses nas literaturas indianas dos séculos XVI, XVII e XVIII." *Boletim da Sociedade de Geografia de Lisboa* (July-September 1955): 367–384.

Portugal. *Portugal Japão: 45 anos de memórias*. Tokyo: Embaixada de Portugal no Japão, 1993.

———. *Rumo à Índia*. Lisbon: Ministério do Exército, Direção dos Serviços do Ultramar, 1956.

Queirós, José Maria Eça de. *A cidade e as serras*. 1901. Reprint, Oporto, Portugal: Lello e Irmão, 1955. Translations as *The City and the Mountains* by Roy Campbell (London: Carcanet, 1955) and Margaret Jull Costa (Sawtry, England: Dedalus, 2011).

———. *A correspondência de Fradique Mendes*. 1900. Reprint, Mem Martins, Portugal: Publicações Europa-América, 1990. Translation by Gregory Rabassa as *The Correspondence of Fradique Mendes: A Novel* (Dartmouth, MA: Tagus Press, 2011).

———. *O mandarim*. Oporto, Portugal: Livraria Internacional de Ernesto Chardron, 1880. Translation by Margaret Jull Costa as *The Mandarin and Other Stories* (Sawtry, England: Dedalus, 2009).

———. *Obras de Eça de Queirós*. 3 vols. Oporto, Portugal: Lello e Irmão, 1979.

Ramos, João de Deus. "A província do Japão da Companhia de Jesus após o século cristão: Uma 'informação' do Arquivo da Évora." In *O século cristão do Japão*, edited by Carneiro and Matos, 95–104.

Ramos, Jorge Leitão. *Dicionário do cinema português: 1895–1961*. Lisbon: Caminho, 2012.

Rebelo, Luís de Sousa. "Language and Literature in the Portuguese Empire." In *Portuguese Oceanic Expansion, 1400–1800*, edited by Francisco Bethencourt and Diogo Ramada Curto, 358–389. Cambridge: Cambridge University Press, 2007.

Reis, Maria Firmina dos. 1859. *Úrsula*. Florianópolis, Brazil: Editora Mulheres, 2004.

Resende, Garcia de. "Miscelânea e variedade de histórias." Coimbra, Portugal: França Amado, 1917. http://www.archive.org/stream/miscellaneaevariooreseuoft#page/64/mode/2up.

———. *Cancioneiro geral*. 1516. 5 vols. Reprint, Coimbra, Portugal: Imprensa da Universidade, 1910–1917.

Ribeiro, Aquilino. *Portugueses das sete partidas: Viajantes, aventureiros, troca-tintas. 1969*. Lisbon: Livraria Bertrand, 1992.

Ribeiro, Manuel Ferreira. *Homenagem aos heróis que precederam Brito Capello e Roberto Ivens na exploração da África austral: 1484 a 1877*. Lisbon: Lallemant Frères, 1885.

———. *A província de S. Tomé e Príncipe e suas dependências*. Lisbon: Imprensa Nacional, 1877. http://babel.hathitrust.org/cgi/pt?id=uc1.$b576899;view=1up;seq=9.

Rocha, Edmundo. *Angola: Contribuição ao estudo da génese do nacionalismo moderno angolano. Período de 1950 a 1964*. 2d revised edition. Lisbon: Dinalivro, 2009.

———. "A Casa dos Estudantes do Império nos anos de fogo." In *Mensagem: Número especial*, edited by P. Borges, A Freudenthal, Tomás Medeiros, and H. Pedro, 103–114. Lisbon: Associação Casa dos Estudantes do Império, 1997.

Rocha, Hugo. *Poemas exóticos*. Oporto, Portugal: Editora Educacional Nacional, 1940.

Rocha, Manoel Ribeiro. *Etíope resgatado, empenhado, sustentado, corrigido, instruido, e libertado. Discurso teológico-jurídico, em que se propõem o modo de comerciar, haver, e possuir validamente, quanto a um, e outro foro, os pretos cativos africanos, e as principais obrigações, que correm a quem deles se servir*. Lisbon: Franciso Luiz Ameno, 1758.

Rocha, Paulo, dir. *A ilha de Moraes*. Film. Suma Filmes, Lisbon, 1984.

———. *A ilha dos amores*. Film. Suma Filmes, Lisbon. 1982.

Rodrigues, João, and Hiroshi Hino. *Arte breve da língua japoa*. Bilingual edition. Tokyo: Shin-Jinbutsu-Orai-Sha, 1993.

Rodrigues, João Pedro, and João Rui Guerra da Mata, dirs. *A última vez que vi Macau*. Film. Blackmaria, Instituto do Cinema e do Audiovisual and Epicentre Films, Lisbon, 2012.

Romero, Sílvio. *História da literatura brasileira*. 5 vols. Rio de Janeiro: Garnier, 1888.

Rosas, Fernando. "A CEI no contexto da política colonial português." *Mensagem: Número especial*, edited by P. Borges, A Freudenthal, Tomás Medeiros, and H. Pedro, 13–21. Lisbon: Associação Casa dos Estudantes do Império, 1997.

Ross, Andrew C. *A Vision Betrayed*. Edinburgh: Edinburgh University Press, 1994.

Rubiés, Joan-Pau. "The Oriental Voices of Mendes Pinto, or the Traveller as Ethnologist in Portuguese India." *Portuguese Studies* (1994): 24–43.

————. *Travel and Ethnology in the Renaissance: Southern India through European Eyes: 1250–1625.* Cambridge: Cambridge University Press, 2000.

Ruffato, Luiz. *Estive em Lisboa e lembrei de você.* São Paulo: Companhia das Letras, 2009.

Rugendas, Johann Moritz. *Viagem pitoresca através do Brasil.* 1835. Reprint, São Paulo: Livraria Martins, 1941.

Russell-Wood, A. J. R. *A World on the Move: The Portuguese in Africa, Asia, and America, 1415–1808.* New York: St. Martin's Press, 1993.

Sadlier, Darlene J. *Brazil Imagined: 1500 to the Present.* Austin: University of Texas Press, 2008.

————. "Modernism and Modernity: The 'Questão Coimbrã' and the Generation of 1870." *Nineteenth-Century Prose* 32, no. 1 (2005): 159–185.

————. *The Question of How: Women Writers and New Portuguese Literature.* Westport, CT: Greenwood Press, 1989.

Said, Edward. *Orientalism.* New York: Pantheon, 1978.

Salles, Walter, and Daniela Thomas, dirs. *Terra estrangeira.* Film. Videofilmes, Rio de Janeiro, 1996.

Santiago, Diogo Lopes de, and José António Gonçalves de Mello. *História da guerra em Pernambuco e feitos memoráveis do mestre de campo João Fernandes Vieira, herói digno de terna memória, primeiro aclamador da guerra.* Recife: Companhia Editora de Pernambuco, 2004.

Santos, Boaventura de Sousa. "Between Prospero and Caliban: Colonialiam, Postcolonialism, and Inter-Identity." *Luso-Brazilian Review* 39, no. 2 (2002): 9–43.

Santos, Maria Emília Madeira. "Das travessas científicas à exploração regional em África: Uma opção da Sociedade de Geografia em Lisboa." Série Separatas. *Boletim da Sociedade de Geografia de Lisboa* 222 (1991): 113–122.

Saraiva, António José, and Óscar Lopes. *História da literatura portuguesa.* 6th edition. Oporto, Portugal: Porto Editora, 1982.

Saramago, José. *A jangada de pedra: Um romance.* Lisbon: Editorial Caminho, 1986.

Sardessi, Laxmanrao. "O barco da África." In *A literatura indo-portuguesa,* vol. 2, edited by Vimala Devi and Manuel de Seabra, 355–359. Lisbon: Junta da Investigação do Ultramar, 1971.

Sayers, Raymond. *The Negro in Brazilian Literature.* New York: Hispanic Institute in the United States, 1956.

Senos, Nuno. "The Arts of Brazil before the Golden Age." In *Encompassing the Globe,* edited by Jay Levenson, *Essays,* 131–137.

Serpa Pinto, Alexandre de. *Como eu atravessei a África.* 2 vols. Vol. 1, *Do Atlântico ao mar Índico, viagem de Benguela à Contra-Costa, através regiões desconhecidas; determinações geográficas e estudos etnográficos.* Vol. 2, *A família Coillard.* London: Sampson Low, Marston, Searle, and Rivington, 1881. Reprint, Lisbon: Publicações Europa-América, 1998. Translation by Alfred Elwes as *How I Crossed Africa: From the Atlantic to the Indian Ocean, through Unknown Countries; Discovery of the Great Zambesi Affluents, etc.* 2 vols. (Philadelphia: J. B. Lippincott, 1881).

Serrão, Joel, and A. H. Oliveira Marques, eds. *Nova história da expansão portuguesa: O império luso-brasileiro, 1750–1822.* Vol. 8. Lisbon: Editora Estampa, 1986.

Silva, António Dinis da Cruz e. *Poesia de António Dinis da Cruz e Silva.* Vol. 4. Lisbon: Tipografia Lacerdina, 1814.

Silva, Douglas Mansur. "Portuguese Writers and Scientists Exiled in Brazil: Exclusion, Cosmopolitanism, and Particularism (1945–1974)." Translation by Mark Carlyon. *Vibrant* 10, no. 2 (2014). http://vibrant.revues.org/1619.

Silva, Thiago Rodrigo da. "Padre Fernando Oliveira: Uma proposição utópica em *A arte da guerra do mar* ao belicismo lusitano das Grandes Navegações." Master's thesis, Universidade Federal de Santa Catarina, Brazil. 2009. http://www.nelool.ufsc .br/palestras/thiagorodrigodasilva.pdf.

Silveira, Francisco Rodrigues. *Memórias de um soldado da Índia.* Lisbon: Imprensa Nacional–Casa da Moeda, 1987.

Sobral, Luis Moura. "The Expansion and the Arts: Transfers, Contaminations, Innovations." In *Portuguese Oceanic Expansion, 1400–1800*, edited by Francisco Bethencourt and Diogo Ramada Curto, 390–459. Cambridge: Cambridge University Press, 2007.

Sousa, Pedro António de Sousa. "Goa." In *Poets of Portuguese Asia: Goa, Macau, East Timor.* Bilingual edition, translated and edited by Frederick G. Williams, 100–101. Provo, Utah: Brigham Young University Press, 2013.

Spínola, António de. *Portugal e o futuro: Análise da conjuntura nacional.* 5th ed. Lisbon: Arcádia, 1974. Translation as *Portugal and the Future* (Johannesburg: Perskor, 1974).

Subrahmanyam, Sanjay. *The Portuguese Empire in Asia, 1500–1700: A Political and Economic History.* London: Longman, 1993.

Sweet, James. *Recreating Africa: Culture, Kinship, and Religion in the African-Portuguese World, 1441–1700.* Chapel Hill: University of North Carolina Press, 2003.

Tavares, Miguel Sousa. *Equador.* Lisbon: Oficina do Livro, 2003.

Teixeira, Manuel. "Japoneses em Macau." In *O século cristão do Japão*, edited by Carneiro and Matos, 201–216.

Tinhorão, José Ramos. *Domingos Caldas Barbosa: O poeta da viola, da modina e do lundu (1740–1800).* São Paulo: Editora 34, 2004.

———. *História social da música popular brasileira.* 2d edition. São Paulo: Editora 34, 1988.

———. *Os negros em Portugal: Uma presença silenciosa.* Lisbon: Editorial Caminho, 1988.

Vanzelli, José Carvalho. "Uma leitura da China em 'Chineses e japoneses' e *O mandarim* de Eça de Queirós." *Revista Estação Literária* 10B (January 2013): 126–141. 2013. http://www.uel.br/pos/letras/EL/vagao/EL10B-Art9.pdf.

Varanda, Jorge. "A saúde e a Companhia de Diamantes de Angola." *História, Ciências, Saúde—Manguinhos* 11, no. 1 (2004): 261–268.

Vasconcelos, José Carlos. "Lusofonia: Uma palavra nova, uma realidade em construção." In *Literatura e lusofonia 2012*, edited by Maria do Rosário Rosinha, 99–104. Lisbon: Imprensa Municipal, 2014.

Vasconcelos, Simão de. *Crônica da Companhia de Jesus*. Lisbon: H. Valente de Oliviera, Impressor del Rey, N.S., 1663.

Vendrell, Fernando, dir. *Fintar o destino*. Film. David e Golias, Lisbon, 1998.

Vicente, Gil. *Three Discovery Plays: Auto da barca do inferno, Auto da Índia, Exortação da guerra*. Bilingual edition. Translation by Anthony Lappin. Eastbourne, England: CPI Anthony Rowe, 2007.

Vieira, António. *Obras escolhidas*. 12 vols. Notes and introduction by António Sérgio and Hernâni Cidade. Lisbon: Livraria Sá da Costa, 1951–1954.

———. *Sermões do Padre António Vieira*. Introduction by Margarida Vieira Mendes. Lisbon: Editorial Comunicação, 1987.

Vieira, Luandino. *A vida verdadeira de Domingos Xavier*. Lisbon: Edições 70, 1974. Translation by Michael Wolfers as *The Real Life of Domingos Xavier* (London: Heinemann Educational, 1978).

Vieira, Nelson H. *Brasil e Portugal: A imagem recíproca*. Lisbon: Ministério da Educação, Instituto de Cultura e Língua Portuguesa, 1991.

Vilhena, Ernesto de. "*Aventura e rotina* (Uma crítica de uma crítica)." (Lisbon) *Diário de Notícias*, July 16, 1953, pp. 4, 6. http://www.erealizações.com.br/livros/aventura _e_rotina.

Vilhena, Luís dos Santos. *A Bahia no século XVIII*. 3 vols. Salvador: Editora Itapuá, 1969.

Villiers, John. "The Portuguese and the Trading World of Asia in the Sixteenth Century." *Portuguese Voyages to Asia and Japan in the Renaissance Period*, edited by Peter Milward, 3–14. Renaissance Monograph 20. Tokyo: Renaissance Institute, 1994.

Wilkinson, Xenia Vunovic. "Tapping the Amazon for Victory: Brazil's 'Battle for Rubber' of World War II." PhD diss., University of Georgetown, 2009. https://reposi tory.library.georgetown.edu/bitstream/handle/10822/553116/WilkinsonXeniaV .pdf?sequence=1.

Wiseman, Paul. "Macau Ranks No. 1 in Economic Performance among World Cities." *New York Times*, January 23, 2014.

Yamasaki, Tizuka. *Gaijin: Os caminhos da liberdade*. Film. Rio de Janeiro: Ponto Filmes, 1980.

Zurara, Gomes Eanes de. *Crónica da tomada de Ceuta*. 1915. Reprint, edited by Alberto Pimenta, Oporto, Portugal: Livraria Clássica Editora, 1942.

Index

Sepúlveda, Manoel de Sousa, 50–51

Sérgio, António, 166, 169

Serpa Pinto, Alexandre, 4, 118–123, 126, 131, 139, 240nn7–8, 241n10; *Como eu atravessei a África* (*How I Crossed Africa*), 117, 118–123, 235n22, 239nn2–3, 239–240n6; studio portrait, *119*. *See also* Lupi, Miguel Ângelo: *Os pretos de Serpa Pinto* (*The blacks of Serpa Pinto*)

Shakespeare, William: *The Tempest*, 239n5

shipwrecks, 3, 29, 48–51, 58–59, 233n59

Siam, 25, 41, 231n42

Sierra Leone, 15–16, 54

Silva, António Dinis da Cruz e: "A José Basílio da Gama, Autor do poema intitulado Quitubia" (To José Basílio da Gama, author of the poem entitled Quitubia), 60

Silveira, Francisco Rodrigues, 229n22

slavery: abolitionism, 61–65, 84–86, 131, 235n14; and Angola, 5, 57–59, 66; and Asia, 40–41, 230n32, 232n42, 237n4; and Brazil, 2–4, 56–92, 104, 118, 235n14, 245n20; *cabeça de negro* (black slave's head), 4, 54–55, 234n4; emancipation, 82, 84–89, 118, 135–136; in fiction, 129, 131–136, 236n28, 242n21, 242–243n26, 246n27; and Freyre, 89, 165–166, 169, 171, 173, 244n8; images of, 4, 30, 54–57, 73–74, 161; and Jesuits, 46, 49, 51, 61; in poetry, 74–89, 155–156, 236n27; and racial mixing, 181; and religious conversion, 29, 43, 234n6, 245n20; slave trade/trafficking, 1–2, 16, 51, 53–56, 63, 66, 74–77, 84, 117, 121, 131–136, 221, 228n15, 233n60, 233n1; treatment of slaves, 4, 61–69, 75, 79, 81, 88, 136, 235n14, 236n28

Smith, Adam, 237n7

Sobral, Luís de Moura, 51, 229n15, 230n31, 233n55

Sociedade de Geografia de Lisboa (Geographical Society of Lisbon), 4–5, 120, 122

Society of Jesus (Jesuits), 1, 20–1, 29–30, 45–51, 61, 65–66, 93, 229n18, 232n44, 232n50; expulsion of, 40, 46; Kraak porcelain bottle with Jesuit emblem, *plate 8*; in Macau, *110*; presence in far east, 33–41, 93–94, 99, 101, 109, 218, 230n33, 231n38–42; Universidade do Espírito Santo (University of Espírito Santo), 141

Sousa, Martim Afonso de, 43

Sousa, Noémia de, 151, 160. *See also* Micaia, Vera

South Africa, 17, 118, 120, 225

Spinola, António de, 193, 253n5

Staden, Hans: *Warhaftige Historia*, 121–122

Stanley, Henry Morton, 118, 239n2; studio portrait, *119*

Subrahmanyam, Sanjay, 233n57

Suma Oriental, 10, 27–28

Tarrafal, 181, 185, 249n40, 252n25

Tavares, Miguel Sousa: *Equador* (*Equator*), 221

Teixeira Pinto, Bento, 49

Tenreiro, Francisco José, 151, 247n31

Teppo Ki (later translated as *Crónica da espingarda* [*Chronicles of the musket*]), 38

Thomas, Daniela: *Terra estrangeira* (*Foreign Land*), 7, 210–216

Timothy, Dallen J., 2, 242n25

Tinhorão, José Ramos, 53, 234n6, 235n16, 235n23

Tourneur, Jacques: *I Walked with a Zombie*, 181

Treaty of Tordesilhas (1494), 1, 3, 12

UCCLA (União de Cidades Capitais de Língua Portuguesa [Union